The Confidence Trap

THE CONFIDENCE TRAP

A History of Democracy in Crisis from World War I to the Present

David Runciman

with a new afterword by the author

PRINCETON UNIVERSITY PRESS

PRINCETON AND OXFORD

Published by Princeton University Press, 41 William Street, Princeton, New Jersey 08540
In the United Kingdom: Princeton University Press, 6 Oxford Street, Woodstock,
    Oxfordshire OX20 1TW

press.princeton.edu

Second printing, first paperback printing, with a new afterword by the author, 2015

Paperback ISBN 978-0-691-16583-7

The Library of Congress has cataloged the cloth edition as follows

Runciman, David.
The Confidence Trap : a History of Democracy in Crisis from World War I to the Present /
    David Runciman.
        pages cm
        Summary: "Why do democracies keep lurching from success to failure? The current
financial crisis is just the latest example of how things continue to go wrong, just when
it looked like they were going right. In this wide-ranging, original, and compelling book,
David Runciman tells the story of modern democracy through the history of moments
of crisis, from the First World War to the economic crash of 2008. A global history with
a special focus on the United States, The Confidence Trap examines how democracy
survived threats ranging from the Great Depression to the Cuban missile crisis, and
from Watergate to the collapse of Lehman Brothers. It also looks at the confusion and
uncertainty created by unexpected victories, from the defeat of German autocracy in 1918
to the defeat of communism in 1989. Throughout, the book pays close attention to the
politicians and thinkers who grappled with these crises: from Woodrow Wilson, Nehru,
and Adenauer to Fukuyama and Obama.The Confidence Trap shows that democracies are
good at recovering from emergencies but bad at avoiding them. The lesson democracies
tend to learn from their mistakes is that they can survive them--and that no crisis is as bad
as it seems. Breeding complacency rather than wisdom, crises lead to the dangerous belief
that democracies can muddle through anything--a confidence trap that may lead to a crisis
that is just too big to escape, if it hasn't already. The most serious challenges confronting
democracy today are debt, the war on terror, the rise of China, and climate change. If
democracy is to survive them, it must figure out a way to break the confidence trap"—
Provided by publisher.
    Includes bibliographical references and index.
    ISBN 978-0-691-14868-7 (hardback)
    1. Democracy—History—20th century. 2. Democracy—History—21st century.
3. World politics—20th century. 4. World politics—21st century. I. Title.
    JC421.R86 2013
    321.8—dc23
    2013019899

British Library Cataloging-in-Publication Data is available

This book has been composed in Chaparral

Printed on acid-free paper. ∞

Printed in the United States of America

10 9 8 7 6 5 4 3 2

For Bee

The trouble with political life is that it
is either too absorbing or too tame.
—ALBERT HIRSCHMAN, "ON DISAPPOINTMENT" (1982)

Try again. Fail again. Fail better.
—SAMUEL BECKETT, "WORSTWARD HO!" (1983)

CONTENTS

PREFACE

TWO STORIES CAN BE TOLD ABOUT DEMOCRACY OVER
the last hundred years. One is the obvious success story.
Democracies have shown that they win wars, recover from
economic crises, overcome environmental challenges, and
consistently outperform and outlast their rivals. There were
very few democracies at the start of the twentieth century
(on some counts, requiring an open franchise, there were
none). Now there are plenty (Freedom House currently puts
the number at around 120). Of course, the progress of democracy over this period has not been entirely smooth or
consistent. It has been haphazard and episodic: in Samuel
Huntington's famous image, it has come in "waves." Nevertheless, whatever the intermediate ups and downs, there
can be little doubt that democracy was the overall winner
during the past century, to the point where it was possible
to argue, as Francis Fukuyama did more than two decades
ago, that liberal democracy is the only plausible answer to
the fundamental problems of human history.

But alongside this success story there is another to be
told about democracy: one of pessimism and fear. No matter
how successful in practice and over time, democracies have
always been full of people worried that things are about to

go wrong, that the system is in crisis and its rivals are waiting to pounce. The onward march of democracy has been accompanied by a constant drumbeat of intellectual anxiety.
Maybe all the good news is just too good to be true. Maybe
democracy's run of luck is about to come to an end. The political history of democracy is a success story. But the intellectual history of democracy is very hard to reconcile with
this. It is preoccupied with the prospect of failure.

You can see both these views of democracy at work in the
world today. There is still plenty of optimism around. It is
not hard to fit the overthrow of autocratic governments in
Tunisia, Egypt, and Libya and the popular appetite for reform across the region into an "end of history" narrative.
It may take time, and it may not be pretty, but democracy
is spreading to those areas of the world that had previously
seemed resistant to it. This is not just true of the Arab world.
Democratic government is stabilizing in much of Latin
America. It is taking root in parts of sub-Saharan Africa.
There are even glimmers of progress in previously frozen re-
gimes, such as Burma.

On the other hand, there is plenty of gloom about. For
every success, it is possible to identify equivalent setbacks:
in Russia, in Zimbabwe, in Thailand.[1] Some of the gloom
comes from commentators who warn that events in North
Africa and the Middle East are not what they seem. The fall
of an autocratic regime in response to popular protests does
not necessarily herald the arrival of democracy: sometimes
it heralds the arrival of another autocracy, or of civil war.
But there is a further anxiety at work too, one related to
the recent performance of the world's established democracies. For while it is true that the last century has been good

for them, the last decade has not. Many of the leading democracies have been fighting long and difficult wars (in Iraq
and Afghanistan) that they do not seem to know how to win
or how to exit successfully. Most Western democracies are
heavily in debt, thanks in part to these wars but also to a
global financial crisis they did much to bring about. In Europe, some of them have come close to default, and there are
fears that the United States may be heading the same way.
All democracies have found it very difficult to know what, if
anything, to do about climate change. And they have been
watching with a mixture of resignation and fear the seemingly inexorable rise of China. These are the four fundamental challenges a system of government can face: war, public
finance, environmental threat, and the existence of a plausible competitor. It is not clear that the established democracies are doing well in meeting any of them.

So there is a puzzle. History indicates that democracies
can cope with whatever is thrown at them. Yet here are the
most successful democracies struggling to cope. Things look
bad, but the historical record of democracy suggests that
nothing is as bad as it seems. This is why we find it so hard to
know how seriously to take the current crisis of democracy.
We can't be sure whether it is really a crisis at all. Are we
in trouble or not? This book is about how we should think
about this question. I believe we are in trouble, but not for
the reasons usually given. The real problem is that democracy is trapped by the nature of its own success.

Inevitably, as so often in politics, there is a temptation
to take sides when thinking about the prospects for democracy. We are faced with what look like either/or questions. Should we heed the good news or the bad news? Was

Fukuyama right or wrong? Is America finished, or are the doomsayers going to be proved wrong this time as they have every time in the past? Is the real story the enthusiasm for democracy in the places that haven't had it before, or the seeming exhaustion of democracy in the places that have had it for a while? If you are an optimist, the long-term benefits of democracy trump the short-term hiccups. But if you are a pessimist, the problems we see around us give the lie to the long-term success story. A lot depends on what counts as "long term." A bad ten years is just a blip in the face of a good hundred years. But a good hundred years is just a blip in the face of two thousand years—from ancient Greece to the mid-nineteenth century—in which democracy was written off as a failure. The critics of democracy over that period always said that in the end the democratic taste for debt and instant gratification, along with a penchant for fighting stupid and impulsive wars, would be its undoing. How can we be sure they weren't right?

In this book I want to show how the two stories about democracy go together. It is not a question of choosing between them. Nor is it a question of disaggregating the problem into a series of smaller problems so that we no longer talk about democracy in general, but only particular democracies in particular times and places, some doing well, some doing badly. I still want to talk about democracy in general. The mistake is to think that the news about democracy must be either good or bad. When it comes to democracy good news and bad news feed off each other. Success and failure go hand in hand. This is the democratic condition. It means that the triumph of democracy is not an illusion but neither is it a panacea. It is a trap.

The factors that make democracy work successfully over time—the flexibility, the variety, the responsiveness of democratic societies—are the same factors that cause democracies to go wrong. They produce impulsiveness, and short-termism, and historical myopia. Successful democracies have blind spots, which cause them to drift into disaster. You cannot have the good of democratic progress without the bad of democratic drift. The successes of democracy over the past hundred years have not resulted in more mature, far-sighted, and self-aware democratic societies. Democracy has triumphed, but it has not grown up. Just look around. Democratic politics is as childish and petulant as it has ever been: we squabble, we moan, we despair. This is one of the disorientating things about the predicament we find ourselves in. All the historical evidence that we have accumulated about the advantages of democracy has seemingly left us none the wiser about how to make best use of those advantages. Instead, we keep making the same mistakes.

In this book I focus on particular points of crisis in the history of modern democracy to show why we keep making the same mistakes, even as we make progress. Crises are often perceived as moments of truth, when we discover what's really important. But democratic crises are not like that. They are moments of deep confusion and uncertainty. Nothing is revealed. The advantages of democracy do not suddenly become clear; they remain jumbled together with the disadvantages. Democracies stumble their way through crises, groping for a way out.

Yet it is this capacity to stumble through crises that gives democracy the edge over its autocratic rivals. Democracies are better at surviving crises than any alternative system because they can adapt. They keep groping for a solution, even as they keep making mistakes. But democracies are no better at learning how to avoid crises than their rivals, and nor are they better at learning from them. It may be that certain types of autocratic regimes are actually the faster learners, particularly when it comes to avoiding the mistakes of the recent past. (Where autocracies tend to fall down is in the assumption that the future will continue to resemble the past.) Their experience of crisis is more likely to make democracies complacent than it is to make them wise: what democracies learn is that they can survive their mistakes. This could still be their undoing if it leads them to make one mistake too many. We have not yet reached the end of history. This is not because Fukuyama was wrong. It is for some of the reasons that Fukuyama was right.

The idea that success and failure go hand in hand is not unique to democracy. It is part of the human condition. It is the essence of tragedy. Hubris can accompany any form of human achievement. The most gifted individuals are often the ones who overreach themselves. Having great knowledge is no guarantor of self-knowledge: intelligent people do the stupidest things. What is true of individuals is also true of political systems. Empires overreach themselves. Successful states become arrogant as they revel in their successes, and they become complacent as they rely on past glories to see them through present difficulties. Great powers decline and fall.

However, the democratic predicament cannot be reduced to the general run of human tragedy, and it is not just another stage in the great cycle of political decline and fall. Democracies suffer from a particular kind of hubris. In ancient

Rome, triumphant generals were accompanied into the city by slaves whispering in their ears that they too were mortal. Democracies don't do this to their heroes, because they don't need to. Successful democratic politicians are constantly being reminded of their own mortality. They can hardly get away from it: the most common experience in a democracy is to suffer abuse, not idolatry. No democratic politician can reach the top without getting used to the catcalls of the crowd. That is why no one in a democracy should ever be taken unawares by failure. If democratic politicians become complacent, it is because they have become inured to the whispers of mortality, not because they have been shielded from them. Autocrats are the ones who are taken by surprise.

The definitive image of a modern autocrat confronting the catcalls of the crowd came when Nicolae Ceauşescu stood on the balcony of the Central Committee Building in Bucharest on December 23, 1989, three days before he and his wife Elena were executed by firing squad. He looked genuinely puzzled: what *is* that noise? No democratic politician ever looks puzzled like that. The look that sums up democratic complacency is different. It is the face that defeated incumbents wear on election night (think George H. W. Bush in 1992). They don't look surprised but they do invariably look hurt. Yes, they seem to be saying, I heard the abuse you have been directing my way. How could I not? I read the newspapers. But that's democracy. I didn't realize you really meant it. That look is one reason why democratic life is more often comic than it is tragic.

What is true of individual politicians is also true of democratic societies. Modern-day America is sometimes compared to imperial Rome, since it has some of the trappings of an empire with its best days behind it. But the United States is not Rome because as well as being an empire it is also a functioning modern democracy. That makes it too restless, impatient, querulous, self-critical to qualify as a candidate for late-imperial decadence. Democracies are hardly oblivious to the impending prospect of catastrophe. If anything, they are hypersensitive to it. One of the hall-marks of present-day American democracy is its endless questioning of its own survival prospects. The problem for such democracies is not that they can't hear the whispers of their own mortality. It's that they hear them so often they can't be sure when to take them seriously.

Successful democracies have plenty of institutional safe-guards against the hubris of individuals. In an autocracy the danger is that a crazed or self-aggrandizing leader will lead the state over a cliff. In a democracy it is much more diffi-cult for a mad leader or a mad idea to take hold for long. Before they go over the cliff, democracies will vote mad lead-ers out of office. Regular elections, a free press, an indepen-dent judiciary, and professionalized bureaucracy all provide protection against being dragged down by the worst kinds of personal misjudgments. In the long run, mistakes in a stable democracy don't prove calamitous because they don't become entrenched. That doesn't stop democracies from making mistakes, however; if anything, it encourages it. It is some consolation in a democracy to know that nothing bad lasts for long, but it is no answer to the question of what should be done in a crisis. Moreover, consolation can pro-duce its own kind of complacency. Knowing that they are safe from the worst effects of hubris can make democracies reckless—what's the worst that could happen?—as well as sluggish—why not wait for the system to correct itself? That is why the crises keep coming.

The person who first noticed the distinctive character of democratic hubris—how it is consistent with the dynamism of democratic societies, how democratic adaptability goes along with democratic drift—was Tocqueville. He provides the starting point for the story I want to tell in this book. Ever since Tocqueville wrote nearly two hundred years ago, people have been arguing about whether he was really an optimist or a pessimist about democracy. The truth is that he was both, and therefore neither. The grounds for democratic optimism were the source of Tocqueville's fundamental worries about democracy. This is what made him such an original thinker in his own time and what makes him such an important thinker for ours. He did not share either the concerns of the traditional critics of democracy or the hopes of its modern champions. In the first chapter I explain what is different about Tocqueville's approach, and why he is the indispensable guide to the ongoing relationship between democracy and crisis.

I then examine a series of crises for democracy from the past hundred years to explore how functioning democracies cope with crises and to see what they learn from them. I have chosen to look at seven critical years, regularly spaced out across that period: 1918, 1933, 1947, 1962, 1974, 1989, 2008. This list is not meant to be exhaustive. There have been other crisis points for modern democracy: 1940, 1968, 2001. There have also been plenty of years that seemed like crises at the time but have since faded from memory. This is one of the distinctive features of democratic life that Tocqueville noticed: it exists in a semipermanent state of crisis, which makes it hard to know when the crisis needs to be taken seriously. The crises I have chosen reflect some of this uncertainty and offer a foreshadowing of some of the uncertainty we feel at present. That, for instance, is why I do not write about 1940, which was perhaps the ultimate existential crisis for modern democracy; the problem that year was not uncertainty, it was the unambiguous threat of destruction. In their very different ways, 1968 and 2001 were also one-offs. The crises I study form part of a sequence in which various patterns emerge. It is a story of uncertain fears, missed opportunities, and inadvertent triumphs. It is a tale of contingency and confusion.

Nonetheless, for all the uncertainty, each of the crises I write about was real. These were important years, with a great deal at stake. In studying how established democracies coped with these crises, I am looking for echoes of Tocqueville and links forward to now. My aim is to understand how we got to where we are. Then, in the final chapter of the book, I explore where we might be heading. I do not suggest any easy ways out of our current predicament. We are caught in a trap. If there were an easy way out, it would not be a trap. But seeing how we are trapped is an essential part of understanding what the future might hold.

Two final remarks. This book is about how established democracies cope with crisis. It is not about how societies become democratic, or about what happens when democracies revert back to autocracy. There is a vast literature on what is called democratic "transition," and political scientists have made considerable progress in understanding how it comes about. I am interested in what happens to societies that have completed the transition to democracy but still find themselves in crisis situations. For that reason, my focus in the book is on the United States and Western Europe, particularly during the early crises I discuss. During the first half of the twentieth century there were very few established democracies. As democracy has spread, so the scope of the story I tell spreads, to include established democracies elsewhere, including in India, Israel, Japan. Nonetheless, the United States remains at the heart of it. Tocqueville first identified the ambivalent character of democratic progress by studying America. The United States remains the place where it can still be seen most clearly. I am not suggesting, any more than Tocqueville was, that America *is* democracy, nor that democracy is only possible on the American model. But if the American model is being undone by its own success, that has significant implications for democracies everywhere.

This book is a mix of political and intellectual history. I am interested in how democratic societies have coped with crises, but also in what has been written and said about the crises as they have unfolded. Beliefs matter: what people think about the strengths and weaknesses of democracy helps shape how democracies perform in practice. For instance, if it is widely believed that democracies are prone to panic, then different strategies will be adopted in a crisis than if it is believed that democracies are made up of rational agents. This book is not a work of political science. But political science provides the basis for some of the beliefs that people have about democracy, and it plays an important role in the story I want to tell. We know a lot more than we used to about how democracies succeed and why. What we don't know is what to do with this knowledge. That is the problem.

A Note on Terminology

In this book I draw a primary contrast between "democracy" and "autocracy," following the current convention. By democracy I mean any society with regular elections, a relatively free press, and open competition for power. These societies are often referred to as "liberal democracies," though some are more liberal than others. By autocracy I mean any society in which leaders do not face open elections and where the free flow of information is subject to political control. Strictly speaking, autocracy means the self-sustaining rule of a single individual, though in some cases individuals rule as part of a small coterie of power holders (for instance, the Greek military junta of 1967–74, also known as "the Regime of the Colonels," is characterized as an autocracy by political scientists drawing broad democratic/antidemocratic comparisons). Some autocracies are dictatorships and some are not. Some are more authoritarian than others. Where necessary I specify these differences.

Contemporary political science tends to plot the transition from autocracy to democracy on a spectrum, with an extensive middle ground where some of the key distinctions get blurred (as in the case of authoritarian states that hold regular elections). I discuss the question of these "hybrid" regimes in the final chapter. In general, though, I stick to the basic contrast between democracy and autocracy and to the core differences between them. This is in keeping with most of the writers I discuss, starting with Tocqueville, who treated "democracy" as an all-purpose concept. For Tocqueville, however, the fundamental contrast was between "democratic" and "aristocratic" societies, that is, between societies in which the principle of equality has taken hold and those in which it has not. I discuss some of the implications of this in the chapter that follows.

In other respects, Tocqueville was notoriously vague in what he meant by democracy. He used the term interchangeably, sometimes to refer to a way of doing politics, sometimes to a set of political and moral principles, sometimes to a way of living altogether. I have not deliberately set out to follow him in this vagueness. However, I have tried to leave my use of the term open and adaptable. The hallmark of the modern idea of democracy is its adaptability. It can accommodate forms of politics that are hierarchical as well as inclusive; it can be identified with leaders as well as citizens; it can combine egalitarianism with many different forms of inequality. In this book I treat democracy as a recognizable entity. But sometimes I use the word in relation to individual politicians (FDR, Nehru), sometimes in relation to particular institutions (elections, a free press), and sometimes in relation to general habits of mind (impatience, inattentiveness). I hope that nonetheless it is clear throughout what I am talking about.

The Confidence Trap

INTRODUCTION

Tocqueville: Democracy and Crisis

WHEN THE YOUNG FRENCH ARISTOCRAT ALEXIS DE TOC-
queville arrived in America in May 1831, he was not much
impressed by what he found. He had traveled to America
with the ostensible aim of writing a book about the country's prison system, but he also wanted to see for himself
what a functioning democracy was really like.

Tocqueville got off the boat in New York, and as so often with first-time visitors, he felt overwhelmed and dis-
orientated. There was too much going on. No one paused
to reflect on what they were doing. No one was in charge.
He soon wrote back to friends in France of his amazement
at the instability of American life, "the absolute lack that
one notices here of any spirit of continuity and durability."[1] The Americans he met were friendly enough, but they
struck him as careless and impatient. He was shocked by the
ease with which they changed their homes, their jobs, their
situations. He was also taken aback by the chaotic state of
American politics, which seemed to reflect this restlessness.

America's elected politicians had no more apparent sense of purpose than the people who elected them. Like most men of his class and generation, Tocqueville was a bit of a snob. What he encountered in America chimed with his instinctive distrust of democracy. There was something childish about its mindless energy. Where was the discipline? Where was the dignity? If this was democracy in action, he didn't see how it could work.

However, Tocqueville was an unusual sort of snob: he was capable of changing his mind. As he left New York City behind and continued his journey around the country, he came to feel that his first impressions had been mistaken. American democracy did work. It had an underlying stability and durability that could not be seen in its day-to-day activities. The democratic way of life had its own strengths, but it took patience to discover them. As Tocqueville wrote in volume one of *Democracy in America*, which he published in 1835: "Its faults strike one at first approach, but its qualities are only discovered at length."[2] The key to making sense of American democracy was to learn not to take it at face value. It worked despite the fact that it looked as though it shouldn't work. Its advantages were hidden somewhere beneath the surface and only emerged over time.

This was the most important thing Tocqueville discovered on his travels: democracy is not as bad as it looks. It represents his crucial insight into modern politics—in some ways it is *the* crucial insight into modern politics. In any durable democracy there will always be a gap between what seems to be happening and what it means in the long run. Democracy appears to be an up-front form of politics—everything is so raw and accessible. But the long-term advantages of democracy are not readily apparent. They can't be grasped in the moment. They need time to reveal themselves.

No one had quite seen democracy in this light before Tocqueville did.[3] It really was his discovery. As he worked through its implications, he found many of them deeply troubling. He felt that the hidden strengths of democracy also represented its most serious weakness, precisely because they were hidden. You can't grasp them when you need them. Trying to do so often makes things worse. Yet giving up on trying to grasp them is liable to lead democracies into a state of passivity and drift. Democracies are caught between their impulse to precipitate action and their instinct to wait. There is no equilibrium between these two states of mind.

This line of thought is what makes Tocqueville such an original and important thinker. He is the best guide to the peculiar character of democracy in crisis. In this chapter I hope to show why.

THE RIVAL VIEWS

Tocqueville was certainly not the first visitor to the United States to conclude that American democracy was not what it seemed. Many travelers learned to mistrust their early impressions. But that was because they usually decided Americans were hypocrites. The common complaint against American democracy was that the reality did not match up to the fine principles: Americans preached the language of dignity and freedom but underneath it all they were a coarse, vulgar, money-grubbing people. Plenty of European visitors were initially enthusiastic about the unstuffy, egalitarian ethos they encountered: America often seemed like a breath of fresh air. But the more they traveled, the more they came to think it was just for show. At bottom America revealed itself to be a materialistic, exploitative society, with everyone out for himself. Worse, it was impossible to get past the fact that the apostles of liberty kept slaves, or if they didn't keep them, they tolerated the fact that other Americans did. Slavery made a mockery of American democracy.

A more typical American journey than Tocqueville's was the one made by another young European writer, Charles Dickens, a decade later. Dickens was no snob and he had an instinctive liking for democracy. He adored America to begin with, particularly since Americans appeared to adore him. He was greeted as a kindred spirit, the great champion in his novels of the poor and the oppressed. (Tocqueville was also feted when he first arrived, but he took this as a sign of how unworldly Americans were, since back in France almost no one had heard of him.) Dickens's enthusiasm did not last. As he traveled around he got sick of the attention, and also of the fact that for all their fine sentiments, Americans had no real interest in living up to their high ideals. The more he saw of them, the more he found them to be ill mannered and self-satisfied. He also felt they were ripping him off, since lax American copyright laws meant his novels were being routinely pirated. In the two books he published about his American experiences—*American Notes for General Circulation* (1842) and the novel *Martin Chuzzlewit* (1843–44)—Dickens made it clear that he felt betrayed. He mocked the hypocrisy of his hosts, and he excoriated them for their tolerance of slavery.

What is so unusual about Tocqueville's intellectual journey is that it went in the opposite direction. Tocqueville loathed slavery as much as Dickens did. But he did not conclude that Americans were hypocrites. Instead, he came to believe that the distinguishing characteristic of American democracy was its sincerity. One of the defining moments of his trip came on July 4 when he and his traveling companion, Gustave Beaumont, arrived in Albany, the fledgling capital of New York State, where they took part in the Independence Day celebrations. Tocqueville found the ceremony pretty ridiculous, with its marching bands and solemn speeches. The provincial self-regard made him want to laugh. But when the evening culminated in a public reading of the Declaration of Independence, he admitted, to his surprise, that he was deeply impressed. "It was as though an electric current moved through the hearts of everyone there. It was in no way a theatrical performance. . . . Here was something profoundly felt and truly great."[4] Democracy in America was not a sham. It was more like a true religion.

Faith was the lynchpin of American democracy. The system worked, Tocqueville decided, because people believed in it. They believed in it despite the fact that it looked like it shouldn't work; from moment to moment it remained a mess. Democracy was an inadvertent form of politics, haphazard, uncoordinated, occasionally ridiculous, but somehow on the right track. Americans muddled through, sustained by their confidence in the future. This was not just blind faith, however. Time showed that American democracy did produce results, and that the messiness of democratic life had a cumulative power that no rival system could match. Democracy, Tocqueville wrote, "does each thing less well, but it does more things." He went on:

> Democracy does not give the most skilful government to the people, but it does what the most skilful government is powerless to create; it spreads a restive activity through the whole social body, a superabundant force, an energy that never exists without it . . . [it] can bring forth marvels. These are its true advantages.[5]

The semimystical language is deliberate. There is, Tocqueville says, something "insensible" or "occult" about the way a democracy functions. By this he did not mean that democracy was sinister or fraudulent. He simply meant that it was not fully transparent. At any given moment you could not see how it worked. But you could be confident that it did.

Tocqueville came to believe that American democracy had hidden depths. That is what made him so different from other European travelers who got fixated on the mismatch between the promise of American democracy and the grubby reality. But it also marked him out from more than two thousand years of European political philosophy. The traditional complaint against democracy had always been about its hidden shallows. According to the philosophers, what lay beneath the surface of democratic life was not stability and durability, but ignorance and foolishness. The accusation went beyond hypocrisy. Democracies could not be trusted because at root they had no idea what they were doing.

Plato had set the template for this line of thought, which helps to explain its long hold over the Western political imagination. Democracy, Plato said in the *Republic*, was the most alluring of political regimes, "like a coat of many colors." But the colorful appearance was profoundly misleading. Democracy was shiny up front, rotten underneath. In other words, it was much worse than it looked. Democracies put on a good show, but there was always something unpleasant lurking in the shadows: the people themselves, in all their greed and stupidity.

The problem was that democracy pandered to desire. It gave people what they wanted from day to day, but it did nothing to make sure they wanted the right things. It had no capacity for wisdom, for difficult decisions, or for hard truths. Democracies were founded on flattery and lies. Democratic politicians told the people what they wanted to believe, not what they needed to hear. As Plato put it, they took their failings and dressed them up as though they were virtues. If the people were ill disciplined, the politicians told them they were brave. If they were profligate, the politicians said they were generous. This would work for a while, as flattery often does. But in the long run it spells disaster, because you cannot hide from your weaknesses forever. Eventually, something will happen to expose them. At that point, democracies will discover the truth about themselves. But by then it will be too late. When the truth catches up with democracy, it tends to destroy it.

Two millennia of European political thought contained endless variations on this theme. Democracies were fickle, credulous, shameless, and lacking in self-control. They ran up debts, because they could not control their appetites. They fought stupid and dangerous wars, because they could not control their passions. They fell for would-be tyrants, because they could not control their craven instincts. Above all, democracy was a form of politics only suited for the good times: in a crisis, it would fall apart. It was a kind of confidence trick, unable to put off forever the day of reckoning. The only certainty about democracy was that it could not last. And if you met a democracy that did last, then you could be certain that it wasn't really a democracy. This was the flip side of the standard critique: genuine democracies couldn't be successful states, so successful states couldn't be genuine democracies. They were hiding an autocratic heart.

Tocqueville broke entirely with this way of thinking. He had no doubts that America was a genuine democracy. But he did not think that American democracy was therefore worse than it looked. How could it be, given its obvious faults? It was the outward appearance of democracy that made it so hard to have confidence in it. Plato had called democracy the most attractive of political regimes. Tocqueville thought it the least attractive, with nothing like the glamour or appeal of an aristocratic society, which really knew how to put on a show. Democracies lacked the necessary discipline and dignity to create a good impression. So yes, at some level it was true that democracies were bound to be a mess. What the philosophers had got wrong was *which* level. That was how things were on the surface. Something different was happening underneath.

By contrasting the outward failings of democracy with its hidden advantages, Tocqueville was turning the traditional arguments of its critics on their head. But it also meant that he was rejecting the argument that was most often made in favor of democracy by its radical champions. Their case depended on the idea that democracy's great virtue is its transparency. It succeeds because, unlike every other system of government, it has nothing to hide. Democracy was the only system that laid bare its inner workings. That meant it could correct its own failings. In the words of Thomas Paine, the great democratic champion of the American and French revolutions: "Whatever are its excellencies and defects, they are visible to all. It exists not by fraud and mystery; it deals not in cant and sophistry." The cant and sophistry, Paine insisted, were all on the other side. It was monarchy that was the sham. "That monarchy is all a bubble, a mere cant artifice to procure money, is evident (at least to me) in every character in which it can be named."⁶ The enemies of democracy were the ones with something to hide.

Paine believed that democracy would succeed once people could see it for what it was, freed from the prejudices of its opponents. When they did, they would see how politics really works. What's more, they would discover that the only thing that really works is democracy. This means there is a cut-off point, or threshold, for having true confidence in democracy. On the wrong side of the line, it will struggle to gain people's trust, because they will not be able to appreciate its virtues. That's where democracy had been stuck for two thousand years. On the right side of the line, it will go from strength to strength, because the truth about politics will have been revealed. Writing at the end of the eighteenth century, Paine was sure that the world was in the process of crossing that threshold. A new order was being born. He conjured up an image for what was happening that has remained the preferred one for democratic optimists ever since. "It is not difficult to perceive," he wrote, "that spring is begun."[7]

Tocqueville did not buy it. This was not because he did not agree that democracy was on the rise. He absolutely did agree. But Paine's belief that the hidden strengths of democracy become increasingly visible over time struck him as a fantasy. Tocqueville could not equate democracy with transparency. There remains something opaque about how a democracy works, no matter how successful it is, because the springs of its success never fully emerge from beneath the chaotic surface of democratic life. Paine wanted democracy to usher in an age of reason. Tocqueville knew the age of democracy would still have to be founded on faith. The lesson he took from his American travels is that democracy never truly reveals itself. There will always be a gap between perception and reality in a society founded on democratic principles.

There will also always be a strong temptation to try to close that gap. Genuine democracy is hard to live with because you have to take so much on faith. Tocqueville rejected the conventional arguments both for and against democracy, but he understood their appeal. Each promised to bring the truth about democracy to the surface: either its underlying strength or its underlying weakness. There is something confusing about the mismatch between the hidden strengths and visible weaknesses of democracy. We want to know which is the real story, for better or for worse. We want closure. What is much harder to live with is the knowledge that the mismatch is the reality of democratic life. That poses a very different set of challenges.

Tocqueville did not think democracy was a confidence trick. You could have genuine faith in it. In that sense, he accepted that American democracy had passed a confidence threshold. His worry was about what lay on the other side. He was afraid that confidence in democracy would prove to be a trap.

DEMOCRACY AND FATE

The name Tocqueville gave to his fears was "fatalism." He worried that the inhabitants of a democracy would drift along with their fate and, as he put it, "follow the course of their destiny weakly rather than make a sudden and energetic effort when needed to address it."[8] There were two reasons why democracies were prone to fatalism. One was the clear evidence that history was on democracy's side. Paine had been right: democracy was indeed the way the world was heading, which meant America was ahead of the curve. For Tocqueville, this was not simply philosophical speculation, nor was it vanity on the part of Americans; it was scientific fact. To know democracy is destiny, he wrote, "it suffices to examine the usual course of nature and the continuous tendency of events."[9] The trend toward what Tocqueville called "equality of conditions" was inexorable. Traditional political elites were being swept away by the idea that no human being is born to rule over another. Nothing could stand in the way of this idea, which meant that ultimately nothing could stand in the way of democracy. It was the providential plan of the universe. "To wish to stop democracy," Tocqueville wrote in the introduction to *Democracy in America*, "would then appear to be a struggle against God himself."[10]

The second reason democracies tended to be fatalistic was that this knowledge of their privileged position in the grand scheme of things required taking the long view. In the short term, democracy often looked as though it was on the wrong side of history: unstable, unreliable, ineffective. You had to put your faith in the future. This meant that although you could have confidence in the strengths of democracy, you couldn't necessarily see those strengths in action in a given political situation. Living with democracy meant surrendering to forces beyond your immediate power to apprehend. Under those conditions, it was hardly surprising if people started to feel a little powerless. Their destiny was in safe hands, but it was not clear that it was in their own hands. Something bigger was at work. A successful democracy had the power to make people feel very small.

But democratic fatalism did not always result in feelings of passivity and inadequacy. If you know history is on your side but beyond your immediate power to control, there are two ways you can respond. You could shrug your shoulders and wait for things to play themselves out. Or you could throw caution to the wind, confident that the future is secure regardless of what you do. It was part of Tocqueville's genius to recognize that democratic fatalism went along with recklessness as well as resignation. What's more, he understood that it could sometimes be hard to tell the difference between the two.

Tocqueville gave an example of what he meant when he recalled a conversation he had had with some American steamboat builders. Tocqueville had been repeatedly struck on his journey by how fragile these boats were, and how dangerous. He and Beaumont almost drowned when the one they were traveling on hit a sandbank on the Ohio River. "I have never heard a nastier noise," he wrote to a friend a few days later, "than the noise that the water made as it rushed into the boat."[11] Still, he behaved with admirable sangfroid in the crisis. But why did the manufacturers of the vessels not make them stronger and more reliable? "They answered that as it was, the boats would last too long because the art of steamboat navigation was making daily progress." This faith in progress, Tocqueville thought, was what prevented Americans "from aiming at the durable in anything."[12] Why take extra pains when something better was around the corner? Nonetheless, the steamboat builders were not simply passive bystanders, watching from the riverbank as the world floated by. Their shoulder-shrugging indifference went along with a kind of heedless energy. They put their inadequate vessels on the water and took big risks in doing so. They were careless of their fate and keen not to waste an opportunity to make money. Fatalists can be impatient as well as patient, active as well as passive. One way of trusting to the future is to act as though it is already here and jump right in.

What was true of the steamboat builders was true of American democracy at large. Democratic man, Tocqueville says, is both "ardent and resigned." Democracies can blow hot and cold. One question that is sometimes asked of *Democracy in America* is whether it is really two different books: volume one, which emphasizes the vitality and energy of American democracy; and volume two, published five years later in 1840, which is a gloomier book and emphasizes the sense of drift. But volume one and volume two simply reflect the two different sides of democratic fatalism. In the first volume, Tocqueville discusses the dangers of "the tyranny of the majority," which makes democracies impatient and vengeful. The examples Tocqueville gives of this tyranny in action—lynching, race riots, war fever—show that he was thinking of the moments when democracies run wild, having become tired of waiting for things to happen. In the second volume, he talks about the "mild despotism of public opinion," which is more insidious and makes people reluctant to challenge conventional ideas. As well as running wild, democracies can stagnate.

Yet both outcomes have the same cause: the knowledge possessed by the inhabitants of a democracy that theirs is the system with the underlying advantages. This can be infuriating. If democracy is such a great idea, why can't we have some action now? Or it can be enervating. Why not settle for a quiet life since nothing we do makes much difference anyway? Or it can be both. Passive democracies are easily roused; active democracies are easily quieted. Democratic fatalism is inherently unstable.

Not everyone appreciated the link between the wildness of democratic life and its tendency to drift: it was a difficult idea to grasp. Volume two got a much cooler reception than volume one. It struck many reviewers as too abstract, too paradoxical. The English philosopher John Stuart Mill was one of the very few people who liked it as much as the first volume. Like Tocqueville, Mill was deeply troubled by the problem of fatalism. In his own writing he had tried to distinguish between the different forms it could take. There was what Mill called "pure fatalism" (or as he sometimes labeled it, "oriental fatalism"), which is the belief that a higher power has mapped out in advance everything that will ever happen to us. This, Mill felt, was a stupefying idea. Then there was what he termed "modified fatalism," which is the belief that we are the products of our circumstances and there is nothing we can do to change that. This was the kind of fatalism that tended to hold sway in the more advanced societies of the West.[13]

Modified fatalism was not an idiotic idea, since modern science showed that we are all in some sense the products of our circumstances: causes have necessary effects (Mill was what is sometimes called a "necessitarian"). Nor did modified fatalism simply make people resigned to their fate, as pure fatalism did. Mill knew that fatalists could be dissatisfied as well as satisfied, whiny and petulant as well as quiet and accepting. Fatalism could produce complacency or it could produce irritability and volatility. Either way, though, it was dangerous. Modified fatalists had still made a basic mistake. They had assumed that because our circumstances shape us, we are powerless to do anything about who we are. But Mill insisted we can do something about it. We can change our circumstances.

When Tocqueville read Mill on fatalism, he wrote to tell him that it captured what he had been trying to say about American democracy. When he got his copy of volume two of *Democracy in America*, Mill wrote to Tocqueville to express his relief at finally finding someone who understood his concerns.

One of your great general conclusions is exactly what I have been almost alone in standing up for here, and have not as far as I know made a single disciple—namely that the real danger in a democracy, the real evil to be struggled against, and which all human resources employed while it is not yet too late are not more than sufficient to fence off—is not anarchy or love of change, but Chinese stagnation and immobility.[14]

Democracies did not really suffer from oriental fatalism, however. They suffered from the modified version. They could be volatile. But alongside the volatility went a tendency to stagnate. The danger for a democracy was that no one would try to address the underlying circumstances of its politics. Instead, everyone fixates on the surface activity of political life—all the squabbling and mudslinging—as a focus for their anger and frustration, while beneath the surface nothing is really changing. In a democracy, all the energy is liable to be directed toward the effects of politics, while the underlying causes are ignored. This is how democracies get stuck.

How do they get unstuck? The basic cure for democratic fatalism, as for any other kind of fatalism, was education. Democracies needed to grow up. Fatalism was an essentially childish state of mind, since children are the exemplary modified fatalists: they spend a lot of time whining and engaged in frenetic activity, but that's because they know nothing really depends on them. They are waiting for someone to take charge. Children grow up when they learn to take responsibility for their own fate. But from whom do they learn? Mill says it is our parents and teachers who show us "how to influence our character by appropriate circumstances." The problem was that democracies do not have parents and teachers, or at least they ought not to have them. Monarchies are ruled by father figures. Democracies are meant to rule themselves. The risk for a democracy was that in allowing anyone to fill the role of parent or teacher, they weakened their resolve to take responsibility for their own circumstances. Tocqueville was afraid of this. "When I think of the small passions of men of our day," he wrote, "I do not fear that in their chiefs they will find tyrants, but rather schoolmasters."[15]

There was also the problem of what to teach a democracy. Tocqueville worried that simply explaining the truth about political trends would encourage people in their fatalism, since the facts pointed toward the inexorability of democratic progress. It was one of the reasons why Tocqueville believed that democratic societies needed a strong dose of religion to sustain them: democracy was best served when individuals had a personal faith that could undercut the general truths of political science. This meant that secular history was a particularly dangerous subject for democracies. Historians in the age of democracy were liable to be infected with what Tocqueville called "the doctrine of fatality" (*fatalité*). "It is not enough for them to show how the facts have come about; they also take pleasure in making one see that it could not have happened in any other way."[16] What democracies needed instead was a sense that the future lay open, and that their choices still mattered. The only way outside of religion to do this was to make sure their choices had real consequences for them. Book learning wouldn't achieve this. Democracies had to learn from experience.

The best way to learn from experience was to make mistakes. Mill and Tocqueville believed that a key part of education was the freedom to experiment and if necessary go wrong. However, there is a big difference between telling an individual to make his or her own mistakes and saying the same to an entire political society. When politics goes wrong, the consequences can be catastrophic for everyone. Democracies might benefit when individuals take chances and make mistakes, since this is the best way to keep politics open to new ideas. But when whole democracies take chances and make mistakes, individuals are the ones to suffer. Moreover, when democracies get things wrong, there is often no coming back.

Tocqueville was acutely conscious of this, and also conscious of why it made the United States unique in human history. American democracy could afford to get things wrong. "The great privilege of the Americans," he wrote, "is the ability to make repairable mistakes."17 America was big enough and isolated enough from the rest of the world that its political misjudgments need not be calamitous. There was both time and space to undo any damage. This was not true in Europe, where pressures of population and competition between states meant that a democracy that tried to learn from experience was liable to be eaten up by its rivals. The same applied to South America, where no democracy had ever lasted, because one mistake was invariably fatal. Only the United States was able to experiment with democracy without fear for the consequences.

However, the problem for American democracy was that the knowledge that it could make reparable mistakes came perilously close to the idea that its mistakes didn't really matter. Tocqueville recognized the moral hazard at work here. If you don't fear the consequences of your choices, how can you learn to take your choices seriously? This was the difference between Europe and America. Europeans were unable to take a chance on democracy because of their fear of the consequences. As Tocqueville said, the only way any European state could be truly confident that its democracy would survive was if every European state was a democracy. Until that happened, Europeans would be stuck on the wrong side of the confidence threshold, frightened to put their trust in democracy. But American democracy, having crossed the confidence threshold, was in a different predicament. It was prone to get stuck in a childish state of mind, because nothing really bad ever happened. If anything, Americans were in need of a real fright. Since the crisis of its birth, American democracy had never had to confront another genuine crisis. "Americans have no neighbours," Tocqueville wrote, "and consequently no great wars, financial crises, ravages or conquests to fear."[18] That was their biggest advantage. It was also their biggest weakness.

DEMOCRACY AND CRISIS

Tocqueville could not be sure what he wanted for American democracy. He wanted it to take responsibility for its fate. But he knew that democracy in America had flourished in large part because this had not had to happen for a long time. Americans had been able to avoid the really tough choices for more than a generation. As a result, Tocqueville was torn as to what he thought about the prospect of some future crisis for American democracy. Crises could be good for a democracy if they woke them up to their circumstances and gave them an incentive to take charge of their destiny. But they could be bad for democracy if they undermined confidence in the future and spread panic and fear. A crisis is by definition a dangerous time. If you wished a crisis on a democracy serious enough to get it to take its choices seriously, you also risked presenting it with a challenge that it didn't know how to solve.

There was no easy way around this problem. A crisis bad enough to do good for a democracy would also have to be bad enough to threaten real evil. What made the problem more acute was that crises are moments of danger, and yet democracies do not perform well from moment to moment. That is when they reveal their weaknesses. Democracies find it much harder than other systems of government to coordinate their actions in the short term: the haphazard and volatile quality of democratic life makes reaching timely decisions difficult. Aristocracies, Tocqueville said (meaning politically inegalitarian or autocratic regimes), are much better at focusing their resources on a single moment in time; there is, by contrast, something about a democracy that is always "untimely." In that sense, aristocracies are going to be better at the immediate demands of crisis politics: speed and decisiveness. Wishing a crisis on a democracy to shake it out of its torpor meant asking it to face a challenge that played into the hands of its rivals. How could that be a good idea?

One way it might work was if the crisis were a long one. Then the advantages of democracy could be given time to reveal themselves. Even if aristocracies are good at swift decisions, they soon get stuck with the choices they make. They are not adaptable. Democracies, because they are always doing more, constantly experimenting, keeping on the move, will do better in the long run by finding different ways to meet a really difficult challenge. Given time, democracies can adapt their way out of a crisis in a manner that no autocratic system can. But does it make sense to wish a long crisis on a democracy? There are two problems. One is that crises that drag on for a long time will be full of dangerous moments. These are, after all, the crises that no one knows how to solve: the longer they last, the more scope there is for something really bad to happen. Long crises contain plenty of room for short-term disasters. The second problem is that crises are meant to shake democracies out of their fatalistic tendencies. But if they last a long time, there is a risk democracies will start to drift again, waiting for history to rescue them.

You can see some of Tocqueville's uncertainty about these questions in his treatment of the prospects of democracy at war. Tocqueville says that democracies ought to be suited by certain sorts of wars: long, difficult, arduous ones. Only then do the democratic advantages of adaptability and versatility come to the fore. Tocqueville thought that democracies were bad at the immediate challenges of international relations: they were jittery, impatient, quick to take offense but also ready to let things slide. As a result, they were prone to avoid the wars they should fight and to fight the ones they should avoid. Aristocratic societies are much better at knowing when and how to pick a fight. But once the struggle gets going, aristocracies tend to get stuck. They are too inflexible. "An aristocratic people which, fighting against a democracy, does not succeed in bringing it to ruin in the first campaign always runs the risk of being defeated by it," Tocqueville predicted.[19]

Democracies have a vitality and an experimental quality that suits them to an extended contest. Apart from anything, they keep shuffling their military leaders until they find ones who are up to the challenge. They do not get hung up on tradition and reputation. (Though one difficulty for a democracy is that after the crisis is over, they often do get hung up on reputation: they have a tendency to reward their military heroes with political office.) Yet even long wars pose their problems for democracies. Just as democracies don't know when to start fighting, they don't know when to stop. "There are two things that a democratic people will always have trouble doing," Tocqueville wrote. "Beginning a war and ending it."[20]

Tocqueville could not be confident that a really serious war would be good for a democracy like the United States. There was always the risk that the short-term weaknesses of democracy in action would prove fatal. But there was also the risk that in a long war, a democracy would resume its tendency to drift. American democracy had only fought one major war by this point in its existence, the War of Independence, and the evidence was mixed.[21] The United States won that war against an aristocratic rival, but it was a close-run thing. Moreover, Tocqueville writes, "as the struggle was prolonged, one saw individual selfishness reappear." Taxes dried up, and so too did volunteers for the army. Wars, especially long wars, are dangerous because they can breed fatalism as well as challenge it. As a result, Tocqueville says that it is very hard to be sure "what degree of effort a democracy is capable of in times of national crisis." It would depend not only on how long the crisis went on, but also on the extent to which individuals were willing to see their own fate bound up with the fate of their nation.

> To judge what sacrifices democracies know how to impose on themselves, one must therefore await the time when the American nation is obliged to put half the revenue from goods into the hands of government, like England, or throw a twentieth of its population on the field of battle at once, as France has done.[22]

That time would come, and sooner than Tocqueville might have imagined.

Wishing a long crisis on a democracy to allow it to display its advantages was inherently dangerous. But there was another problem with the idea that a crisis might wake a democracy up to its strengths. Democracies are very bad at knowing when a real crisis is upon them. This was not because they are oblivious to danger. It was because they are oversensitive to it. The secure position of the United States did not stop Americans from treating every little drama as though it were a crisis. Democracies always include plenty of people who think disaster is just around the corner. Freedom of speech includes the freedom to panic needlessly. As Tocqueville discovered on his American journey, democratic life is a succession of crises that turn out to be nothing of the sort.

The most visible of these fake crises come around as regularly as clockwork: they are called elections. In a chapter in *Democracy in America* titled (with deliberate irony) "The Crisis of the Election," Tocqueville describes the ritualized hysteria that accompanied these events.

As the election approaches, intrigue becomes more active, agitation more lively and more widespread . . . The entire nation
falls into a feverish state; the election is then the daily text of
the public papers, the subject of particular conversations, the
goal of all reasoning, the object of all thoughts, the sole interest of the present.

As soon as fortune has pronounced, it is true, this ardour is
dissipated, everything becomes calm, and the river, one moment overflowed, returns peacefully to its bed. But should one
not be astonished that the storm could have arisen?[23]

This is the other side of democratic drift: it goes along with
a lot of surface activity. If drift were simply a passive state
of mind, it would be easier to argue that crises might be
useful in waking up democracies. But Tocqueville knew that
democracies never really go to sleep. If anything, they are in
a state of near permanent wakefulness, which helps to give
them their manic, jittery quality. It means they are always
on the lookout for a crisis. But it also means that almost all
the crises they anticipate turn out to be illusions.

Elections remain the characteristic sham crises of democratic life, both for their regularity and for their transience.
It is routine to describe any election as a turning point ("the
most important choice for a generation," etc.). It is also routine to discover, once the election is over, that nothing much
has changed. Every now and then an election comes along
that really is a turning point. But it is also characteristic of
democracies, as we shall see, that these are the changes they
tend not to notice at the time.

As Tocqueville says, the main culprits in this charade are
the newspapers. It is the job of any newspaper (at least, any

newspaper that wants to attract readers and make money) to talk up a crisis. You can't have a democracy without a lively, argumentative press. But the very liveliness of the press made it hard for people to know when they should really be paying attention. Tocqueville found American newspapers horribly vulgar and extremely excitable. "The spirit of the journalist in America," he wrote, "is to attack coarsely, without preparation and without art, the passions of those whom he addresses, to set aside principles in order to grab men." He went on: "One must deplore such an abuse of thought . . . but one cannot conceal that the political effects of the license of the press contribute indirectly to the maintenance of public tranquillity." After a while, people get so used to the noise of a free press that they hardly notice it. Each little explosion of anger soon passes, to be replaced by another one. As a result, "the views expressed by journalists have so to speak no weight in the eyes of readers."[24] Newspapers, like elections, underscored how much crisis talk was a part of the routine of democratic life, and therefore how little it signified.

Newspaper hysteria was only part of the general problem: crisis might be good for a democracy, but democracies are not good at recognizing crises. They overreact; they underreact; they lack a sense of proportion. That is why it was so hard to know what sort of crisis would enable a democracy to learn its lesson. If the crisis turned out to be so bad that no one could doubt it was real, then there was always a risk that it would end in disaster. If it did not end in disaster, then there was always a risk that it would be filed along with all the other overblown crises of democratic life as a false alarm. And even the real crises—the ones no one could doubt—were hard to learn from. If democracy doesn't survive, you've learned your lesson, but at an unacceptable cost. If democracy does survive, then you may learn the lesson that democracy can survive any crisis. Instead of making you wise, recovering from your mistakes can make you reckless.

There was another way democracies might learn from a crisis, however. It did not have to be their crisis. They could learn their lesson from other people's mistakes. They could look at democratic disasters happening elsewhere in the world and think: we need to make sure that doesn't happen to us. Tocqueville thought that American democracy might benefit in this way from greater knowledge of what was happening in Europe, just as he hoped that Europeans could learn from the experience of America.

One reason he had written *Democracy in America* was to allow his French readers to see democracy at work in circumstances different from their own, in order to gain a sense of perspective. They would at least see that it *could* work. America, with its ability to survive its mistakes, might teach Europeans that democracy was still possible. Europe, with its enduring monarchies and its history of democratic failures, might teach Americans that democracy was not inevitable. They would see that it doesn't *always* work. A world in which democracy existed at different stages of development, and with very different chances of success, helped to break up the view that God's plan for the universe was a done deal. The future still lay open.

But were democracies capable of learning from other people's mistakes? American democracy, in consequence of being isolated from the rest of the world, was insular, provincial, self-regarding. It had real difficulty seeing beyond its own immediate horizons. When democracies run up against foreign experiences, they are liable to view them as a threat, rather than as an education. What's more, there was no guarantee that any democracy could be entirely isolated from the ill effects of democratic failure somewhere else. Even the United States, cut off from the rest of the world, could not assume that the problems of other states were simply morality tales. It was always possible that the effects of a European crisis might spill over into the United States. And then it would be America's crisis too.

Was it worth taking a chance on crisis politics in order to inject a sense of purpose back into a democracy? In the end, Tocqueville and Mill fell out over the answer to this question.[25] The break came not because of anything that happened in America, but because of what was happening in Europe. In late 1840 Britain and France came to the brink of war in an imperial dispute over Sudan. Mill was dead against the war. Tocqueville was enthusiastic. Mill thought any such war between two fledgling democracies was stupid and the politicians who were stoking it criminal. He reserved his greatest contempt for the bellicose British foreign secretary Palmerston, of whom he wrote to Tocqueville, with real venom: "I would gladly walk twenty miles to see him hanged, especially if Thiers [his counterpart in the French foreign ministry] were to be strung up with him."[26] No democracy could possibly be educated at the hands of scoundrels like these and their hysterical supporters in the press.

Tocqueville saw things very differently. Like many Frenchmen, he did not think Britain, for all its liberal traditions, was much of a democracy anyway. It was still a fundamentally aristocratic society, and men like Palmerston were its typical representatives. France was much more of a real democracy (that is, further along the path toward equality of conditions) but one that had got stuck in a rut and lost all sense of its own powers in the long, miserable hangover from the revolution. It needed something to shake it out of a torpor that came all too easily to the French cast of mind. This was not going to be achieved by a spirit of international cooperation. As he wrote scoldingly to Mill in 1841: "One cannot let a nation that is democratically constituted like ours . . . take up early the habit of sacrificing its grandeur to its repose. It is not healthy to allow such a nation to console itself by making railroads."[27] Tocqueville thought that democracies need a real crisis now and then to show them what they are capable of. Mill thought that wishing a crisis on any democracy was deeply irresponsible, knowing what they are capable of in a crisis.

Tocqueville and Mill were on opposite sides in this dispute, but the argument reflected the two sides of their shared view of democracy. The things that democracies are good at (commerce, comfort) are bad for democracy, because they breed narrow-mindedness and complacency; the things that democracies are bad at (crisis management, international confrontation) are good for democracy, because they might broaden its horizons and shake that sense of complacency. There is no easy way out of this dilemma. The reason Mill and Tocqueville could not agree about war between Britain and France was not simply because they were on different sides. It was because in a crisis there are always two sides to a democracy—good and bad—and it can be very hard to reconcile them.

A Guide to the Future

A lot of what Tocqueville said about democracy and crisis was unsystematic: his thoughts on the subject are scattered haphazardly across his writings. He is not always clear and he is not always consistent. Moreover, what he said was essentially guesswork. There was simply not the evidence to know how democracies would cope in critical situations. America had the functioning democracy but not the crises. Europe had the crises but not the functioning democracies.

Nevertheless, Tocqueville's reflections provide a relatively clear set of predictions about how democracies might fare in future. In general, democracies ought to be better at coping with crises than rival systems because they are more adaptable. But there are three problems. First, democracies are not good at recognizing crisis situations: all the surface noise of democratic politics makes them insensitive to genuine turning points. Second, crises need to get really bad before democracies can show their long-term strengths, but when they get really bad, there is more scope for democracies to make serious mistakes. Third, when democracies survive a crisis, they may not learn from the experience. All crises generate lessons about the mistakes to avoid in future. But democracies are capable of taking a different lesson: that no matter what mistakes they make, they will be all right in the end.

The nineteenth century provided limited opportunities to put these hypotheses to the test. The great crisis of French democracy came in 1848, the year of revolutions across Europe. Tocqueville, who had by now become a moderately successful politician, was close to the heart of these events (he ended up, for a brief time, as France's foreign minister). Nonetheless, the crisis turned into a disaster, both for him personally and, as he saw it, for his country. It woke up French democracy in the wrong way: not to its potential, but to its inadequacies. French politics was caught between the promise of revolutionary transformation and a hankering for autocratic certainties. Tocqueville felt himself buffeted by political forces beyond his power to control. He ended up caught by the thing he most despised: fatalism. He wrote in 1850, having abandoned his political career: "I see myself without a compass, without a rudder and without oars on a sea whose coast I no longer perceive, and, tired from my vain agitation, I crouch at the bottom of the boat and await the future."[28]

Tocqueville died in 1859 and so he did not live to see the great crisis that engulfed American democracy two years later. In *Democracy in America*, he had been quite confident that the festering sore of slavery would not end up in a prolonged civil war. Democracies, he felt, were insulated from the worst effects of civil conflict because the population would not tolerate the disruption: here democratic passivity was a blessing in disguise.[29] Nevertheless, passivity was only one side of democracy. As time went on, Tocqueville became increasingly dismayed by the other side of American political life: its petulance and its volatility. Far from learning from its mistakes, American democracy seemed to be becoming more and more childish and obstinate. As he wrote to an American friend in 1856: "What is certain is that for some years you have strangely abused the advantages given to you by God, advantages which have allowed you to commit great errors with impunity. . . . Viewed from this side of the ocean, you have become the untamed child."[30] American democracy looked increasingly uneducable. Its childishness was allowing it to drift toward the abyss.

The crisis, when it came, turned out to be far longer, bloodier, and more destructive than anything Tocqueville could have imagined. Fours years of civil war could have proved fatal to American democracy, but in the end they did not. The republic adapted and it survived. Was this the moment when American democracy grew up? In 1888 the British lawyer and diplomat James Bryce published a book called the *American Commonwealth*, which was intended as a fifty-years-on update of Tocqueville, designed to take account of all the things that Tocqueville either couldn't have known about or had ignored. Bryce decided that American democracy had become more stable, equable, and mature than the one Tocqueville had encountered. Tocqueville had only known American democracy when it was still young, and, as Bryce puts it, "flushed with self-confidence, intoxicated with the exuberance of its own freedom." This had given Tocqueville the wrong idea.

> The masses were so persuaded of their immense superiority to all other peoples, past as well as present, that they would listen to nothing but flattery, and their intolerance spread from politics to every other sphere. . . . As the nation grew, it purged away these faults of youth and inexperience, and the stern discipline of the Civil War taught it sobriety, and in giving it something to be really proud of, cleared away the fumes of self-conceit.[31]

It had been a hard school, but civil war had taught American democracy its lesson.

Now Bryce detected a different problem. American political life had settled to a new, more stable pattern. The threat it faced was from what Bryce called "the fatalism of the multitude," which was Tocqueville's tyranny of the majority stripped of its anger and impatience. Americans had acquired sufficient evidence of the underlying strength of their political institutions that they tended to take their success for granted. This had produced an "optimism which has underrated the inherent difficulties of politics and the inherent failings of human nature."[32] Americans were no longer wild and arrogant. But they had grown complacent about their ability to survive whatever the world might throw at them. They had acquired a renewed faith in their democratic destiny that was the more robust for having been put to the test. In that sense, American democracy had not really learned its lesson. Bryce's update of Tocqueville takes us back to where Tocqueville ended up.

As Bryce shows, it is possible to read the great crises of nineteenth-century democracy as confirmation of some of Tocqueville's insights into the democratic predicament. It is very hard to learn the right lesson. Failure breeds despair; success breeds complacency. The line between the two is a fine one. Both are manifestations of democratic fatalism, which means success and failure often go hand in hand. But Bryce was not typical. Late nineteenth-century views of democracy more often conformed to the radical extremes. People were still looking for the underlying truth about democracy and waiting for the crisis that would reveal it. From a European perspective, 1848 was unfinished business and the American civil war remained a sideshow. This was the age of revolutionary socialism and of rising nationalism, of extreme democracy and extreme antidemocracy. The political thinkers from this period who still get read are the world-historical Germans, Marx and Nietzsche, the apostles of democratic transformation and exposure, the sham smashers. These men are treated as the prophets of the coming century of revolution and war. No one reaches for Bryce's *American Commonwealth* looking for the key to the future.

Yet Bryce's view from the late nineteenth century proved to be the truly prescient one. Marx and Nietzsche between them helped to shape the crises of the twentieth century: theirs are the ideas people turn to when they are looking for political transformation. But the cumulative effect of these same crises fits the pattern laid out by Bryce and by Tocqueville before him: failure leads to success, success leads to failure and the truths that might close the gap between the two are always somewhere out of reach. We still read Marx and Nietzsche because we want crises to be moments of truth. What Tocqueville reveals is that moments of truth for democracy are an illusion. Democracy muddles on through war and revolutionary change, its confusions ineradicable and its progress inexorable. It never fully wakes up and it never fully grows up. And it leads to where we are now.

To see how we have arrived at this point I am going to tell the story of seven crises for established democracies over the past hundred years. The democratic crises of the nineteenth century were too haphazard to bear Tocqueville out: democracy was not yet established enough to reveal the ways in which it was set in its ways. It was the twentieth century that would prove him right, starting with the war to end all wars and the world-historical triumph of democracy of 1918, which turned out to be nothing of the sort.

CHAPTER 1

1918

False Dawn

THE CRISIS

ON JUNE 30, 1918, THE EXACT HALFWAY POINT OF THE year, the French writer Édouard Estaunié declared that the struggle for civilization was over. The Great War, which had been dragging on for nearly four years, was lost. The Germans had achieved a decisive breakthrough and advanced to within fifty miles of Paris, near enough to set up an incessant bombardment of the city. Soon Paris would fall, since there was nothing to stop the German army from pressing home its advantage against demoralized opponents. The Germans would find themselves entering a ghost town; already many Parisians had fled and the city increasingly felt like a morgue. *Plus ça change*. Victory went to the people who wanted it more and were prepared to do whatever it takes to get there. In the struggle between barbarism and civilization throughout history, Estaunié lamented, barbarism always triumphed in the end.[1]

But Estaunié was wrong on two counts. First, this was not a fight between civilization and barbarism. Instead, it had turned into something different, a fight between democracy and autocracy. Civilizations are not always democracies; democracies are not always civilized. Second, the fight was not lost. In fact, it was just about to be won. Within a few weeks the German advance would be decisively checked, and within a few months the German army would be in full-blown retreat. Well before the end of the year the German and the Austro-Hungarian Empires had both collapsed, their leadership in disarray, their political systems overthrown. France, Great Britain, and the United States were about to win a crushing victory. Democracy was on the verge of the greatest triumph in its history.

What Estaunié's cosmic gloom captures is just how unexpected this triumph was. During the first half of 1918 there existed a widespread feeling that in the final struggle between autocracy and democracy, autocracy was proving itself the stronger. The democracies were not gripped by panic or outright defeatism, but by a sense of debilitating drift. There was a long-standing suspicion that they lacked the resolve for total war. Paris was not being depopulated in a mad rush; instead, people were melting away, taking trips to the country from which they did not return. The British and French armies were not in outright retreat; they were simply being pushed back step-by-step. The politicians appeared powerless to turn the tide. The best they could do was cling on, hoping for better days. How could they match the remorseless sense of purpose of Germany's military rulers?

As it turned out, they did not need to. The democracies won the war by being better able to withstand defeat and disappointment than their enemies. They survived their setbacks in 1918 and turned them to their advantage in ways the German regime could not. Not knowing how to force the issue went along with not knowing when they were beaten. The sense of crisis is permanent in democracies and for that reason rarely definitive. When crisis engulfed the German state, it proved terminal.

The feeling some experienced during the first half of 1918 that the failings of democracy were being definitively exposed was therefore an illusion: the democracies were stumbling toward victory rather than defeat. However, this meant that the idea victory represented a moment of truth for democracy was also an illusion. The democracies had not seized hold of their destiny at a time of crisis. They had simply held on. The truth about successful democracies is that they never arrive at their moment of truth.

Still the temptation to see victory for democracy in 1918 as a historical watershed proved almost irresistible, especially for the people whose intervention in the war had done most to turn it into a struggle for democracy: the Americans. If some French intellectuals had a tendency to view the prospect of defeat in cosmic terms, some American intellectuals had a tendency to see victory in the same light. This was an opportunity to remake the world: to make it safe for democracy. The best known of these intellectuals was the American president, Woodrow Wilson. Yet Wilson had few illusions about democracy. Before becoming a politician he had been a full-time political scientist. He was a student of Tocqueville and a colleague of Bryce. He knew how hard it was to capture the truth about democracy at any given moment, and he understood the pitfalls of trying. But this knowledge was not enough to save him from disaster. Recognizing the pitfalls did not prevent Wilson from falling into the trap.

The year 1918 remains one of the defining crises in the history of modern democracy. The experiences of that year show how quickly extreme democratic pessimism can turn into unjustified optimism. Both are the product of the quest for the underlying truth about democracy. Democracies tend to overreach themselves when they outlast or defeat autocratic rivals, because they assume the truth about democracy has finally been revealed. It hasn't. What eventually gets revealed instead is the inherent difficulty democracies have in seizing the moment. The triumph of democracy in 1918 was not illusory, but it was inaccessible. Democracies turn defeats into victories. However, because they misapprehend what they have done, they also turn victories into defeats.

AUTOCRACY VERSUS DEMOCRACY

For the First World War to result in a triumph for democracy it first had to turn into a crisis for democracy. In order to turn into a crisis for democracy it first had to turn into a fight for democracy. That is what had happened in 1917.

The original conflict that began in August 1914 did not make sense as a fight for democracy because the democracies were not all lined up on one side and the autocracies on the other. The world's preeminent democracy, the United States, had remained neutral under the leadership of Wilson, who had no pressing wish to get dragged into Europe's atavistic blood feuds. The vast majority of the American people felt the same. One reason why most Americans had little appetite to join in was that Britain and France were fighting in alliance with the most autocratic state in Europe, czarist Russia. Russia's presence on the "democratic" side made a mockery of the idea that this was a war of political principle. Indeed, fighting the czar helped to persuade many German democrats that theirs was the true struggle for European freedom against Asiatic barbarism. From both an American and a German perspective, the British and French were not democrats. They were just imperialist hypocrites.

The Russian revolution of February 1917 changed all that. The abdication of the czar and his replacement by a provisional constitutional government committed to holding free elections was heralded as a victory for democracy. It made sense of the wider conflict in a way that even its critics could understand. The Irish playwright George Bernard Shaw, who had been against the war from the beginning, wrote to his friend, the Russian writer Maxim Gorki: "I regard the revolution as such a gain to humanity that it not only at last justifies the Franco-Anglo-Russian alliance (which in the days of tsardom was a disgrace to Western democracy) but it justifies the whole war."[2] The Russian revolution helped to precipitate America's entry into the contest. The immediate trigger was the German High

Command's decision in January 1917 to resume sinking American ships. But the moral impetus came from Russia. As Woodrow Wilson told Congress in April when he made the announcement that America was taking up arms on the side of democracy: "Does not every American feel that assurance has been added to our hope for the future peace of the world by the wonderful and heartening things that have been happening in Russia?"[3] This was the speech in which Wilson declared that America's aim should be to create a world made safe for democracy.

In a war that had lasted far longer than anyone expected, the Russian revolution looked like the denouement. The journalist Walter Lippmann, who was about to leave the staff of the *New Republic* to start work at the White House, wrote after he heard Wilson's speech: "When Russia became a Republic, and the American Republic became an enemy, the German Empire was isolated before mankind as the last refuge of autocracy."[4] Russia's provisional government was now pledged to continue the war in the name of democratic freedom. The revolution had thrown up a fresh democratic hero in its youthful, idealistic leader, Alexander Kerensky. In the West, there was a brief cult of Kerensky, who became the symbol of a new democratic optimism. Almost everyone found something to admire in him. The always-hyperbolic Bernard Shaw, somewhat ominously, said that what he liked about "the boy braggart" Kerensky was that he reminded him of himself.

In reality, Kerensky was a thirty-six-year-old lawyer with little political experience who had been propelled to power on the back of his oratorical gifts. He had a mesmerizing speaking style, which drove crowds into paroxysms of delight, especially the women, who would wail and swoon along with their idol. But he lacked political judgment. In the summer of 1917 Kerensky decided to gamble everything on a military offensive against the encroaching Germans, putting his faith in the power of democratic ideals to motivate his forces. He called on Russia's soldiers to prove "there is strength, not weakness, in freedom."[5] Unfortunately, they did just the opposite. The campaign turned into a disaster, as the Germans routed the ill-equipped and poorly led Russian troops. It turned out that the Russians were not drunk on freedom; many of them were simply drunk.

After this fiasco, the democratic optimism of the spring began to shrivel, in the West as well as the East. Kerensky's new democracy seemed to confirm the old prejudices about democratic ill discipline and recklessness. He represented the triumph of democratic hope over experience. His failure opened the door for Lenin's much more hardheaded Bolsheviks to take over. Lenin announced that he would give the Russian people what they really wanted, an end to the war, and he commenced peace negotiations with the Germans. A Russian exit from the war in the East greatly increased the chances that the democracies would lose in the West, since the Central powers would no longer be fighting on two fronts. Russia's democratic revolution was turning out to be a disaster for democracy.

While the Kerensky cult faded in the West, another cult was on the rise: the cult of Erich Ludendorff, the implacable quartermaster of the German war effort. Ludendorff came to symbolize what the democracies were lacking. As the war dragged on through 1917 the performance of the Western democracies appeared increasingly shambolic. There were mutinies in the Allied armies, endless squabbling among the politicians, and repeated changes of personnel at the top (France went through three prime ministers in a matter of months). For all his fine words, Wilson was proving very slow at getting American troops and equipment to Europe. In November, the ill-disciplined Italian army broke and ran in the face of an Austro-Hungarian advance at Caporetto, seeming to show once again that there was weakness not strength in freedom. (The resolve of the Austro-Hungarian forces, which had been notoriously flaky, was stiffened by the presence of German troops.) Meanwhile, the German state, by now effectively a military dictatorship under the control of Paul von Hindenburg and Ludendorff, began to gather its forces for the final assault. Democracy was on the retreat. It was autocracy that was on the march.

Earlier in the year, the *Atlantic Monthly* had sent the journalist H. L. Mencken to Germany to profile Ludendorff. Mencken was a self-styled political iconoclast, on the model of his hero Nietzsche, whose ideas he had first introduced to the American reading public a decade earlier. Mencken revered Nietzsche as the great "sham-smasher" of democratic pieties. When the war began in 1914 Mencken came out on the side of the Germans, whose political system he admired for rewarding men on the basis of strength of will, not passing popularity. Ludendorff's rise to supremacy confirmed this. As Mencken happily noted: "The 1914 edition of *Wer Ist's*, the German *Who's Who*, does not mention Ludendorff at all. At the time it was published he was a simple colonel on the German staff."[6] Now he was "the real boss of the country—perhaps the best man Germany has produced since Bismarck." But still very little was known about him. "He is credited with no apothegms, no themes, no remarks whatever. He remains a man of mystery."[7] The contrast Mencken wanted to draw was with Wilson, a politician he despised. Wilson, the democratic man of many slogans, was all crowd-pleasing talk, all sententious philosophizing, but no action.

Mencken was touching on an anxiety that had been building throughout the war. How could the democracies, which chose their leaders on the basis of their ability to pander to the public, match the meritocratic German system, which rewarded success on the battlefield, not in the charade of electoral politics?[8] War had brought Ludendorff to the top. The United States was still being led by a man who had won reelection in 1916 by promising to keep America out of the war. Wilson had shown himself to be adaptable to the point of absurdity. In a straight confrontation between the systems of government these two men represented, Mencken felt sure which was going to come out on top.

Anxiety about the inadequacies of democracy reached its peak in early 1918. Were the democracies ruthless enough to compete with their rivals in a fight to the death? Did they have sufficient will to power? Or would the democratic propensity to patch up and make do and muddle along destroy them in the end? In the East the men of action, Hindenburg and Ludendorff, Lenin and Trotsky, were deciding their own fate and perhaps the fate of the entire world. In the West, the democratic politicians were waiting to see what would turn up. The autocrats were in charge. What else did the democrats have to offer?

Two Speeches

To start with, they had what democratic politicians always have in limitless supply: more words.

As 1917 turned into 1918, the world's attention was focused on the Belorussian city of Brest-Litovsk, where German and Russian representatives were negotiating the terms of Russia's exit from the war. The leaders of the Western democracies had two overriding fears about what might emerge from these discussions. The first was that the Bolsheviks would give too much away to the Germans, thereby shifting the balance of power in the military conflict. The second was that the Bolsheviks would demoralize the democratic war effort by pouring scorn on it. The Bolsheviks had contempt for Western democracy, which they saw as an obvious sham. Trotsky used the occasion of the peace negotiations to publish details of the secret treaties between the czarist regime and its Western allies in an attempt to show that all the belligerents were as bad as each other: scheming, devious and acquisitive. "In exposing to the entire world the work of the ruling classes," Trotsky had announced back in November, "as expressed in the secret diplomatic documents, we address the workers with the call which forms the unshakeable foundation of our foreign policy: 'Proletarians of all countries, unite!'"[9]

In early January 1918, *Pravda* spelled out where it stood on Wilson's professed aim of making the world safe for democracy. It was a sick joke. The American government had entered the war not for the sake of "right and justice" but to promote "the cynical interests of the New York stock market."

Mr. Wilson serves American war industry just as Kaiser Wil-
helm serves the iron and steel industry of Germany. One gives
his speeches in the style of a Quaker Republican—the other
wraps himself in the mists of Prussian-Protestant-Absolutist
phraseology. But at bottom it is all the same.[10]

Democratic leaders in the West were not worried that their
populations might be reading *Pravda*. But they did fear the
destabilizing effects of the basic Bolshevik message: that the
war was a conspiracy against democracy. In both London
and Washington it was decided that the moment had come
to restate the reasons why the democracies were fighting this
miserable war. They had to counter the idea that beneath the
surface the belligerents were all as bad as each other.

The British made their case first. On January 5 the prime
minister, David Lloyd George, gave a speech to a gathering
of trade unionists in which he set out the Allied war aims.
He emphatically rejected the Bolshevik claim that there was
no moral difference between the two sides in this war. The
Central powers were seeking territorial gain and material
rewards for violence. The democracies were simply trying
to defend themselves. Lloyd George declared that "the democracy of this country means to stand to the last by the
democracies of France and Italy and all our other Allies."[11]
So this was a war of democratic solidarity. The aim was
to undo the wrongs done to them all, which required the
restoration of territorial or material losses caused by the
war. It had to be made clear that no democracy could be the
victim of military aggression.

Lloyd George's speech was designed to sound quite reasonable: who could object to democracy defending itself? In

that spirit, he paid lip service to many ideas that were usually associated with Woodrow Wilson, including national
self-determination and an international league to resolve
future conflicts. But Wilson was not fooled. On January 8
he delivered his own statement of war aims to Congress, in
which he listed fourteen principles for a democratic peace.
It was intended as a rebuff to Lloyd George as much as
to Lenin.

Wilson's "Fourteen Points" speech retains its reputation
as one of the twentieth century's defining statements of
democratic idealism. Yet nowhere in his list of proposals
did Wilson actually use the word *democracy* (unlike Lloyd
George, who peppered his speech with it). Lloyd George had
wanted to explain why democracy would only be safe if it
emerged victorious from the war. For Wilson, this made the
cause of democracy too dependent on its short-term prospects. He still wanted to win the war, of course. But he did
not want anyone to think that a victory *by* the democracies
was the same thing as a victory *for* democracy. That would
come later, and would take time. Democracy was the path to
peace—Wilson was confident that established democracies
would never go to war with each other—but it was a long
road. Nothing would happen in a rush.

Throughout the shifts in his political stance on the war,
Wilson had retained a core political philosophy, which had
been with him since his days as a student of politics. Wilson had never believed in sudden moments of democratic
transformation. Instead, he thought democracy needed
time to establish itself and take advantage of its underlying
strengths. He felt that Americans instinctively recognized
this. Much of the rest of the world did not. There was a racial

strain to this line of thinking: Anglo-Saxons had the temperament for democracy, but more excitable groups got carried away with it and went too far. Americans, for all their restless energy, understood that democracy required patience. However, Wilson did not simply believe it was enough to trust in what he, like Tocqueville, called "democratic providence." He also believed that democracy needed strong leadership. The steady progress of American democracy was liable to get bogged down in mediocrity. Whereas excitable democracies needed calming down, stable democracies needed waking up to their true potential. To this end, Wilson believed in putting crises to use. They were an opportunity to reassert the terms of democratic progress.[12]

The Fourteen Points speech fitted with this political philosophy. It was an act of strong leadership by a man who did not want to be boxed in. The fourteen points themselves were designed to provide the framework for peace: a space in which democracy could grow. It would be achieved by "public diplomacy" (that is, no more secret treaties) (point 1), freedom of the seas (point 2), free trade (point 3), disarmament (point 4), national self-determination (point 5), the settlement of territorial disputes (points 6–13), and a new "association of nations" to resolve future conflicts (point 14).[13] In essence, Wilson was trying to set a threshold for a new democratic world order that was neither too high nor too low. Lenin's threshold was clearly far too high: on the Bolshevik worldview democratic transformation could only be achieved by means of a revolutionary rupture from everything that had gone before. But Lloyd George had set the threshold too low. He had tied too much to the mere fact of victory and to the restitution of wrongs done to the democracies currently in existence. Wilson was interested in the democracies yet to come.

For a while, it seemed to work. Wilson's long-term vision struck an immediate chord. It was well received by the war-weary populations of Europe, who were attracted by its flexible, accommodating conception of what might come after the misery was over. It allowed people to dream a little. But it had no impact on the people who had first provoked it: the Russians negotiating at Brest-Litovsk. In the end, the Bolsheviks did one of the two things the Allies had feared. They gave up the fight. When a peace treaty was finally signed on March 3, it became clear that the Germans had insisted on total surrender, and that Lenin had complied with their wishes. The ultimate price of peace for the Russians was the loss of huge swaths of territory, including much of their industrial base. The Central powers were now in a position to turn their attention westward in the pursuit of final victory.[14]

This was very bad news for the democracies. But it had one benefit. It meant the other fear of the Western allies, that the Bolsheviks would undermine the will of their populations to fight, receded. Brest-Litovsk made it abundantly clear why the democracies needed to continue the struggle: to avoid being on the receiving end of a peace like that. As the British socialist intellectual Beatrice Webb wrote in her diary a few days after the terms of Russia's surrender had been announced: "The Tolstoyans [that is, the pacifists] will blindly and fanatically continue their cry for peace at any price. But the men and women who are believers in democratic equality between man and man and race and race will become more and more in favour of continuing the war."[15]

On the day war had been declared in August 1914 Webb had confided to her diary: "The best result would be that every nation should be soundly beaten and no-one victorious. That might bring us all to reason."[16] Nearly four years later, peace without victory was a luxury democracy could no longer afford.

The prospect of disaster gave the democracies a renewed sense of purpose, which helped to trump some of the differences between them. Wilson speeded up the deployment of American troops to Europe and put his peace plans on hold. The Russian catastrophe had clarified what was at stake. But clarity came at a price. Nicer distinctions got lost. It was no longer possible to distinguish between democracy's short-term goals and its long-term prospects. For now, there was nothing to choose between them: if democracy could not hold on in the short term, its long-term prospects were moot. But something else that became increasingly hard to see was the distinction Lloyd George had insisted on between the conduct of the democracies and that of their enemies. This was total war in the pursuit of final victory, which made the belligerents difficult to tell apart. Democracy was starting to look a lot like autocracy, or perhaps it was the other way around. The Allies and the Central powers were mimicking each other in their reliance on censorship, propaganda, and the mass mobilization of their populations.

The war had become a contest between public relations machines alongside the military machines. Much of the battle focused on the effort to persuade civilians to do their duty by buying war bonds. In early 1918 the Germans launched their eighth bond drive, which was needed to fund the spring offensive that Ludendorff told the German people would bring them final victory. The success of the war loan, Ludendorff announced, would "prove our will to power, which is the source of everything." The US Treasury responded with a massive publicity campaign to persuade American citizens to fund the war to the limit of their resources, in the run-up to the third Liberty Bond auction in April 1918. The Committee on Public Information (CPI) (the newly founded propaganda wing of the US government) quoted Ludendorff back to the American people, telling them "to prove our own will to power. . . . The failure of a single issue of government bonds would be worse for America than a disaster on the field of battle."[17] CPI publicists went out of their way to emphasize that democracy needed to be as tough as autocracy if it wanted to defeat it. "I am Public Opinion," one Liberty Bond poster declared. "All men fear me! If you have the money to buy and do not buy, I will make this 'No Man's Land' for you." Here was Tocqueville's tyranny of the majority, co-opted by the government's propagandists to ensure the majority did what it was told.

This melding of the two rival political systems into one was noticed on both sides. Randolph Bourne, Wilson's most eloquent critic on the American left, complained that American democracy was being Germanized. By 1918 Uncle Sam had become just another version of the idealized *Vaterland*. "A people at war," Bourne wrote, "have become in the most literal sense obedient, respectful, trustful children again, full of that naïve faith in the all-wisdom and all-power of the adult who takes care of them."[18] This wasn't democracy any more. It was a palliative designed to keep people quiet while their fate was being settled for them.

Meanwhile, in Germany, the novelist Thomas Mann com-plained that the German state was being Americanized. It was turning into just another mass political regime, with all its attendant tricks and idiocies. "Only mass politics, demo-cratic politics,'" Mann wrote in early 1918, "that is a politics that has little or nothing to do with the higher intellectual life of the nation, is possible today—this is the knowledge that the government of the German *Reich* has acquired in the course of the war."[19] Mann was contemptuous of the idea of some future "democratic peace," which he regarded as an obvious absurdity. "The rule of the people ensures peace and justice?" he asked scornfully. "The most certain safe-guard of peace is 'democratic control'? That's what I'd like to know. . . . Did you see August 1914, the London mob dancing round Nelson's Column? . . . Responsibility!"[20] Still, he had no doubt that democracy was the wave of the future. And what did that mean? "Affairs, scandals, political-symbolic conflicts of the times, magnificent crises that inflame the burgher in alternating dances, a new one every year—this is the way we will have it, the way we will live every day."[21] De-mocracy would be the winner in this war, but only because the war had turned politics into a giant, empty charade.

THE TURNAROUND

What Mann did not believe possible was that Germany might actually lose the war. Democracy would triumph by default, not on the battlefield. Like many German nationalists, Mann's worst-case scenario in early 1918 was some botched peace negotiated on the basis of Wilson's idiotic fourteen points. After Russia's capitulation, the idea of military defeat had become unthinkable. It seemed more remote than ever when, on March 21, Ludendorff launched his spring offensive. For the first time in the war the Central powers now had more divisions massed on the western front than the Allies. This concentration of forces enabled the German army to break through the British and French lines. The Allies suffered heavy losses in fighting that was bloody even by the standards of this ghastly conflict. Within a few weeks the situation was sufficiently desperate that the British field marshal, Douglas Haig, issued his famous order: "With our backs to the wall and believing in the justice of our cause, each one of us must fight on to the end." The cult of the omniscient Ludendorff grew. In the words of the *New Republic*: "Never since the war began have the Germans seemed so much like Supermen as they do at this moment."[22]

The German advances of March and April were eventually checked. But that was not the end of it. A massive new offensive was launched in May, and soon the German forces were closing in on Paris. While Parisians fled their city, in London tales of conspiracy and paranoia abounded. Defeatism was in the air, which was being preemptively blamed on anarchists and homosexuals. In the United States serious consideration was given to postponing the midterm elections scheduled for November, something that had never happened before (not even during the Civil War). Pessimists were beginning to wonder whether the game was up. Optimists were hopeful that if the Allies could hold on for a year or more, then maybe in 1919, more likely in 1920, they could start to turn the tide, once the weight of American manpower and resources was able to tell.

Then in July the turnaround occurred, perhaps the most dramatic in the history of modern warfare. The speed of the German collapse took both sides by surprise. Ludendorff, certainly, could not believe it. On August 8 his troops suffered their biggest reverse of the war, losing thirty thousand men at the Battle of Amiens. Ludendorff christened this "the black day of the German army," and he was plunged into immediate despair. Within the space of a few weeks the master strategist was exposed as a fraud: when his military offensive failed to achieve the decisive breakthrough, it turned out he had no plan B, just endless, futile reiterations of plan A. In September he suffered a nervous breakdown and had to be packed off to a sanatorium, where his doctors encouraged him to sing folk songs to keep his spirits up. It did not work.

But if Germany's military rulers were unprepared for defeat, the democratic leaders of the West were unprepared for victory. As late as September strategists on both sides of the Atlantic were sticking to plans that envisaged the war going on at least into 1919, and probably into 1920, by which time massed American reinforcements would be able to ram their advantage home. No one had any desire to see the American war machine, which was only now cranking into top gear, switched off prematurely. In late September the fourth Liberty Bond sale took place. The popular rallies that preceded it were greater than ever, and the propaganda was no less emphatic in its insistence that the fate of democracy hung in the balance. The life-and-death struggle for democracy continued, unaffected by the fact that German autocracy was already in its death throes.

It is a cliché of twentieth-century history that the spectacular turnaround in military fortunes in 1918 proved too much for the German people to cope with and laid the seeds for the stab-in-the-back legend that grew up afterward. How could an army that they had been told was about to win the war suddenly lose it, unless Jews and socialists had betrayed it? But the speed of the German collapse was hard for the winners to take in as well. How could the democracies that had been in such disarray in the late spring—displaying all their traditional weaknesses of indecision, backbiting, and incipient despair—have emerged so completely dominant by the autumn? On this side too it was tempting to look for some hidden explanation.

One possibility was that this had not been a victory for democracy at all. The democracies had only emerged on top by ditching their principles and behaving in a way that was as cruel and oppressive as their rivals. The conduct of the democracies in the final months of the war was certainly fearsome, both on and off the battlefield. The Allies were by now producing more, and more efficient, chemical weapons than the Central powers, and were showing no qualms about using them. It was the prospect of being obliterated by gas that did much to destroy the morale of the German army. At the same time, by this point in the conflict all the combatants were having to fight a new enemy: a deadly flu pandemic that was spreading rapidly through armies and civilian populations. It had become apparent to those in the know that large gatherings of any kind were deathtraps. Yet the US government continued to hold massive bond rallies, regardless of the dangers to public health. In late September more than two million people assembled in Philadelphia to hear government propagandists extol the virtues of democracy, in one of the biggest rallies of the war. Nothing was said of the risks they were running. Within days thousands of them were dead.[23]

Woodrow Wilson made no mention of the flu in any public pronouncements during 1918, and the Allied newspapers were forbidden from discussing it in detail (it became known as the "Spanish flu" because only in Spain, a noncombatant, was the press at liberty to report on the scale of the disaster). American troops were packed off to Europe in ships that made the spread of the disease inevitable; many became floating charnel houses. Ludendorff briefly became convinced that the flu would save him because it would sow panic among the Allies. His doctors, rightly, took this as further evidence that he had lost his mind. The democracies were by now far more disciplined and far more ruthless fighting machines than the Germans.

Whenever democracy survives a genuine crisis, it is tempting to think that this has only been achieved by a betrayal of democratic principles: it survives by ceasing to be itself. But this is too simplistic. The democracies did not win in 1918 merely by being more brutal than their enemies. They won by being more adaptable. In this respect, Tocqueville was right. In a long war two democratic tendencies will be in competition with each other: the tendency toward drift, which makes democracies passive and hard to rouse to the effort needed for victory, and the tendency toward experimentation, which makes democracies restless and eager to try something new. In the First World War, though it was a close-run thing, experimentation won out over drift.

The democracies proved themselves more adaptable militarily. Their armed forces performed poorly in the first three years of the war. They were badly led and set in their ways. But they did not remain like that. They were finally able to turn things around in 1918 by being far better than the Central powers at learning from their mistakes.[24] The democracies were also much more adaptable politically. They were able to accommodate the simmering discontent of their populations. This might cost them in the short run—democracies cannot focus their resources in the way autocracies can, because there are always so many different demands on them—but it was an advantage in the long run. Democracies are forced to make concessions to shifts in the public mood, however inconvenient. This means they have no choice but to be flexible.[25]

As Tocqueville said, nondemocratic regimes are good at achieving their short-term goals, but then they get stuck. They also get stuck with their leaders, which can be disastrous when things go wrong. Democracies often shuffle their leaders, which looks like indecision, but means they can keep going until they find the right one. France's fourth prime minister of 1917, Georges Clemenceau, was elevated to power late in the day and under chaotic circumstances (one reason for the delay was that France's president, Raymond Poincaré, disliked and distrusted him). He turned out to be the savior of his country. In the desperate spring of 1918 Clemenceau held his nerve and helped inspire the Allies to victory. Ludendorff, the silent master, was the destroyer of Germany. By the summer of 1918 it was clear he had run out of ideas, but there was no one to replace him. Democracies adapt in the fact of their weaknesses. Autocracies plow on with theirs to the bitter end.

One of the crucial lessons of 1918 was that democracies can experiment with autocracy in ways that autocracies cannot experiment with democracy. The French, British, and American governments all wielded near dictatorial power toward the end of the war in the pursuit of ultimate victory, but they did not destroy their democracies in doing so. The German High Command, meanwhile, committed everything to military conquest because they could see no other way of dealing with their public's desire for the war to end. The German people were as sick of the fighting as anyone and had suffered more than most (the Allied naval blockade had come close to its professed aim of starving them into submission). But Ludendorff was not willing to provide any political outlets for this resentment, for fear of where it might lead. So he doubled down on his military gamble in the West, and ended up losing everything. He had to remain in character. Wilson, Lloyd George, Clemenceau could all do a passable impersonation of an autocrat when required, not least because as democratic politicians they were well versed in shifting their positions.[26] Ludendorff could not successfully impersonate a democrat, because that was an act he could not control. Mencken was wrong to think he was a man of mystery. In the end, like any tyrant, he was not mysterious enough.

Yet the fact that the victory for democracy was a triumph of adaptability over rigidity also highlights the difficulty of treating it as a moment of truth. The democracies made a mess of the war, but they won because they did not get stuck with the messes they made. Nevertheless, the temptation to rewrite history existed on the winning side as well as the losing one. The war, which had been a desperate, disjointed, deeply compromised and compromising struggle, suddenly produced a decisive outcome that trumped all that had gone before it. A complicated story became simple again. The principles of democracy had triumphed. Reason had prevailed. Now was the moment to secure a democratic peace that would make the horrors of the last four years worthwhile.

For democracy, the time is never right to capture its long-term destiny. Something about it always remains elusive. Democracies keep adapting to their circumstances, which means the mistakes keep coming. As Tocqueville said, there is something about a democracy that is always "untimely." For that reason, as he also said, there are two particular moments of crisis when democracies will find it hard to do the right thing. One is at the beginning of a war. The other is at the end of one.

Two Elections

Once it became clear the war was not lost, the midterm elections were back on. They were scheduled to take place on November 5. This meant Wilson spent the preceding weeks in the sort of bind that can only afflict a democratic politician. On the one hand, he was trying to bring an end to the greatest military conflagration in history and secure the future peace of the world. On the other hand, he had to worry about how this would play with ordinary Americans, whose local gripes and grumbles were often a world away from the epic events taking place in Europe. The midterms presented Wilson with a golden opportunity and a looming threat. The opportunity was to secure a vote of confidence from the American people for his long-term vision of a democratic peace. The threat was that the American people would make it clear they were not interested in long-term visions. They wanted more immediate rewards for the sacrifices they had been making. Any democratic politician who asks the voters for an open-ended commitment to the peace of the world risks being greeted with a shrug of indifference.

Wilson grappled with these dilemmas throughout October. It was by now clear that an end to the fighting was in sight. Wilson drafted an electoral message to the American people in which he asked for a clear mandate to pursue the principles he had set out in his Fourteen Points address. "If in these critical days," he wrote, "it is your wish to back me with undivided minds, I beg that you will say so in a way which it will not be possible to misunderstand either here at home or among our associates."[27] However, this message was never released. Wilson's advisers thought it made him sound arrogant. Wilson tried again in a second draft, in which he requested the voters, more modestly: "If you wish other leaders, please say so in unmistakable terms."[28] But this too was cut from the final draft. It was a hostage to fortune for what was not, after all, a presidential election. Wilson could not find a way to ask for the thing he wanted.

Meanwhile, some of Wilson's friends tried to warn him about the risks he was running by expecting too much of the voters. On October 14 he met with Henry Ashurst, a Democratic senator from Arizona who had come to voice his fears about the forthcoming elections. Wilson responded with his own shrug of indifference. He explained that he had grander things to worry about than what might happen in three weeks' time. "I am now playing for a hundred years hence," he told Ashurst.[29] For Wilson, the long-term prospects of democracy trumped its short-term convulsions. But there is no easy way to say this at election time. It is very hard to get people to vote for the idea that their votes don't really matter.

Wilson's other problem was that although the war was clearly approaching its end, the fighting was not yet finished. In this respect, and for perhaps the first time in his life, democratic providence let him down. The elections were held just a few days before the final armistice. Austria had agreed its own separate peace on November 3, but news was slow to arrive back in the United States, and with Germany still fighting, Wilson's opponents hammered to the last their message that now was not the time to be talking about future accommodations with the German people. Throughout October the Republicans had campaigned on the theme that the man who had once championed peace without victory now risked squandering the prospects of a final victory with premature talk of peace. The Republican campaign managers used Wilson's Fourteen Points speech to portray him as a dangerous idealist who needed to be reminded that the American people had more down-to-earth concerns. As one historian has put it, by painting Wilson as "a dictatorial, pacifistic, socialistic, anti-American, pro-German internationalist," the election of 1918 "cut the pattern for Republican campaigns for the rest of the century."[30]

When the results came in, it was quickly apparent that the public had not given Wilson the vote of confidence he wanted. The Democrats lost twenty-two seats in the House and seven in the Senate. But Wilson was not downhearted for long. He took comfort from the fact that election day had arrived at just the wrong moment, which meant it could be put down to bad luck as much as anything. As his campaign managers told him, just a few more days would have allowed the news of Austria's surrender and Germany's impending collapse to filter through from Europe, which might have made all the difference. This is what campaign managers always tell their defeated candidates: if only the election hadn't come when it did, we could have won it! Wilson's advisers also told him that his opponents had exploited the credulity of the voters, who had been tricked into believing Wilson was going to let the Germans off the hook. As one of them reported: "A [Republican] campaign based on the slogans 'Unconditional Surrender' and 'No Negotiated Peace' proved surprisingly effective."[31] Wilson consoled himself with the thought that the voters would come around once they understood what he really stood for: a victory that would last.

When would that be? The first thing that had to happen was for all the fighting to stop, so that it would not be so easy for unscrupulous politicians to jumble up the issues of war and peace. However, the British general election that took place a month later showed that even when the fighting had stopped, unscrupulous politicians could still have a field day. Lloyd George scheduled the election for December 14. It was the first to take place in Britain since 1910 and also the first to be held since the passage of the Representation of the People Act earlier in the year, which had extended the vote to almost all men aged over twenty-one and to most women over thirty. Britain was now a genuine mass democracy. Many of those who were entitled to vote were still serving as soldiers, despite the fact that the war had ended a month previously. Nonetheless, the end of hostilities and the collapse of Germany meant this was a definitively postwar election. The question was no longer how to win. The question was what to do with the victory.

The 1918 general election soon acquired a number of different names from contemporaries. It was christened the "coupon" election, in reference to the letters sent out by Lloyd George and the leader of the Conservatives, Andrew Bonar Law, endorsing their favored candidates at the expense of rival Liberals (the Liberal prime minister that Lloyd George had deposed in 1916, Herbert Asquith, christened these "coupons" in a disparaging reference to wartime rationing). It was also a "khaki" election because of the number of soldiers voting and the patriotic themes that dominated.[32] Finally, this was the "Hang the Kaiser!" election, because of the virulent and jingoistic newspaper headlines that proliferated throughout the campaign. The press, dominated by newspaper magnates like Northcliffe (who had been Lloyd George's director of propaganda) and Beaverbrook (who had been his minister of information), were in no mood for talk of reconciliation and aiding German recovery. The priority was to make the losers pay for the war. Lloyd George tapped into these sentiments with election addresses promising "to demand the whole cost of the war from Germany." The voters returned his government with an overwhelming majority. Asquith's Liberals were crushed.

Nonetheless, these nicknames are misleading. Participants in the election did not experience it as a festival of patriotic enthusiasm and vindictiveness. More remember the mood as sullen, resentful, bemused. The war had been long and hard. The victory had been swift and overwhelming. Now the election was an added burden. The Liberal politician Charles Masterman, a friend of Lloyd George, described what he encountered during the campaign:

> The Election was hopeless. I addressed thirty meetings, mostly in the open air. The rain fell steadily on us, the crowd gazed open-mouthed and silent. They cheered nothing, not even Lloyd George's name. They hissed nothing. They only intelligible sentence they responded to with a slight rumble distantly resembling approval was that there ought not to have been an election.[33]

It was a miserable affair, not because the mob was out for revenge, but because the public was in no mood to be co-opted into any more grand schemes. They wanted a return to normality. The sudden influx of women into the electorate did not fulfill either the hopes or the fears of those who anticipated that their presence would have a transformative effect. Most women voters, like most men, had no strong views about what to do with their victory. They simply knew they didn't want to pay for it. The politicians and the public embraced the vitriol of the press as a displacement activity in lieu of discussing more difficult subjects. The war had been funded by huge amounts of public borrowing, which had fueled an incipient inflation. No one wanted to talk about retrenchment or repayment. So instead they talked about punishing the Germans.

All this gave the election an air of unreality. It certainly looked like the worst of democracy. As the *Economist* noted in its December 14 issue, "the election and all its circumstances have been a grisly example of the manner in which politics should not be conducted."[34] Yet it was also a charade: the vengefulness and hysteria were just a contrivance, a way of avoiding making tough decisions. So what was the true face of democracy? There were two prevailing views. One, optimistic, said that behind all the noise and distortion of election time lay the good sense of the public, which would come through in the end. The *Economist* professed to believe this: "The country is not nearly so base as those who appeal to its baser feelings seem to think." Democracy would "stumble through this valley" and eventually "reach the heights" where it could think for itself.[35] Then it would choose peaceful coexistence. But the other view said that the crass, sometimes absurd business of electoral politics was the reality of democracy. There was nothing hidden behind it. Instead, it was Wilsonian idealism, which purported to see beyond mere elections, that was the fantasy.

On this second view, it was only the extremity of the crisis of 1918 that had hidden the true face of democracy. When everything was on the line, it was possible to believe that democracy had arrived at its moment of truth. But as soon as the crisis was passed, then democratic politics returned to its familiar pattern of missteps and muddling on. Walter Lippmann reported a conversation he had with an Italian politician in December 1918, when, as he put it, "the British elections were at the bottom of their deepest depression." The Italian told him to take note of what these elections said about the real condition of democracy in Europe:

> We have been through a frightful illness and thought we were going to die. Our minds turned in those days to higher things, and along came the Americans with a perfect bedside manner, entrancing self-confidence, the strength of youth, and a gospel of the simple life. We made good resolutions. . . . You know—no more city life, but the country, a cow, rise at dawn, to bed early, exercise, fear God and listen to Woodrow Wilson. It was sincere at the time. Then Europe recovered. It put off going to the country. It paid a visit to the old haunts, met the old cronies, and felt most awfully bored with the everlasting morality of the Fourteen Commandments. A little of that goes a long way.[36]

THE AFTERMATH

In December Wilson decided to take matters into his own hands. He traveled to Europe, the first sitting American president to do so, in order to prepare the ground for the peace conference that would be held in Paris the following year. He was greeted by huge, enthusiastic crowds in London and Paris, and similarly vast gatherings in Rome, where he went in January. Wilson was greatly cheered by this: even if the American voters had failed to give his peace plans their endorsement, the goodwill of the European public was unmistakable. The people who came out in their millions to greet him and to wave banners in praise of the Fourteen Points and of their author, whom they dubbed "the Savior of Humanity," clearly wanted a stable democratic peace as much as he did. The results of the British election did not deter him. Wilson took these crowds to signal that there existed a groundswell of democratic optimism that could not find expression through the messy business of elections. It had been distorted by rabid newspaper opinion. The people of Europe were behind him, and their politicians and pressmen would have to come around.

He was wrong. The huge crowds that welcomed him to Europe were a reflection of the fact that he was by now the most famous man in the world (his only plausible rival in early 1919 would have been Charlie Chaplin). This was the power of celebrity, not democracy, in action. A cult of Wilson had replaced the earlier cults of Kerensky and Ludendorff, and had much of Europe in its grip. It proved just as evanescent. George Bernard Shaw, always a good weather vane, had put aside any earlier doubts about Wilson to embrace the new hero of the hour. He published his own guide to the forthcoming peace conference, in which he declared: "Mr Wilson, as a Great Man standing for a Great Idea, must depend on sheer intelligence and moral superiority, without regard to election figures."[37] This was very bad advice. Europe's politicians were well versed in the results of the November midterms and knew that Wilson's grand schemes did not necessarily represent American public opinion. Since this meant that there were no guarantees he would be able to deliver on his promises, it gravely weakened his negotiating position.

Meanwhile, the British elections had shown that whatever banners the cheering crowds might hold up, national electorates were much more concerned about what they might lose in the Paris negotiations than by what they stood to gain by crossing over into Wilson's promised land of democratic peace. The costs of the war were not something any democracy wanted to take on to itself. Every European state had exited the war burdened with debt: they owed money to their own citizens, to each other, and, crucially, to the United States. No state was willing to honor those obligations unless it received what it was owed first.

Wilson came face to face with this hard reality in April. It was the Italians who revealed it to him. Italy had only joined the war on the Allied side in 1915, on the basis of the secret treaty of London that had promised the Italians territorial gains from a dismantled Austro-Hungarian Empire. This was just the sort of clandestine deal making the Bolsheviks had used to embarrass the democracies, and Wilson was pledged in the Fourteen Points to abolish it. But to his intense frustration, the Italian prime minister, Vittorio Orlando, and his foreign minister, Sidney Sonnino (who had negotiated the original treaty), were determined that they should get what they had been promised, above all the Adriatic port of Fiume. Exasperated by their refusal to budge and remembering the ecstatic reception he had received from the crowds in Rome a few months earlier, Wilson decided to appeal over the heads of the politicians and speak directly to the Italian people.

On April 23 he issued a statement through the Italian newspapers calling on the Italian public to give up their territorial demands and join him in creating a new order

built on "the rights of peoples and the right of the world
to peace." This too brought the crowds out onto the streets.
They tore down street signs that had been erected in honor
of Wilson's visit and replaced the word *Wilson* with the word
Fiume. Orlando immediately returned to Italy where he was
greeted with a popular outpouring of support, and banners
declaring: "Viva Orlando! Viva Fiume! Viva Italia." The national parliament gave him its unequivocal backing. Mussolini's recently founded fascists attached themselves to this
sudden upsurge in nationalist sentiment and did what they
could to exploit it. They also found an early hero in Gabriele
d'Annunzio, the poet and rabble-rouser, who made Fiume
his personal cause and Wilson the object of his ridicule
("That Quaker," as he told parliament, "with his long equine
face and his thirty-two false teeth.").[38] Mussolini followed in
his footsteps. The cult of Wilson was over. The much longer-
lasting cult of Mussolini was about to begin.

Wilson discovered there was no reliable way to access the
democratic goodwill of the people of Europe. Whenever he
tried to grasp it, it slipped through his fingers. So he had no
choice but to deal with the politicians instead. For month
after miserable month he met with Lloyd George and Clemenceau (and Orlando when he was not back in Italy stirring
up trouble), and he grappled with their demands and their
fears. The basic gulf remained the one that had existed at the
start of 1918. The British and French governments wanted
security for the victorious democracies. Wilson wanted to
leave the door open for democracy to grow and to achieve
its long-term potential.

The British and French position was not simply backward
looking and vindictive. The French in particular did not

trust Germany's new democracy to behave itself in the future. At the start of 1919 Clemenceau saw a Europe in which
all the major states bordering Germany had been dimin-
ished by war—Russia had collapsed, the French were morally and materially exhausted, the Austro-Hungarian Empire was splintered—while Germany had been left relatively
unscathed, with her industry intact and her economic potential undiminished, save only for the loss of her national
pride. In these circumstances, any democracy was liable to
seek revenge.

Wilson's belief was that in the long run, and given the
chance, German democracy could evolve and mature. Clemenceau thought that before that happened, German democracy was capable of anything, and he was not prepared to
take any chances. So what he wanted were concrete guarantees: a promise of American armed support in the event
of renewed German aggression, and American financial support to help rebuild the French economy. In the absence of
these, he would only sign up to Wilson's League of Nations
if the remainder of the peace treaty did what it could to keep
Germany on her knees.

The peace that eventually emerged from the Paris Conference had two faces, reflecting the two sides of democracy:
the hopeful and the fearful. The victorious European democracies were afraid they might still end up the losers from the
conflict. Their peace was enshrined in the war guilt clauses
of the Treaty of Versailles: Germany had to accept moral
blame for the conflict, to pay large reparations, to cede significant amounts of territory, and to dismantle its military.
The other face of the peace was contained in the provisions
made by the treaty to establish a League of Nations, to over-

see the peaceful settlement of international disputes, and to coordinate worldwide disarmament. These parts of the Versailles treaty looked forward to a secure democratic future.

Wilson was confident that over time the good side of the peace would undo the bad. He believed that the long-term advantages of democracy would eventually trump its short-term failings. But his critics thought he had got this entirely the wrong way around. The bad bits of the treaty would make a mess of all its good intentions, since they would poison the new world order before it got going. The Treaty of Versailles was a patch-up job. It redrew the map of Europe to accommodate a whole series of burning national demands and resentments. Yet Wilson's League of Nations was committed to defending these arrangements in the name of democracy. Wilson was assuming that so long as the world is geared toward its democratic destiny, nothing bad can last for long. He was forgetting that even the bad things that do not last long can play havoc with political destiny. Like the American steamboat builders Tocqueville had written about, Wilson's faith in the future had persuaded him to put an unsafe ship out to sea. Soon he would have to watch his ship go down.

One of Wilson's most savage critics was Lippmann, who like many progressive young men on the fringes of power saw the Versailles treaty as a personal betrayal. He had more cause than most. Lippmann had made his name before the war as the author of *Mastery and Drift*, a book that argued for strong, scientifically minded political leadership to arrest the democratic tendency to muddle along aimlessly. These views had served to bring him within Wilson's orbit. He had helped Wilson draft his Fourteen Points speech. Now he saw

Wilson attach those open-ended, flexible, accommodating principles to a treaty that was narrow-minded and inflexible and punitive. Wilson had abandoned what for Lippmann had been his shining virtue: his patient resolve. He had become impatient and thereby had lost control of events. Lippmann believed that Wilson had betrayed his own principle that creating a world safe for democracy took time. You could not simply make a peace and call it democracy. If you did, you were liable to force the world's already established democracies to defend the indefensible.

The focus of this anxiety was Article X of the new League of Nations charter, which committed the members of the league to defend other members against external aggression. Given the Versailles peace had created all sorts of unstable and volatile "self-governing" entities across Europe, this was a hostage to fortune. The league had bound itself to treat the arrangements that had been agreed in Paris in 1919 as though they were set in stone, when in reality they were lines in the sand. Lippmann argued that Article X constituted a form of political arrogance: it was "an effort to be wiser than the next generation."[39] No one could know which nations would prosper, which boundaries would endure, and which democracies would survive. Committing the United States to defend an entirely arbitrary point in the evolution of global democracy undermined the ability of democracies to make their own fate. Wilson had made the mistake of trying to second-guess democratic providence.

Lippmann's attack on Article X was joined from the other side by American Republican leaders in the Senate, who wanted to know why the United States was being asked to put its fate in the hands of others. If the League of Nations existed to make the world safe for democracy, why was American democracy being prevented from making its own choices about whom its friends and enemies were? In July Wilson had traveled back to the United States to sell his peace to the American people. On August 19 he agreed to appear before the Senate Foreign Relations Committee to tackle his critics head on. One of them, a pompous, blustering senator from Ohio called Warren Harding, wanted to know whether Article X was binding or not. If it was, how could the elected representatives of the American people sign up to it? If it wasn't, what was the point of it?

Wilson, increasingly bad tempered, tried to explain that it was neither binding nor nonbinding: it was a kind of moral signpost, designed to guide the world toward its better future. But pressed, he had to admit that America's democratic politicians were bound to express "the judgment of the American people." He went on: "If the unhappy time should come when that judgment is against the judgment of the rest of the world, we would have to express it."[40] This little exchange was a portent of things to come. Wilson was trying to speak for democracy in general. Harding spoke for one democracy in particular. Wilson was much smarter and better informed than Harding. He had a wealth of knowledge and experience on his side. But Harding won the argument.

Exasperated by his mauling at the hands of his opponents in the Senate, Wilson decided once again to appeal over the heads of the politicians to the people, who he believed were on his side. In September Wilson embarked on a speaking tour across the country, heading west to where he believed the strongest support for the League of Nations was to be found. He appeared before increasingly large and enthusiastic crowds, to whom he portrayed a vision of two possible futures for American democracy. In one, full participation in the new institutions of the democratic peace would guarantee for the United States a secure and prosperous future. It would take time but it would be worth it: all it required was a leap of faith. In the other, American democracy, resolved to reserve its own judgment on international affairs, becomes a paranoid and militaristic society, indistinguishable from its enemies. Short-term security would have been bought at too high a price.

By the end of September, after nearly a solid month of travel and public speaking, Wilson was on the brink of collapse (he was almost certainly still suffering from the after-effects of an attack of the flu that had struck him in Paris in April). He was taken back to Washington to recuperate. On October 2 he suffered a severe stroke, which almost killed him. More dead than alive he remained in office and in his enfeebled state refused all talk of a compromise with the Senate on the ratification of the treaty. He remained convinced that the crowds that had come out to listen to him in September were the true representatives of American public opinion. But he was deceiving himself. By now he was trapped, in body and in mind. He had been trying to grasp something that was out of reach. He wanted to access the better instincts of the people, over and above the distortions of elections and newspapers and all the day-to-day noise of democratic politics. He was determined, somehow, to capture the democratic future in the present. But the democratic future cannot be captured in the present. Democracy lives from moment to moment. That is its strength, and its weakness.

In mid-November Wilson rejected a proposal from his Republican critics in the Senate to endorse the treaty with reservations on certain provisions, including Article X of the charter of the League of Nations. Wilson insisted that the choice was an all-or-nothing one: either ratification or the wilderness. As a result the United States never signed the Treaty of Versailles and never joined the League of Nations. Wilson served out his time in office bitter, sick, and isolated from the outside world. In the presidential election of 1920, the Democrats chose as their candidate the governor of Ohio, James Cox, a strong supporter of the League of Nations, and as his running mate Franklin D. Roosevelt, the assistant secretary to the navy and another internationalist. The Republicans chose Warren Harding, and for vice president, Calvin Coolidge. Harding won. His margin of victory in the popular vote—60 percent to 34 percent—was the largest ever recorded. The American people did not make a wise choice. In a competitive field, Harding proved himself to be to be one of the more useless presidents in American history.

Harding is now more or less forgotten, but Wilson remains a deeply divisive figure. He is easy to caricature. He has been variously portrayed as a fantasist, an academic dreamer, a hyperrationalist, an unthinking believer in providence, a hypocrite, and a fool—the horse-faced Quaker with his thirty-two false teeth. For a new generation of twenty-first-century rabble-rousers like Glenn Beck, Wilson has been cast the schoolteacher-tyrant, a type that Tocqueville warned against. He is the professorial president who enmeshed America in his schemes of a managed world order and a managed currency (President Obama is, on these accounts, his obvious heir). But none of these characterizations is remotely fair. Wilson was certainly a professorial type, and as a working professor he had come to an understanding of some truths about democracy. Its future was secure and something to trust in, but its present was messy and to be handled with caution. He did not think it was a good idea to tempt providence. But then he became a working politician, and he eventually discovered that the temptation could prove irresistible. For most of his political career he resisted it, and he was remarkably successful. Cautious, ambitious, insightful, adaptable, confident, taking nothing for granted: his political skills were formidable. But his extraordinary experiences in 1918 made him want to speed up the passage of time in the year that followed, particularly as time started to run out for him personally. That was his undoing. He tried to pin democracy down, and it got away from him.

CHAPTER 2

1933

Fear Itself

The Crisis

THE YEAR 1933 WAS TRULY GRIM FOR DEMOCRACY. WE know this now, of course, and can sum up the reason why in a single word: Hitler. People who lived through 1933 also thought it was a terrible year for democracy, though for most of them Hitler's arrival in power was only a small part of it. Events in Germany were more a symptom than the cause of what had gone wrong. The real problem was the failure of the established democracies to stem the tide of history as it appeared to be flowing against them. The democracies had lost control of their destiny and were floundering. If contemporaries had been asked to sum up in a single word their sense that things were spiraling out of control, they would have said: London.

As seen at the time, the great political calamity of 1933 was the World Economic Conference, which took place in London over six hot and miserable weeks during June and July. It began with a great fanfare of expectation. After nearly four years of economic depression following the crash of 1929, this was a final chance for the world's leading economies to arrest the slide into chaos. The aims of the conference were to stabilize exchange rates, restore international cooperation against a rising tide of protectionism, and revive economic confidence. All this was far easier said than done, however. The conference took place in the dusty and overcrowded chambers of the London Geological Museum, a setting that didn't do much to convey a sense of urgency. There were sixty-six countries in attendance, which made the whole event ridiculously cumbersome. By no means all of these countries were democracies: most weren't, since by 1933 democracy was in retreat all over the world. Of the seventeen new democracies that had been set up in the hopeful aftermath of the First World War, only a few were left. Italy, Portugal, Poland, Brazil, Argentina, Uruguay, Japan, and Germany had all reverted to forms of authoritarianism. Each of them was represented at the London conference anyway. Of the big powers only the Soviet Union stayed away. Nevertheless, the three leading players were still democracies: the United States, Britain, and France. It was generally accepted that however chaotic and confused things got in the main body of the conference, its success or failure would depend on these three coming to an understanding among themselves. If they couldn't agree, then what hope was there for the rest?

As it turned out, they couldn't agree. The conference ended in failure, accompanied by plentiful recriminations and a widespread sense of betrayal. The British and French felt betrayed by the Americans, above all by the actions of the new American president, Franklin Roosevelt; the Americans felt the British and French had been betrayed by their false expectations; the British and French, as is traditional, felt betrayed by each other. Stalin was delighted. So too were Hitler's representatives in the German delegation, who felt that the conference had fulfilled its purpose of showing that democracy was a busted system. All that remained, one of them reported back to Berlin, was to ensure "that the odium for the failure is heaped onto others while ensuring that Germany reaps the benefit."[1] In the middle of the worst economic crisis of the century, the established democracies had been given an opportunity to seize the moment and save themselves. They had blown it. Now was the time for their rivals to show what they could do.

However, not everyone on the side of the democracies was downhearted. The conference was only a calamity for democracy if you believed that democracy had arrived at its moment of truth. If, on the other hand, you believed that the great advantage of democracy was that it never reaches its moment of truth, then the failure of the conference was a price that had to be paid for allowing the democracies to carry on muddling through. Roosevelt, by keeping his options open, did what a democratic politician must. Their rivals wanted to pin the disastrous state of the world in 1933 onto the democracies. But democracy cannot be pinned down so easily. This was why even at the height of the crisis the democracies were unable to agree on what needed to be done. But it was also why the crisis did not finish them.

The year 1933 showed what can be at stake for democracy when confronted with a worldwide economic crisis. In Germany, the failure of democracy was absolute. In a country where democracy had not yet passed the confidence threshold, muddle and confusion simply bred toxic mistrust of democratic institutions and paved the way for a ruthless autocratic takeover. In the United States, by contrast, muddle and confusion prepared the ground for a recovery of sorts. German experiences before and after 1933 confirm how dangerous it is to assume that democracies can improvise a solution to every crisis they face. Improvisation destroyed the Weimar Republic, because it unraveled the authority of the state. But the demise of Weimar was not the whole story. Democracy looked to be in deep trouble almost everywhere in 1933. Yet that impression was ultimately misleading. No one can know for sure when established democracies have finally run out of road. Sometimes, despite the risks, improvisation remains the best bet.

THE RIVALS

By 1933 democracy was engaged in an ideological battle on two fronts. It faced twin rivals in Soviet Bolshevism and Italian fascism. Both these systems had been in place for more than a decade, but during the relatively prosperous 1920s they tended to be seen in the West as political curiosities. Stalin and Mussolini were not exactly figures of fun, but nor were they taken entirely seriously. That changed after 1929. The Great Depression turned Bolshevism and fascism in many people's eyes into standing rebukes to Western democracy. These new autocracies suddenly appeared to have some of the virtues the democracies so conspicuously lacked. They were decisive. They were resolute. Their leaders were not hamstrung by the need to compromise and to pander to their electorates. They could make the political weather. The democracies, by contrast, appeared in danger of being blown away by forces beyond their power to control.

Democracy revealed its relative weakness in two ways. First, democratic politics was too slow for a world that increasingly required rapid responses. The presiding impression that had been left by four years of economic turmoil and mismanagement was of Western politicians struggling to keep up with the speed of events. While they were debating what to do next, the crisis would take another turn, so that they were left proposing solutions to yesterday's problems. Jan Smuts, the South African leader and one of the original architects of the League of Nations, came to London in 1933 and articulated fears that many shared: "The pace of events is such as to demand swift action, decisive action at almost every point. I wonder whether we can be as decisive as the dictators. Yet it is only in that way that democracy will be able to defend itself."[2] At the same time, democracy appeared too fickle to generate lasting solutions to problems that required a long-term perspective. Too much about democracy seemed piecemeal, hasty, rushed. Decisions would be made and then unmade, solutions proposed and then abandoned, as governments came and went. It was a sobering fact that by the time of the London conference Russia and Italy were the only major countries not to have experienced a change of government since the start of the depression. Stalin and Mussolini represented continuity in an unstable world. Every democracy—the United States, Britain, France, Germany, Spain, every republic in Latin America, every republic in central and eastern Europe—had changed its government at least once since 1929. Plenty had abandoned democracy altogether.

Too slow to act, too quick to change its mind: this was the double trouble with democracy. The contrast the new autocracies provided was symbolized by Stalin's decision to modernize the Soviet Union through a series of five-year plans. The first five-year plan had been unveiled in 1928. Its aim was to drag the Russian economy into the twentieth century by means of a rapid expansion of heavy industry. Wildly ambitious targets were set and all the coercive machinery of the state employed to ensure they were met on time. To start with, the response in the West was generally derisive, both of the scale and the specificity of the targets. But as the Western economies went into a nosedive after 1929, and the Soviet economy moved inexorably toward those targets, the tone changed. Across the democracies, references to five-year plans started to proliferate, as politicians cited them in evidence of what might be achieved with a little foresight and determination. In 1932, the future British prime minister, Clement Attlee, told the House of Commons:

> If I had put forward a suggestion of this need of a national plan quite a short time ago, such Members as were present . . . would all have said: "Oh the Russians, with their ridiculous Five-Year Plans!" As a matter of fact, the times have changed entirely, and in every country the people are now beginning to say, "Is not the Russian Five-Year Plan going to succeed, and what are we going to do about it?"[3]

Another speaker in the same debate called the five-year plan "the most vital and important economic and political fact in the world at the moment." It showed the sort of resolve that democracy was lacking.

Some commentators believed that unless democracy could compete with the grandiosity of Stalin's schemes, it was doomed. The Spanish philosopher José Ortega y Gassett argued that given the "vegetative" condition of Western democracy, the emotional and spiritual pull of the five-year plan would prove almost impossible to resist.[4] The only thing that might rival it was a grand plan to create a United States of Europe, something that would have seemed absurdly ambitious in 1933. Others thought that Bolshevism gave democracy a glimpse of its own destiny. In the early 1930s plenty of Western intellectuals traveled to the Soviet Union and came back with tales of having seen the future. One was Bernard Shaw, who decided that Stalinism was not the alternative to Western democracy; it was its crowning achievement. He told American audiences they should not be afraid of the ruthless determination of the Bolsheviks because it was a necessary feature of any genuinely democratic revolution, including their own ("Jefferson is Lenin," he explained helpfully, "Hamilton is Stalin"). Stalinism was ultimately America's reward for having fought a war to make the world safe for democracy: "The USSR is what you got for your liberty loans and the blood of your young men. It was not what you intended to get but it seems it was what God intended you to get."[5] If you really believe in democracy, Shaw seemed to be saying, then don't complain about the way democratic providence pans out.

Attempts were likewise made to turn fascism into the true face of democracy. The British trade consul in Rome reassured a London audience in 1933 that Mussolini was neither a tyrant nor a fool; he was a democratic visionary. He had invented a "new form of democracy" that used the power of the state to reconcile competing interests while commanding popular support. It was this revitalized democracy that explained why "Italy was holding her head above water" while the rest of Europe was drowning. True, Mussolini looked like a dictator, but the fact that he had abolished the old Italian parliament showed he was not one:

> If Signor Mussolini had wished to be a dictator for life he would have kept the old inefficient Parliament in being. Everybody would have supported him against it. The fact that he created a new chamber which enjoys so much of the confidence and backing of the people is a proof of his disinterestedness, and that he wishes not to override the will of the people, but to guide and educate it.[6]

Shaw, never one to be left out, also praised Mussolini as a leader whose decisiveness showed "what is really possible and what is real in a genuine democracy."[7]

It was not only the useful idiots who thought that democracy needed to learn from its rivals. In a 1932 BBC radio address the economist John Maynard Keynes described Soviet Bolshevism and Italian fascism as "the two most extraordinary political movements of the modern age," and he told his audience: "Let us not belittle these magnificent experiments or refuse to learn from them."[8] Still, Keynes did not confuse them with democracy, which continued to possess the crucial long-term advantages. Bolshevism and fascism were enjoying the benefits of being young movements. Over time, these benefits would fade and the two fatal weaknesses of any autocratic system would emerge: first, a growing dissatisfaction on the part of the general population with being told what to do; second, sclerotic leadership (only in the early days, Keynes insisted, "when those who rule have carved their own way to power," did autocracies have a mechanism for picking out "the best talent"). In the long run, neither system could compete with Western democracy. Nevertheless, Keynes was famously skeptical about putting too much weight on how things would play out in the long run. ("The long run is a misleading guide to current affairs. In the long run we are all dead."[9]) For now, Russia and Italy had shown the advantages of what he called "intelligence and deliberation at the centre" in organizing the life of the state.

The challenge for the democracies was to maintain their long-term advantages while taking action to address their present failings. Keynes thought the way to do it was for "state planning [to] be carried out in the same sort of way and with the same kinds of instruments of administration under a democratic as they would under an autocratic government."[10] This would be possible because democracies could experiment with autocracy without letting it take over: they still retained the capacity to kick out their administrators if they went too far. Administrative expertise would rescue democracy from its short-term inability to make the best use of its own resources; democratic judgment would then rescue the administrators from their inevitable tendency to accumulate too much power over time.

It was a nice idea but there were two problems. The first was elections. Keynes hated elections. He couldn't bear having to listen to all the rubbish politicians were required to utter in order to get elected. When really important decisions had to be made, he thought elections could do great damage. He had seen it happen twice in his lifetime. Once was the British general election of 1918, which Keynes thought had done much to poison the Paris peace conference. The other was the British general election of 1931, which had returned a National government promising austerity and a balanced budget at a time when what was needed (Keynes was convinced) was more public spending. In both cases, it disgusted him to see how easily votes could be harvested with scaremongering and idiotic slogans ("Hang the Kaiser!" "Save the Pound!"). "General elections are always dismal affairs," he wrote to a friend during the 1931 campaign, "but I do not think I remember any election in which more outrageous lies were told by leading statesmen."[11]

In Keynes's ideal world, elections would only take place at moments of calm. In a crisis, when ordinary people tend not to be thinking straight, it was better to leave things to the experts (that is, to people like him). This was wishful thinking, of course—as Tocqueville had noted, there is no such thing as a calm election. But it also made it hard to see how democracy could be relied on to sort things out once the experts overreached themselves, given that democracy would be being asked to pass judgment at a moment when things were going wrong. This is the unresolved tension in attempts to combine autocratic efficiency with democratic accountability. We give power to experts because democracy can't be relied on in the short term. We think it's safe to give them that power because democracy can be relied on in the long term. Yet at some point the long-term reliability of democracy will have to be put to the test in a crisis if it is going to make any difference. And when that happens, people are liable to ask themselves why they needed the experts in the first place.

The other problem for Keynes was the one that has haunted democracy throughout its modern history: gold. The conventional view had been that only a gold standard could give democracies the stability they needed. This idea went back to the nineteenth century and to the traditional criticism of democracies: they had no self-discipline. Without the external discipline of a gold standard, democracies would always be prey to their fickle tendencies and free to inflate away their obligations. For Keynes the discipline gold bought came at the price of flexibility: it left decision makers unable to adapt to the requirements of the moment, particularly in an economic crisis. It squeezed the room experts needed to exercise their judgment. Keynes thought the obsession with gold was a kind of fetish. Nevertheless, he recognized its power. Democratically elected politicians had to bow down before it if they were not going to appear crazily irresponsible and cavalier. In a world where gold signaled discipline, any rejection of gold signaled ill discipline. No democracy could afford that.

What to do? The crisis of the First World War had forced the leading combatants (including Britain) to suspend the convertibility of their currencies to gold. The Bank of England insisted that this was a temporary measure, brought on by an emergency.[12] Gold payments had to be resumed if the country was to be restored to its former preeminence. After some dithering Britain had rejoined the gold standard in 1925 at a punitive rate, suffered six years of grinding deflation and rising unemployment, then had given up the struggle. In the autumn of 1931 Britain once again suspended gold payments, its politicians having done everything in their power to avoid that fate. It took an emergency National government to throw in the towel: the Labour administration that preceded it hadn't dared (as one of its outgoing members, Sidney Webb complained when told that Britain was coming off gold: "Nobody told us we could do that!").[13]

Permitting the pound to float was a decision of last resort, taken by politicians who were for the most part deeply fearful of the consequences. So even though the consequences proved broadly beneficial—the devaluation of sterling helped to kick-start the British economy, driving up exports and easing the squeeze on wages—the whole episode was not a great advertisement for democracy. The National government that enjoyed the benefits of coming off gold was made up of "sound money" men who repeatedly claimed the whole thing was a disaster and would require much more belt-tightening to stave off its ill effects. If they really believed what they said, Keynes felt, they were fools. If they didn't, they were liars. What Keynes most hated about the 1931 election was that it was these fools and liars who were returned with a thumping majority. This was definitely not an example of intelligence and deliberation at the center. It was what made democracy such a frustrating system of government: the right solution stumbled across by the wrong people, who didn't understand what they were doing.

Nor was it an example that could easily be copied by other democracies. The outside view was that the British were being reckless and cavalier, and that a general retreat from the gold standard would produce global instability and a beggar-thy-neighbor round of competitive devaluations. It was typical British hypocrisy to preach the virtues of monetary discipline while selfishly enjoying the benefits of having breached them. Especially appalled were the French, who were terrified of abandoning gold. The French government had only resumed gold payments in 1927 after an inflation that nearly bankrupted the French economy and wiped out personal savings. The French public and politicians alike were convinced that gold was all that stood between democracy and disaster; without it, their political system could not be trusted to show any resolve. Britain had come off gold when it felt it had no choice. France had gone back on gold when it felt it had no choice. At this point in its history French democracy was frightened of itself.

The respective condition of British and French democracy—incompetent and fearful—showed how hard it would be to reach any agreement about what needed to be done to get the world out of its slump. In 1933 Keynes would have liked a meeting of independent economic experts, freed from the rivalries and neurotic pressures of their national governments, to sort out the mess. What he got was the London conference instead. But at least it wouldn't just be down to the British and French. The Americans were coming.

CONFERENCE SEASON

During the 1920s many Americans had turned their back on international affairs, preferring to surf along with the tide of rising domestic prosperity. But after 1929, the mood shifted dramatically. The economic catastrophe showed that international affairs could not safely be left to take care of themselves. By 1931 the Hoover administration, partly in response to the pressure of public opinion, had begun a process of reengagement with the institutions of the League of Nations, though stopping short of formal American entry. American representatives started to play their full part in a succession of international conferences on disarmament, on free trade, and on other steps to revive the world economy. A meeting at Lausanne in the summer of 1932 had attempted to lay down the ground rules for a comprehensive international economic rescue plan, though no consensus could be reached on the key questions of currency stabilization and tariff reduction. At the insistence of the Americans it was decided to organize a make-or-break gathering of all the leading nations for the following year. The British government agreed to act as host. In that sense, the London conference was an American idea.

This was what gave many people hope. It was widely understood that no solution to the world's problems would be possible without American involvement, and now here were the Americans taking the lead. But hope was tempered by caution. There were a number of reasons to doubt the extent of America's commitment. The first was the problem of debt. For the European nations, including Britain and France, the immediate priority for restoring economic confidence was to reduce the crushing burden of debt left over from the war. Germany owed Britain and France in the form of reparations; Britain and France owed the United States in the form of war loans. During the 1920s, the United States had exported capital to Germany, which allowed the Germans to keep paying back the British and French, which allowed the British and French to keep paying back the Americans. After 1929, following the collapse of global trade, all that ceased. The magic circle no longer worked. If America was in no position to help Germany pay its debts, then Britain and France wanted to know how they were going to pay their debts to America. They would only pay what they owed if they were paid what they were owed. Otherwise, they wanted the United States to let them off the hook.

The Americans couldn't do it, because democratic public opinion wouldn't allow it. Back in 1922 the US Congress had passed a bill that was still in force, setting a floor to any restructuring of war debts at 90 cents on the dollar. The American public remained adamant that the Europeans must pay back what they had borrowed. Democracies, then as now, do not like to see other democracies wriggle out of their obligations; it is one of the things that set basic limits to international democratic solidarity. At Lausanne, British and French representatives had pressed hard for a reopening of the debt question, but the Americans refused to budge. Their precondition for taking part in the London conference was that the issue of war debts and reparations should not be on the agenda, because of the toxic domestic consequences of any renegotiation. The conference would have to be restricted to questions of currency, prices, and free trade. That was the only way to reach an agreement that could pass back home. It was not a good omen. For many Europeans it was all too reminiscent of what had happened fourteen years earlier, when American politicians had convened a make-or-break conference to save the world, only to be prevented by domestic opinion from taking the steps that would have made salvation possible.

Memories of 1919 were still fresh at the London conference. One of the best-selling books of 1933 was Harold Nicolson's *Peacemaking, 1919*, which offered a firsthand account
of what had gone wrong in Paris. Nicolson, a diplomat, had
been there in person, another of the progressively minded
young men on the fringes of power who felt personally betrayed by the Versailles treaty. The most famous of these
angry young men was Keynes, who had also been there in
person, as an economic advisor to the British delegation, before quitting in disgust. Keynes had made his international
reputation later in the same year with *The Economic Consequences of the Peace*, in which he had pinned the blame on the
politicians, particularly Wilson and Lloyd George, for allowing personal vanity and pettiness of spirit to get in the way
of what needed to be done. The people of Europe, Keynes
flattered his readers, had been let down by the inability of
their representatives to voice their better instincts. In 1933
Nicolson saw it differently. It wasn't the politicians who had
failed democracy. It was democracy that had failed the politicians. The tragedy of the Paris conference was that it had
to take place against the backdrop of what Nicolson called
"the welter of democracy," with all its impossible demands:
for peace, prosperity, security, the payment of debts, the ex-
traction of revenge, and a quiet life. "Democracy," Nicolson
wrote, "for immediate, as distinct from ultimate purposes,
[is] a fool."[14] It was bound to scupper any attempt to put the
world to rights. No one with high hopes for London 1933
could say they hadn't been warned.

Democracy also posed another difficulty for the London
conference. The gathering had been initiated a year earlier
by the American president, but before it could take place the

American voters had dumped that president and chosen a new one. It was Hoover's conference, but Hoover was gone. His successor, Franklin Roosevelt, was a man of whom much was hoped and much was feared, but about whom relatively little was certain. He was hard to pin down. Lippmann, during the 1932 election campaign, called him "a pleasant man who, without any important qualifications for the office, would very much like to be president."[15] His preelection commitments were studiedly vague. He was resolved to do everything in his power to rescue hard-pressed Americans from the grip of the depression. At the same time, he ran on a platform of relative austerity, promising to balance the budget and to "preserve a sound currency at all hazards." He was also pledged to full participation in "the international monetary conference called on the invitation of our government."[16]

Once Roosevelt had won his handsome victory in November, Hoover pressed him for some joint statement to reassure the world of his plans. Roosevelt would say nothing. He had no intention of tainting himself by association with Hoover's discredited administration, nor of limiting his freedom of action once he assumed office. That meant waiting until March to discover what he was thinking. Hoover, the ultimate lame duck president, became increasingly desperate for Roosevelt to show his hand, but all to no avail. This, too, looked like the worst of democracy. It was a case of the king is dead; the new king will be with you in five months. In the meantime, both the American and the global economy continued their downward spiral.

When Roosevelt finally took the oath of office on March 4, he told Americans that they had nothing to fear but fear itself. He also offered some carefully crafted statements of intent. He insisted that "there must be provision for an adequate but sound currency." As he was to point out at a press conference a few days later, he deliberately ordered this "adequate but sound" rather than "sound but adequate" (though when his questioner persisted by asking "Now you have more time, can you define what that is?," FDR responded "No!").[17] Without specifying the means, Roosevelt was leaving the door open for a devaluation. He would do what he could to raise prices. He also promised to balance the budget. He would work toward a revival of international trade, but he would put national interests first.

> Our international trade relations, though vastly important, are in point of time and necessity secondary to the establishment of a sound national economy. I favor as a practical policy the putting of first things first. I shall spare no effort to restore world trade by international economic readjustment, but the emergency at home cannot wait on that accomplishment.

Above all he pledged himself to speedy action to tackle the crisis, declaring that he would ask Congress for "broad Executive power to wage war against the emergency, as great as the power that would be given to me if we were in fact invaded by a foreign foe." In the short term, democracy might need rescuing from its tendency to prevaricate (many interpreted this to mean that he would force Congress to balance its books). But he also insisted: "We do not distrust the future of essential democracy."[18] In the end, everything would be all right.

During his first hundred days in power, Roosevelt unleashed a flurry of initiatives. One of them came on April
19 when he effectively took America off gold, by suspending the convertibility of paper money into bullion. This was
the beginning of a series of concerted measures to devalue
the dollar and inflate the American economy. The world was
shocked: Roosevelt had not even put up a fight. Unlike the
British, he could not say he had been forced off gold. He had
taken the leap of his own volition. Many economists warned
of disaster: runaway inflation, debt repudiation, national
ruin. Even one of Roosevelt's supporters, the financier Bernard Baruch, declared: "It can't be defended, except as mob
rule."[19] But no one could say it was a complete surprise. Although Roosevelt had not said he would do it, he had repeatedly refused to say that he wouldn't. In a crisis, after all,
"adequate" came before "sound."

His decision completely changed the terms of the London
conference. It had been assumed that the Americans would
join the French in trying to persuade the British back onto
gold; now the French were faced by the Americans having
joined the British in unshackling their currencies from the
discipline of the gold standard. Would this make it easier or
harder to reach agreement in London? The professed goal of
all the participants at the conference, including the American delegation, was currency stabilization, meaning fixed
exchange rates. Were the Americans signaling that they had
given up on that idea, or that they were doing what needed
to be done in order to make it a realistic objective?

A lot depended on whether Roosevelt was seen as having
caved in to American democracy, or as having stood up to it.
If you thought the suspension of gold payments was an act

of political expediency by a president who was concerned only to alleviate the immediate pressure on himself, then it was easy to fear the worst. This was typical democratic recklessness: short-term gain at the expense of long-term stability. It would make any international agreement practically impossible, because no one would be able to trust the Americans to keep to it. On the other hand, if you thought that Roosevelt was asserting his own executive competence in the face of widespread pressure to do what was expected of him (from the right, to maintain the value of the dollar; from the left, to print money), then it might be the prelude to decisive action on the international stage. He had, after all, shown he was his own man and that he had guts, along with a huge amount of charm. (Even now, the transcripts of his press conferences, of which he gave more than sixty during 1933, can make the reader smile.) Perhaps he was the sort of international leader democracy needed: someone who could inspire in his fellow leaders the confidence to take decisive action.

On the eve of the London conference the BBC set up one of its first-ever live transatlantic radio broadcasts, a conversation between two of the leading public intellectuals of the age: Keynes and Lippmann.[20] They were to consider the prospects for the conference. Both were relatively optimistic. Keynes reminded his listeners that "we live miserably in a world of the greatest potential wealth." It would be a terrible mistake to assume that the temporary calamity of the depression represented a permanent reverse. Nonetheless, the situation would not correct itself automatically. What was needed was decisive statesmanship, built on expert advice. To that end, the relative freedom of action the British and American governments had acquired in unshackling their currencies was much more of a help than a hindrance. "I put all my hopes on one possibility," Keynes announced.

> England and America should somehow find a way to get to-
> gether to an agreed program—to do, in fact, just what we failed
> to do in Paris in 1919. For there are few remedies which we could
> not apply, acting together, even if others were to hold back.[21]

The implied rebuke here was to the French, who were cling-ing to gold, fearful of the consequences of allowing demo-cratic politicians to set their own terms for an agreement. The French thought any such agreement would not hold be-cause it would be vulnerable to domestic pressures. Keynes thought any agreement that ignored domestic pressures would not hold either.

Lippmann concurred. He pointed out that the London conference had a significant advantage over the other big international gathering of the time, the disarmament con-ference then taking place in Geneva. The Geneva conference had been dragging on for a year with little to show for it, despite the fact that disarmament was almost the only thing on which international public opinion was agreed. It was by far the most popular cause across all the democracies: no one liked war. Yet reaching agreement was proving impossible. Lippmann thought the difficulty was obvious. Disarmament was a classic chicken-and-egg problem, which unilateral ac-tion could not solve. People wanted disarmament in order to feel safe, but no country would disarm until it felt safe. Security, the goal of disarmament, was also its precondition. So no one dared take the first step, and no agreement was possible unless everyone agreed. But the economic crisis was different. Here unilateral action could aid progress by reviving domestic confidence, which was a precondition of any sustainable international cooperation. The great advantage of the London conference, Lippmann said, was that the actions needed to tackle the depression—"to raise prices, to relieve debtors and the unemployed, and generally to enhance the capacity of their own people to buy goods"— were ones "the enlightened leaders of both [Britain and the United States] would wish to pursue, even if there were no World Economic Conference."[22]

But of course, in those words of encouragement there was also an implicit threat. If what needed to be done had to be done regardless of the conference, then the conference was expendable. First things, as Roosevelt had said in his inaugural, must come first. There would be nothing to agree on if the democracies could not agree on that.

THE BREAK

The conference was launched on June 14 with an address from the British prime minister, Ramsay MacDonald, in which he told the delegates that this was a crucial moment in world history, a golden opportunity to show that international accord was possible, even in the most testing circumstances. MacDonald was a committed internationalist who seemed to believe what he said. However, during the course of a long, somewhat rambling speech, he did not help his cause by alluding to the importance of resolving the one subject the Americans had insisted remain off the table, the hangover of debts from the war. The American delegation, led by Secretary of State Cordell Hull, was exasperated. But they were also frustrated by uncertainty about their own role. Roosevelt never had any intention of traveling to London himself (he had the baleful example of Wilson's experiences in Paris before him in case he was tempted), and he sent off the American delegation with deliberately open-ended instructions. They were to reach whatever agreements were possible and not those that were impossible. Already at this early stage of his presidency Roosevelt had established a certain creative ambiguity as his modus operandi. He did whatever he could to keep his options open, even if that meant misleading those closest to him about his ultimate intentions. He did not want to be pinned down, until he had no choice.

The result was that the first weeks of the conference were spent waiting for some clear indication of what the Americans planned to do. There were effectively four conferences going on simultaneously. First, there was the main conference, in which the delegates of sixty-six countries established their early positions on a range of complex questions and then settled in for the long haul. No one here was holding his breath for a speedy resolution (the British chancellor, Neville Chamberlain, was reminded of the Great War; in a letter to his sister, he mocked MacDonald for his belief that the whole thing would be over by Christmas). Second, there were the tripartite discussions taking place between the representatives of the British, French, and American governments, in which the British tried build a bridge between the other two by leaving open the possibility of a return to gold while exploring alternative means of stabilizing their respective currencies. Third, there was a shadow conference, convened by the governor of the Bank of England, Montagu Norman, that gathered together the leading central bankers to press the case for sound money and to discuss among themselves the best means of getting there. The presence of these "goldbugs" behind the scenes of the official conference made Keynes very uneasy. Finally, there was whatever discussions were taking place back in the United States between Roosevelt and his advisors, which would ultimately decide whether any of the other discussions were going anywhere.

Roosevelt hemmed and hawed, forbidding Hull from making any firm commitments while encouraging American bankers to explore the fixed currency options. But when rumors started to circulate that a currency stabilization pact between Britain, France, and the United States was in the cards, Roosevelt was forced to declare his hand. On July 3 he sent a message to the conference in which he rejected what he called "a purely artificial and temporary expedient" to fix the value of the dollar. He contrasted such a scheme with what he called "the larger purposes of the conference," which were to restore confidence in the international system more widely. The best way to achieve this would be for other countries to follow the United States in adopting "domestic price-lifting programs," and to continue working toward tariff reduction. He explained to the delegates that they had been preoccupied with the wrong thing, since "the sound internal economic system of a nation is a greater factor in its well-being than the price of its money in changing terms of the currencies of other nations." He went on, with a nod to Keynes as well as to popular opinion back home: "Old fetishes of so-called international bankers are being replaced by efforts to plan national currencies with the objective to give those currencies a continuous purchasing power which does not greatly vary in terms of the commodities and needs of modern civilization."[23]

It was clear Roosevelt had been spooked: he feared the American recovery would be choked off before it got going if the value of the dollar was stabilized too soon (he had been particularly alarmed to see the dollar start to strengthen on the back of the rumors coming out of London). He had also been piqued; he hated the idea of being bossed around, whether by the British and the French, or by his own economic advisors. Nonetheless, this was a statement of principle. Roosevelt was adamant that temporary fixes should not be mistaken for sustainable solutions. The conference was in danger of confusing its time horizons. It wanted long-term stability but was in too much of a hurry to get there. Roosevelt believed the rest of the world should follow the American example, which meant his personal example. One had to be willing to tolerate some short-term instability for the sake of a more durable settlement. All it took was confidence in the future and steady nerves: nothing to fear but fear itself.

The delegates at the conference did not see it that way. They did not spot that Roosevelt was taking a principled stand. All they detected was political expediency and the whiff of panic. The effect of his communication was to spread outrage and despair, particularly among the British and French, who felt that Roosevelt had played them for fools. Newspapers in both countries castigated him for caving in to American special interests, the curse of American democracy. He was the one who had got his time horizons all wrong: he was fixated on day-to-day price movements in the American markets to the exclusion of everything else.

One of the few people to stand out against this chorus of disapproval was Keynes. In a talk to the London Political Economy Club he defended Roosevelt against the charge of being concerned only with stimulating a bounce in the American markets. "We misjudge him gravely," Keynes told his audience, "if we suppose his object to be to excite Wall Street by the dope of competitive exchange devaluation."[24] When the "bombshell" of Roosevelt's message to the conference arrived on July 3, Keynes went into print the next day with a Daily Mail article headlined: "President Roosevelt Is Magnificently Right." His critics, Keynes insisted, were putting the cart before the horse—proposing arrangements to restore confidence that could only work once confidence had already been restored. Keynes reiterated Lippmann's point that the problem of economic recovery was not at all like the problem of disarmament. Progress did not have to wait on collective agreement. Better for the conference participants to know where they stood than "concocting phrases designed to conceal a fundamental difference of outlook."[25]

The problem now was the conference itself. It was still going on, and Roosevelt had no desire to see himself blamed for its failure. The great weakness of the position he had taken was that it was so undiplomatic: he was lecturing the world on how to achieve lasting international cooperation in a manner that had antagonized even his allies. Lippmann, who like Keynes thought Roosevelt was basically right, criticized him on precisely these grounds. "Mr. Roosevelt's purposes may be excellent," Lippmann wrote about Roosevelt's decision, "but he has completely failed to organize a diplomatic instrument to express them."[26] It was no good pointing out the advantages of doing things the American way if it set public opinion in the other democracies against America.

Roosevelt did what he could to keep the conference going. He made conciliatory noises and indicated that he was still open to agreement on anything else on its agenda. It was too late. The conference dragged on for the best part of another month, but nothing came of it. Too much bad blood had been spilled. The British, as well as being appalled by Roosevelt's cavalier behavior, blamed American cold feet on French intransigence: France's blind attachment to gold had scared off the Americans. The French blamed American behavior on British duplicity; why should Roosevelt agree to stabilize the dollar when the British had done what they could to devalue their own currency. The French did not believe the British government had any intention of rejoining the gold standard anyway, and they were probably right. Roosevelt's intervention had merely cemented the growing distrust between the leading democracies.

The conference finally collapsed without agreement on July 27. This time around Keynes joined in the general chorus of lamentation. He recognized that whatever the benefit for the United States of having retained its relative freedom of action, it had come at a huge cost. It was no good trumpeting fearless confidence in the future if the immediate effect was to spread a sense of inadequacy and betrayal. The world was an intensely dangerous place in 1933, and it was not clear how much time was still available for democracy to prove its long-term worth. In the meantime, it could not afford many more failures like this one. This is what Keynes wrote on the day the conference was put out of its misery:

> The Conference's lamentable end is a matter for dismay, if not for surprise. There will be no protest from the public. But the facts are duly noted. The fiasco of the Conference merely increases the general cynicism and the lack of respect towards those in power. This growing lack of respect is, as results elsewhere have shown, one of the most serious things that can befall a democracy. For when a real emergency arises, the responsible authorities, having no firm roots in the confidence of their country-men, go down like a pack of cards.[27]

In the long run, democracy still had the crucial advantages. But the long run is a misleading guide to current affairs.

Despite this, Keynes retained considerable personal confidence in Roosevelt. All his diplomatic reverses were compensated by his restless energy and his willingness to try almost anything to revive the American economy. He was the prisoner of no doctrine and in the grip of no fetish. He was open to expert advice, even if he didn't always take it. He was adaptable. At the end of 1933, in a slightly patronizing open letter to the president, which mixed stern economic advice about the mistakes he had made with a certain amount of unctuous solicitude, Keynes told him as much:

> You are the only one who sees the necessity of a profound change of methods and is attempting it without intolerance, tyranny or destruction. You are feeling your way by trial and error, and are felt to be, as you ought to be, entirely uncommitted in your own person to the details of a particular technique.[28]

Keynes put it more bluntly when writing to a friend in the aftermath of the London conference. "Roosevelt," he said, "has about as much idea of where he will land as a pre-war pilot."[29] A disastrous crash was still a possibility. But at least, unlike some of his European counterparts, he was up in the air.

THE AFTERMATH

In *The Shape of Things to Come*, which he published at the end of 1933, H. G. Wells identified the World Economic Conference as a turning point in human history. It had inaugurated a new "Age of Frustration." The title of one chapter runs: "The London Conference: The Crowning Failure of the Old Governments; the Spread of Dictatorships and Fascisms." Wells believed that the Great Depression had shown the overwhelming need for "a Five Year or Ten Year plan for all the world."[30] Instead, the London conference had produced nothing but empty words and broken promises. It spelled the end for democracy.

The great mystery of the age was how faith in democracy had been allowed to last so long. Wells, writing from some imagined future, when twentieth-century democracy has long been consigned to the dustbin of history, treats it as a shabby and threadbare religion, founded on mysticism and devoted to the worship of "that poor invertebrate mass deity of theirs, the Voter." The farce of the London conference had exposed "this Divinity [as] altogether too slow-witted for the urgent political and economic riddles, with ruin and death at hand." Democratic politicians could not take decisive action because of their "inability to shake off their life-long habit of speaking to, or at, a vaguely conceived crowd of prejudiced voters, and their invincible repugnance of clear statement." All they could do was wait to see if something would turn up. "Ramsay MacDonald rolled his r's and his eyes over the Conference and seemed still to be hoping that some favourable accident out of the void might save him and his like from the damning verdict of history." It was, Wells said, "an effect of fatuity far beyond even the pompous blunderings of Versailles." These "pseudo-leaders . . . this amazingly ineffective collection of men" were doomed. Fascism ("not an altogether bad thing . . . a bad good thing") stood ready to show what it was capable of.[31]

The Shape of Things to Come, like a lot of science fiction, is both uncanny and absurd. Wells foresees another world war beginning in 1940 with a showdown between Germany and Poland that soon drags in everyone else. The war is finally ended by the London Peace Conference of 1947, though that peace breaks down and new conflicts erupt. The world is by this point in a state of utter decay. Disease is rampant—this war, like the last one, brings in its wake a devastating flu. Conditions everywhere are shabby, unclean, poverty stricken. The United States is more or less ungovernable. It is there that a new movement emerges, called "Technocracy," which draws inspiration from an earlier generation of neglected thinkers, including Keynes. Rule by experts is seen as the only way forward, but the Keynesian version is fatally flawed by its attachment to national boundaries and its naive faith in the compatibility of technocratic government with democratic politics. More wars, more dictatorships, more failed conferences (the First Basra Conference of 1965, the Second Basra Conference of 1978) have to come and go before mankind arrives at its true political destiny: a technocratic World State, founded on efficiency and education, able to manage nature, neutralize religion, and channel human impulses in a healthy direction (the tide of pornography that threatens to sweep the planet is finally reversed). The Age of Frustration is over.

Wells makes the mistake of many futurologists in supposing that the future will be surprising in ways that resemble the surprises of the past. The Second World War that he envisages is too much like the First, the London Peace Conference too much like the Paris Peace Conference, and his 1966 too much like a supercharged version of the miseries of 1933. But he also makes the mistake of supposing that the truth about politics is written on the surface of events. He treats the failure of the World Economic Conference as evidence that democracy has nothing more to offer. The democratic politicians had their chance to show what they could do. If they couldn't rise to the occasion this time, they never would. But that is to assume the test of the strength of any political system is its ability to rise to the occasion. This produces an automatic bias in favor of authoritarianism, which is little more than rise-to-the-occasion politics. The strength of democracy is its ability to turn make-or-break occasions into routine moments of political uncertainty. (One of its weaknesses is a tendency to turn routine moments of political uncertainty—elections—into make-or-break occasions.) Democracy is more durable than other systems of government not because it succeeds when it has to, but because it can afford to fail when it has to. It is better at failure than its rivals.

Roosevelt understood the need for a democracy to refuse to be pinned down and to keep experimenting. Yet that raised a fresh set of doubts about his commitment to democracy. If Roosevelt was "experimenting" with democracy, was he any different from Hitler? Throughout 1933, particularly once it became clear they were likely to be the dominant political figures of the age, it became relatively commonplace to compare the two leaders. Were these the new dictators? The *Economist*, in the week following Roosevelt's inauguration, and six weeks after Hitler had taken power in Germany, set the tone by noting: "The indications are that in the United States, no less than in Germany, democracy, if it is to survive the crisis, may have to surrender some of its traditional sovereignty to executive rulers."[32] Both men were understood to believe in a form of Keynesian technocracy. In May the same newspaper tried to remind its readers this was not the only option.

> Before looking round for our Hitlers and our Roosevelts, and choosing our Economist-Kings, we might do well to consider whether the verdict of the crisis has been so sweeping against democracy as is sometimes supposed.[33]

The democracies should not be too hasty in handing over their powers to "dictators," even temporary ones. There was one caveat, however. Dictators were undoubtedly better at foreign affairs than their democratic equivalents. They had the ability to take decisive action when the occasion demanded it. In the international arena the democracies needed to get their act together. For that reason, the paper predicted, "the forthcoming World Economic Conference is likely to mark a political as well as an economic turning-point."

In reality, 1933 revealed the fundamental difference between Roosevelt and Hitler. One was experimenting with democracy; the other was experimenting on it, like a crazy vivisectionist. In some ways, Hitler was more constrained than Roosevelt in what he could do in 1933. For instance, he did not dare take Germany off gold, because the German people had been even more profoundly scarred by inflation than the French. He needed its totemic value, as a signifier of discipline. The massive indebtedness of the German state also meant that any devaluation of the mark would simply have increased its debt burden, since the money was owed in dollars and sterling and francs. It would have effectively led to an outright repudiation, and in 1933 Hitler lacked the stomach for that.

What he did instead was commit his regime to reviving the domestic economy by means of capital and price controls, centralization of public spending, a rearmament program, and a massive increase in political propaganda. In other words, he gambled everything on the coercive power of the state to keep himself and Germany afloat. It was experimental only in the sense that it would test to destruction the idea that a dictatorship could use force to meet any challenge and adapt to any situation. Of course, Hitler still retained the capacity to change his mind, to be fickle, unpredictable, cavalier, monstrous, insane. In that sense he hadn't boxed himself in. But he had closed off all ways of doing politics except his chosen one. He couldn't have experimented with democracy even if he had wanted to. His form of dictatorship was a one-way bet.

Roosevelt's was the opposite, which is why it wasn't really a dictatorship at all. The American state only had limited coercive capacity in 1933, and its federal system placed significant constraints on what any president could do. Even if he had wanted to, Roosevelt could not simply have imposed his political will on the country. He never got the sort of sweeping emergency powers he talked about in his inaugural, and it is not clear he ever expected to.[34] Instead, he had to find his way through the mess of democratic politics by prompting, cajoling, bamboozling, charming. He turned out to have a genius for it. He could do things in 1933 that Hitler couldn't: he took the United States off gold. But he couldn't bind the country to one course of action, come hell or high water. His form of experimentalism required that he use his executive powers to keep his options open.

There were plenty of short-term risks attached to Roosevelt's approach. He was spreading his bets, like a casino, and was ready to take some losses. Hitler was putting everything on red, like a committed gambler. In the end the casino beats the individual gambler because the casino can survive a longer losing streak. But that takes for granted that the casino always has the greater resources, which can be a risky assumption, especially in the unpredictable world of international politics. Any democracy that assumes it can always survive a run of bad luck may be tempting fate.

The previous year, on June 4, 1932, in an editorial titled "A World Adrift," the *Economist* had offered up another image of how things might play out. For now, democracy was in disarray. However:

> It may be that after a bitter interregnum in which conceptions of Hitlerism, of "authority," and all the other delusive nostra of crisis-begotten unreason and hysteria must be given an opportunity to work themselves out—like infections of the blood which flourish until the phagocytes are sufficiently

stimulated—nations will succeed in placing in power elected representatives who also have the capacity to make the world safe, not for heroes, but for "the common economic man."[35]

Looking back, you could say that the *Economist* was ultimately proved right. Hitlerism did work itself out of the system. Democracy did prove too strong in the end, and far better for its ordinary citizens. But there are two things wrong with this image. First, it holds out the false hope that as well as outlasting them democracy will one day prove its true worth by outdoing the authoritarians: beating them at their own game. That is asking too much. Second, the underlying assumption is still too fatalistic. The body will not always have the time to fight back. Sometimes the infection will win. And even when the body wins, the effects of waiting for the disease to work itself out can be profoundly debilitating. The body does not necessarily end up stronger for the experience. If the leader writers at the *Economist* had been told in 1932 that the illness would last until 1945, they might have been less sanguine about democracy's prospects.

CHAPTER 3

1947

Trying Again

THE CRISIS

NEAR THE END OF 1947 WINSTON CHURCHILL MADE A remark that has since become perhaps the most quoted line about democracy of the twentieth century. On November 11 he told the House of Commons that "democracy is the worst form of government except all those other forms that have been tried from time to time."[1] Churchill's line is now so familiar that it has turned into a cliché, the presiding cliché of democracy in crisis.

Those who first heard him say it might be forgiven for missing its significance. It came during a debate on the 1947 Parliament Bill, which had been introduced by Britain's Labour government to speed up the workings of the House of Lords in order to stop it delaying important legislation (the particular legislation the government had in mind was a plan to nationalize the British steel industry). Churchill, now in opposition, was adamantly opposed to this tinkering with the constitution. He saw it as evidence of an impatience with the ad hoc nature of democratic politics. He wanted to remind his audience that democracy was a clumsy and often tardy way of organizing the nation's affairs. That was the price you paid for avoiding the alternatives, which were more efficient but also, when they went wrong, far more destructive.

Churchill was trying to sound reasonable: he was on the side of democratic pragmatism against the grandiose schemes of those he referred to as "the supermen and super planners." Yet the speech in which he made this remark was not very reasonable. It was filled with wild flights of Churchillian rhetoric. He took Labour's relatively modest plans for the House of Lords as evidence that "we approach very near to a dictatorship in this country . . . dictatorship that is to say without either its efficiency or its criminality." He accused his opponents, through their incompetence and impatience, of leading the country to the brink of utter ruin. "It may well be that not only bankruptcy but actual starvation will come upon this island, largely from their mismanagement."[2] In trying to offer a measured defense of democracy, Churchill came across as slightly unhinged.

He was caught in a rhetorical bind. He wanted to be both restrained and alarmist: restrained about what democracy could achieve, alarmist about the risks it faced. His Labour opponents in the Commons gently and effectively chided him for his speech, treating it as an overworked music hall turn by a performer long past his best. Churchill's predicament in 1947 is of a piece with the tragicomedy of democratic life. Having saved British democracy from the gravest threat in its history, he had been rejected by the British people in an election. Labour's landslide victory in 1945 indicated that the voters wanted practical rewards for the sacrifices they had made. Their new rulers were not would-be dictators, any more than FDR had been. They too were pragmatists. So Churchill was forced to exaggerate the threat they posed in order to restore a sense of proportion to democracy. Had people forgotten just what had been at stake and who it was who had saved them? His problem was that people had not forgotten; they knew only too well, which is why they had plumped for something different. As Tocqueville might have said, democracy is the worst system apart from all the others because democracies lack a sense of proportion. They make mountains out of molehills but they also make molehills out of mountains.

Churchill was not the only one who had difficulty getting things in proportion. His predicament reflects the bind that democracy found itself in after 1945. The end of the Second World War had been very different from the end of the First, in part because people remembered what had happened last time. There was a strong sense that too much had been asked of democracy in 1918, and great hopes had only produced even greater disappointments. What was needed this time around was a more modest, more pragmatic defense of democracy. Yet the Second World War had been a truly cataclysmic event. It left chaos and misery in its wake. Could a modest defense of democracy meet the challenges of the postwar age, with its immediately pressing demands for action? Recognizing democracy as the least worst option is a way of guarding against hubris. But is it any help in a genuine crisis?

The crisis was not long in coming. By 1947 Western democracy was facing two interrelated threats. First, there was the growing threat posed by the Soviet Union, which had emerged from the war as a superpower to rival the United States. If superpower rivalry produced another war, what kind of war could the democracies now be confident of winning? Second, there was the growing threat of political and economic breakdown on the continent of Europe, which remained bankrupt, divided, and traumatized by its wartime experiences. People wanted democracy. But could they be trusted with it? Democracy needed defending. Could it be defended while acknowledging its weaknesses?

One persistent fear was that a pragmatic defense of democracy would leave the door open for anyone peddling political transformation. How could you stand up to the would-be dictators unless you were prepared to meet them on their own terms? But another fear was that pragmatism is just a small step away from fatalism. Citizens everywhere were seeking practical recompense for the sacrifices they had made. Yet if you gave them what they wanted, you would be acquiescing in their limited time horizons and prosaic ambitions. Crises were an opportunity to get things into perspective. How would that be possible if democracies were being encouraged to muddle through?

The crisis of 1947 was an acute one: Europe seemed on the brink of economic collapse; the United States seemed on the brink of war with the Soviet Union. Yet the key question from that year was whether democracies were capable of taking the long view. The most important arguments of

1947 concerned the ability of democracies to see beyond the immediate crisis and find some way of capturing their long-term advantages. These arguments set the terms for the Cold War. They also played a crucial role in its eventual outcome. However, they did not succeed in their ultimate goal of teaching democracies how to control their destiny. That proved beyond them.

Uncertain Victory

In the popular historical memory of the Western democracies, the Second World War is the "good" war. It was an unavoidable fight against an evil enemy that produced a clear-cut outcome. The First World War, by contrast, is remembered much more equivocally. Its abiding symbol is the futility of trench warfare. It was an avoidable contest that caused much suffering and resolved very little. All it did was create the conditions for the disasters to come. Yet seen from the point of view of democracy, this contrast is misleading. The First World War was the contest that became more clear-cut as it went along. It started out as a vast imperial power struggle but turned into a fight between democracy and autocracy, which the democracies won. In the Second World War it happened the other way around.

The conflagration of 1939–45 was really two separate wars. The first, from 1939 to 1941, was a contest between democracy and its enemies, which the democracies effectively lost. Few people looking at a map of Europe in the summer of

1941 could have believed that democracy on its own was any match for Hitler. The second contest, from 1941 to 1945, was a vast imperial power struggle, which the United States and the Soviet Union won. As a result, fascism was destroyed, along with its Japanese equivalent. But it was much harder in 1945 than in 1918 to view the outcome of the war as an unalloyed triumph for democracy. Stalin's subjects died in their tens of millions to defeat Hitler, under conditions of duress that look utterly grotesque from a democratic perspective. The United States, as in the First World War, provided the money and the material resources, but the Soviet Union provided much of the human capital. The democracies had needed this help to withstand the death-or-glory project of Nazism. It had been very difficult to see the 1914–18 conflict as a straightforward battle for democracy until Russia was out of it. It was very difficult to see the 1939–45 conflict as a straightforward battle for democracy once Russia was in it.

Stalin had paid lip service to Western ideas of democracy—including the need for elections in Eastern Europe—at the wartime conferences held to lay the groundwork for a postwar settlement: first in Tehran (1943), then Yalta (1944), then Potsdam (1945). By 1947 it was clear his pledges counted for nothing. Stalin was only interested in elections that the communists would win. Otherwise there would be no elections. These wartime conferences highlighted another fundamental difference between the outcome of the First World War and the Second. In 1945 no attempt was made to convene a single international peace conference to set the terms for a new world order. Memories of what had happened in Paris 1919 were still strong. Instead, the big players had tried to come to some arrangement among themselves. This had two consequences. One was that nothing much was settled, since everything depended on the future relations between the United States and the Soviet Union. The other was that no single pattern for a new democratic order was established. The democracies that were created in the aftermath of the Second World War did not emerge together in a blaze of publicity. They emerged bit by bit, in their own different ways, stumbling into the light. The prospects for democracy lay open and unresolved.

Yet by 1947 there was a sense that time was growing short. The fear was that while the world was waiting to see how democracy might turn out, the Soviets would snuff it out wherever they could. Reasonable caution about the prospects for democracy was better than hubris. But caution was no answer in an emergency. Something more was needed.

Matters came to a head in early 1947. The spur was the growing crisis in Greece and Turkey, where it was feared that political instability and economic distress would allow both countries to fall under the Soviet sphere of influence. In the United States, the Truman administration decided the moment had come to take a stand. The president asked Congress to approve $400 million of aid to support the cause of freedom in Greece and Turkey. In a speech on March 11 he set out the political principle that lay behind this request. "At the present moment in world history nearly every nation must choose between alternative ways of life," Truman declared.

One way of life is based upon the will of the majority, and is distinguished by free institutions, representative government, free elections, guarantees of individual liberty, freedom of speech and religion, and freedom from political oppression.

The second way of life is based upon the will of a minority forcibly imposed upon the majority. It relies upon terror, oppression, a controlled press and radio, fixed elections, and the suppression of personal freedom.

I believe that it must be the policy of the United States to support free peoples who are resisting attempted subjugation by armed minorities or by outside pressures.[3]

This was the bare bones of what soon came to be known as the "Truman Doctrine."

Truman understood perfectly well that Greek democracy was barely functioning in 1947: the country was in a state of incipient civil war and its provisional democratic government was proving brutal and corrupt. Violence was everywhere. The American people were being asked to support a regime that hardly conformed to the ideal of the first way of life he had spelled out. But Truman's message was that if Greek democracy could be preserved from Soviet influence, it would improve. "No government is perfect," he said. "One of the chief virtues of democracy, however, is that its defects are always visible and under democratic processes can be pointed out and corrected." Truman thought Americans could not afford to be squeamish. The time had come to draw a line between democracy and the alternatives. Where democracy was possible, it would evolve into something better. America's job was to make sure it remained possible.

Truman had stated his belief that democracy needed protection in the places where it was most at risk. What he had not said was what this would mean for the democracy that was doing the protecting. Would it also be able to recognize its own defects and correct them once it was engaged in a struggle to preserve other people's freedom around the world? Most commentators greeted the clarity of purpose in Truman's speech with enthusiasm, but not Lippmann, who was by now the most famous journalist in America (his only rival in 1947 would have been H. L. Mencken). Lippmann thought Truman was self-deceived and his argument self-defeating. The Truman Doctrine meant asking Americans to put their trust in the transparent qualities of even the most rickety democracies. Yet this would commit American democracy to a course of action that would not itself be transparent. It would be opaque, like all drawn-out political battles. Its progress would be difficult to judge, never mind to correct. "A vague global policy, which sounds like the tocsin of an ideological crusade, has no limits," Lippmann wrote after hearing Truman's speech. "It cannot be controlled. Its effects cannot be predicted."[4] It was a fight the democracies could not win.

Lippmann was not alone in wondering whether Truman was making a big mistake. The Truman Doctrine was designed to preserve democracy for the long run, by playing to its underlying strengths of durability and adaptability. In its May 17 issue, the *Economist* asked whether it didn't in fact play into the strengths of the Soviet system instead. Democratic adaptability was closely tied to democratic fickleness. The longer the struggle went on, the more chance democracies would have to mess it up. Did democracies really have the stomach for the long game?

> There is a sense in which time is on Russia's side—though it is not the reason that is usually given [i.e., the Marxist reason, that in the long run capitalism is doomed]. It is unlikely that time will raise their strength relative to that of the West—it might even have the contrary effect. But time will bring out some of the inherent weaknesses of the western position, the weaknesses from which any democracy, and still more a collection of democracies, suffers when it comes to the game of power politics. For that game demands patience, resolution, clear sight, a lack of illusions, a refusal to be frightened by tactical moves, a determination not to be taken in by appearances or to yield to emotions.[5]

The paper concluded: "What made Hitler strong was not any great accumulation of economic resources but the flabbiness of the democracies, their lack of clear thinking and courage. The answer to the riddle of Russia's power is to be found in Washington."

INVENTING THE COLD WAR

Washington attempted to supply its answer to the riddle a few weeks later. In July George Kennan, a State Department official writing under the pseudonym "X," published an essay titled "The Sources of Soviet Conduct." It appeared first in *Foreign Affairs*, then in *Life* magazine, where millions read it. In it, Kennan explained why in the long run Russia would lose.

The article was based on the "Long Telegram" that Kennan had sent in the spring of 1946 from Moscow, where he was then posted, to his masters back in Washington, instructing them that the Russians should no longer be thought of as anybody's allies. Roosevelt had held out hopes up until his death in April 1945 that Russia and America could jointly "police" the postwar world. Kennan had wanted the Truman administration to acknowledge that this was a fantasy. The Russians were not interested in doing anything with the United States, except to bring the country to its knees. Theirs was an implacable, ideological regime devoted to the demise of Western democracy. It could not be accommodated. It had to be faced down. Kennan wanted to suggest some of the ways this might be done short of war.

The "Long Telegram" was an internal government document, written for policy makers to acquaint them with the reality of the Soviet mindset. The 1947 article was not intended for public circulation either (it started life as a private report for Secretary of Defense John Forrestal). But Kennan was persuaded that it would suit a wider audience if published anonymously. Coming so soon after Truman's articulation of his doctrine for the defense of freedom, it was inevitably seen as a rationale for that approach. Kennan later felt his words had been co-opted in a propagandist cause. Yet in the article he went further than he had in the telegram. In 1947 he did not simply lay bare the nature of Stalin's regime in order to dispel any illusions about its amenableness. He set its behavior in a framework of historical destiny. "The Sources of Soviet Conduct" depicted the future confrontation between democracy and its enemies as a battle between two different kinds of fate. The Soviets were trapped by theirs. If the Western democracies could recognize this, it was their fate to come out on top.

Kennan felt the Soviets were trapped in two ways. First, they were trapped by their total dependence on coercion and the suppression of free speech. It was simply too dangerous for politicians whose authority was founded on force to explore the alternatives. They were stuck with the path they had chosen: absolute state control. In some ways this made them more adaptable than the democracies. Stalin could get his people to do things, and to put up with things, that no American president would dream of. But in the long run the Soviet system would be unable to adapt. It could not allow its citizens any say in the running of the state without destabilizing the entire regime.

The longer this went on, the worse the problem got. People who are brutalized and infantilized become more unpredictable, not less, because no one can know what they might do given the chance to express themselves. Kennan thought the breaking point would come when the regime had to hand over power from one leader to the next. What would happen, he asked, "if rivals in the quest for higher power reach down into these politically immature and inexperienced masses in order to find support for their higher claims?"[6] Democracies do this all the time, whenever they hold elections. But a routine crisis for a democracy was liable to be terminal for the Soviet system.

The other reason the Russians were trapped was because of their absolute faith that the future belonged to them.

They were committed to a doctrine of historical determinism: capitalism was bound to collapse; communism was bound to replace it. Did the Soviet leaders actually believe in their own ideology? Kennan said it didn't matter. They had to take it seriously, because it was the basis of their power. Whether they believed it or not, they could not afford to doubt it.

Again, this gave them some advantages. They could be patient because time was ostensibly on their side. In the international arena, they could toy with their enemies, and conciliate them if necessary. For Kennan this is what distinguished Stalin from Hitler. Nazism was a fundamentally impatient ideology that had no faith in anything except the use of force to achieve its goals. It was reckless or it was nothing. Stalin, by contrast, could afford to appear reasonable, and he knew when to play it safe. But the Soviet system was still doomed, because while they were deceiving others, its leaders were also deceiving themselves. Kennan borrowed a line from his favorite book, Edward Gibbon's *Decline and Fall of the Roman Empire*: "See how the conscience may slumber in a mixed and middle state between self-illusion and voluntary fraud."

Their ideological commitments meant Russia's leaders could indulge in absurd plans for accelerated growth, which skewed their entire economy, causing some branches of industry to be developed out of all proportion, while others were left to atrophy. It also caused them to mistake the dislocations of Western capitalism for evidence of impending collapse. "The Soviet thesis," Kennan explained, "implies complete lack of control by the West over its economic destiny. . . . The palsied decrepitude of the capitalist world is the keystone of Communist philosophy."⁷ The Soviets took for granted that the chaotic appearance of Western democracy was evidence of its underlying weakness, whereas the decisive appearance of their own system was evidence of its underlying strength. This was a historic mistake.

The way to combat the Soviet threat was to let it collapse under the pressure of trying to sustain its own illusions. It did not have to be crushed; it simply had to be contained. The fake patience of the Soviets would be exposed if it encountered true patience on the part of the democracies. What was required, Kennan wrote, was "long-term, patient but firm and vigilant containment of Russian expansive tendencies." Were the American people up to the task? Kennan had no illusions about democracy, about what he called "its sporadic acts" and "its momentary whims." It was an often chaotic and sometimes foolish way of making decisions, especially foreign policy decisions. But that was why the Soviet challenge was good for it, because it allowed democracy to access its underlying strengths. Kennan's article concluded with an invocation of democratic providence that seemed to come out of another century:

> The thoughtful observer of Russian-American relations will find no cause for complaint in the Kremlin's challenge to American society. He will rather experience a certain gratitude to Providence which, by providing the American people with this implacable challenge, has made their entire security as a nation dependent on their pulling themselves together and accepting the responsibilities of moral and political leadership that history plainly intended them to bear.⁸

"X" no longer sounds much like the prudential author of the "Long Telegram." He sounds more like a prophet. He was Tocqueville, minus the doubts.

When Lippmann read the article by "X," who was soon known to be Kennan, he realized it was what he had been looking for. He went into print straight away, in fourteen short articles for the *New York Herald Tribune*, which were then collected into a single book. Lippmann called this book *The Cold War*, the first time the phrase had reached a wider audience. The name stuck. But in christening the contest, what Lippmann was doing was repudiating it. He thought it was Kennan who had made the historic mistake.

Lippmann believed that Kennan had made the same misjudgment that he was accusing the Russians of having made: he had allowed himself to get trapped in a vision of the future. The best way Kennan could see to combat the Soviet threat was to mimic its resolve: do the same, only do it better. But what reason was there to think that a democracy could do it better? Yes, the democracies were more flexible and more resourceful than the Soviet system, but that was precisely what made them unsuited to a policy of containment, which required that they pick a course and then stick to it. They would be sacrificing their most useful quality: their ability to adapt to changing circumstances. And for what? For an uncertain promise of some distant reward.

Kennan's article purported to give a realistic assessment of the enemy, stripped of any false hopes. But in fact, Lippmann said, it was a piece of wishful thinking. It was not wishful about the Soviets. Lippmann did not disagree that the Soviet system was intrinsically hostile to the West and likely to overreach itself (though he thought that Kennan had overstated the importance of ideology at the expense of geography). Where Kennan was being wishful was in his view of the United States.

Lippmann thought Kennan was expecting too much of American democracy in requiring it to show the necessary patience for a policy of containment ("the Americans would themselves probably be frustrated by Mr. X's policy long before the Russians were," he wrote).[9] He also thought the challenge of funneling aid and support to fragile regimes around the world would simply replicate the worst features of the Soviet system: it would put power in the hands of "the planners," who would skew the operation of market forces in favor of propping up inefficient and corrupt governments. The basic problem, however, was that containment meant fixing democracy's future before it was ready to be fixed. It preached the virtues of patience but in fact it was an impatient doctrine, because it said we have to draw the line *now*. Now—the chaotic circumstances of 1947—was no time to be drawing the line.

Lippmann felt he had been here before. Both Kennan and Truman were confident they had learned the hard lessons of the previous generation and were not going to make the same mistakes: they were not Woodrow Wilson. Yet as Lippmann saw it, they were replicating Wilson's final, fateful error of judgment. They had been tricked by their long-term perspective into jumping the gun. As a result, they would scupper the chances of a durable peace just as surely as Wilson had. They would destroy the prospects for the United Nations, which would simply become an extension of the US-Soviet battleground. Containment, far from giving democracy the room to grow, was boxing it in prematurely. It would freeze democracy at an artificial stage of its development.

What Lippmann wanted instead was what he called "the Marshall Plan purged of the Truman Doctrine"; that is, financial aid to rebuild European economies without the political commitment to defend democracy wherever it was deemed to exist. He thought this political commitment was most obviously unsustainable in Germany. The conclusion of the war had produced a country divided between West and East, the Allied and the Soviet spheres. The Truman Doctrine was promising to defend democracy in the West. But what most Germans wanted was to be a single country once again. At some point, the Russians would be able to exploit the mismatch between American promises for the future (including the distant promise of reunification) and their insistence on the artificial realities of the present. The Soviet Union could offer Germany swift reunification in return for ditching the Americans. The Germans, Lippmann suspected, would take it.

> In an auction for the support of the Germans, the Russians can offer them great prizes, and we can offer them absolutely nothing—except some help in rising from squalor and misery and prostitution to the position of a fifth rate power living a prosaic and stunted national existence.[10]

What self-respecting democracy would want that?

When Kennan read Lippmann's attack he was dismayed. He was also angry. Kennan deeply resented the implication that he was providing the intellectual rationale for the Truman Doctrine, and he came to regret his association with the term *containment*. He had not been saying that the United States should always push back against the Soviets wherever they threatened to encroach into the Western sphere of influence. He had never argued that every nascent democracy around the world should be defended, no matter how fragile or ineffective. He agreed that democracies could be stupid and reckless. He was stating the need for American democracy to be vigilant, to be persistent, and to bide its time. In his own mind, this was an argument for adaptability, not rigidity. So what were he and Lippmann arguing about?[11]

What they were really arguing about was democracy and fate. Kennan thought that a democracy might be galvanized by being given a glimpse into the future. Lippmann thought that if you told democracies that they would win in the long run, you were leading them astray, even if what you said happened to be true.

Kennan's dispute with Lippmann was like Tocqueville's falling out with Mill in 1840. Two men who agreed about the problem with democracy found themselves on opposite sides of the thing they agreed about. Both were conscious of the tension between democracy's short-term failings and its long-term advantages. Kennan thought the only way to access the advantages was to confront democracies with a really serious long-term challenge. Lippmann thought that risked exacerbating the failings. A long struggle with the Soviets was bound to involve a succession of future crises, and in those circumstances the long-term advantages of democracy would be no help. A policy of containment would lead to drift, and to the recklessness that went along with drift. Either Americans would lose interest in the struggle and so be taken unawares by the next crisis, or they would rush headlong into the next crisis, impatient for their reward, and so make things worse.

The question for both men remained the one it had been for Tocqueville and Mill: how could democracies learn from their mistakes? Lippmann feared that the underlying message of the Truman Doctrine was one of impunity: in the long run, mistakes don't matter much. All that mattered was keeping democracy going wherever possible. The moral hazard was clear: democracies would never be required to learn, and so would keep making the same mistakes. Kennan agreed that democracies were likely to keep making the same mistakes. That meant the only way for them to learn was to look at the historic mistake the Soviets were making. Democracies always lack a sense of perspective: it has to be given to them from the outside. Lippmann felt this outside perspective was warped. It turned democracy into a monolithic entity, seen through the looking glass of its monolithic opponent. It ignored all the different ways democracies might still go wrong.

Kennan was trying to provide a pragmatic vision for democracy, one that was sensitive to its failings. All anyone could know for sure was that the ideological alternatives were worse. He thought he was being realistic. Still, he was asking too much. He soon acknowledged this. No long-term vision can ever be truly pragmatic, and no democracy ever really learns from other people's mistakes. Containment came to mean ongoing confrontation and mutual suspicion. It produced a mindset that was both reckless and unthinking. It eventually morphed into something Kennan loathed, the policy known as "rollback," which insisted that the West push back against the Soviets, and push back harder. When that happened, Kennan found that he agreed with Lippmann. The long view is dangerous for democracy. It leads into a trap. The more confident democracies are of their destiny, the more likely they are to veer wildly off course.

Faith in the future, which is meant to breed patience, ends up corroding it.

The View from the Mountain

Lippmann is the Zelig of twentieth-century politics. He turns up everywhere, at all the important moments, though in retrospect it's easy to miss him. It's the people he is standing next to who get remembered.

After the war the Austrian economist Friedrich Hayek was also experiencing an unexpected brush with fame. As with Kennan, it was Lippmann who had provided the spur. Back in 1937, Lippmann had published a book called *The Good Society*, in which he argued that the politics of the New Deal was posing a growing threat to the freedom of the individual: he thought the emergency of 1933 had turned into an excuse for excessive governmental control. Partly inspired by Lippmann's example, Hayek had written a short book of his own for the general public about the threat to freedom central planning posed. He called it *The Road to Serfdom*, a title he took from the closing pages of Tocqueville's *Democracy in America*.[12]

Hayek's book was published in 1944. It was generally well received by his fellow economists, who were starting to think about the possibilities and limits of the postwar world. Keynes told Hayek he was in sympathy with much of it, though he found it quixotic in its certainties. In 1945 the *Reader's Digest* brought out a condensed version, which made its core arguments accessible to the widest possible audience in the United States. For some, it became a kind of bible.

Hayek's theme in *The Road to Serfdom* was that planning might look like a way for democracies to gain control of market forces, but this was an illusion. Instead it results in the total loss of democratic control. No voting public is ever going to agree on a plan for the economy—it would be far too complicated and there would be far too many competing interests—so planning requires an elite cadre of experts to make the relevant decisions about who gets what. Democracy means majority rule, but majorities can't agree on plans. That leaves just two possibilities. Either the majority agrees to let someone else make all the important decisions. Or the majority agrees to give up on the idea of having a plan. Hayek thought the only way to save democracy was to persuade it to take the second option.

From 1945 Hayek started trying to organize a gathering of liberal intellectuals whose job it would be to make the counterintuitive case that democracies could only retain control of their destiny if they stopped trying to control it. People would have to learn to live with uncertainty. Hayek thought the essential task for postwar democracies was to learn to understand their own limits.

Eventually Hayek found a financial backer and put together a program and a guest list for a conference to be held at the Swiss resort of Mont Pèlerin in April 1947. Lippmann was invited but did not come; he was too busy fighting his own battles back in the United States. Hayek's Austrian

colleague, Ludwig von Mises, was there, along with Karl
Popper, Michael Polanyi, and a number of younger European and American economists, including Milton Friedman
from Chicago. Hayek wanted to call the new gathering the
Tocqueville-Acton Society, in honor of his two heroes of
nineteenth-century liberalism (Acton was Lord Acton, the
man who had said that "power tends to corrupt, and absolute power corrupts absolutely"). In the end, it became
known as the Mont Pelerin Society.

The purpose of the Mont Pelerin Society, as Hayek saw it,
was to provide an antidote to the sense of drift he perceived
around him. He identified "fatalism" as the greatest threat
of the postwar age. His fear was that Europe's exhausted and
traumatized democracies would vote for socialism, more or
less by default. Social democracy—welfare states, planned
economies, price controls—seemed to offer a way out of the
horrors of war and a safeguard against repeating the economic chaos that had led to war. Here was the chance of a
fresh start and the hope of a more stable, equitable world.
Who was going to say no to that?

British voters had set the lead in 1945 by ditching their
warrior-king Churchill in favor of the mild-mannered Clement Attlee and his government of administrators. Across
continental Europe, the early evidence suggested that other
electorates were preparing to follow suit, or do something
worse. In France and Italy communists made big gains in
local elections. In Germany, regional plebiscites indicated a
strong public preference for the nationalization of major industries. Most people wanted government to take charge of
their miserable, day-to-day struggle for existence and give
them some security. Hayek thought this appetite for secu-

rity was a political death trap. He felt it was imperative to let people know there was an alternative to socialism. However, they had to want to take it.

It was this belief that democracies could learn how to exercise self-control that made Hayek so different from many of his contemporaries. It was the big difference between him and Lippmann, who did not have nearly so much confidence in the ability of any democracy to understand what it is doing. Hayek's belief in democracy also marked him out from another Austrian economist with whom he is often compared and sometimes confused: Joseph Schumpeter.

Schumpeter had become internationally famous in 1942 with his book *Capitalism, Socialism, and Democracy*, which exploded the idea that democracies were capable of choosing the course they wished to take. There was no such thing as the "general will," Schumpeter insisted, no "common interest." The voters had no real clue what they wanted in the long run; too many of them wanted contradictory things. Instead, democracy was simply a mechanism for replacing one government with another. The means by which this was done—elections—was simply a contest between competing teams of salesmen offering the voters a choice of manufactured products to pick from. In this contest, the politicians who offered the voters the nicest-sounding product would win. Socialism was nicer sounding than capitalism. It promised security, solidarity, peace of mind. These were vapid promises, but that didn't matter, since democracy was a vapid business. The voters would choose socialism by default, because the alternatives were too hard to sell.

That was far too fatalistic for Hayek, who saw himself in the spirit of Tocqueville: someone who could wake European democracy up to its fate and give it the chance to regain some control over it. Unlike Schumpeter, Hayek took democracy seriously on its own terms. It meant that the majority was in charge, not the salesmen. This was extremely dangerous, since majorities could do idiotic, self-destructive things. It was a big mistake to suppose that democracy was valuable for its own sake, given its capacity to go down the wrong path. Democracy was only valuable in conjunction with capitalism. But in conjunction with capitalism, it was extremely valuable. It gave capitalism political legitimacy and public support. Hayek did not want capitalism without democracy. So he was determined to find ways for them to coexist.

Hayek's answer was to juxtapose experimentalism with fatalism and then ask democracy to choose between them. It was one or the other. A democracy that chose to protect and preserve experimentalism would learn that it could not give in to its appetite for security. It would insist on limits to the power of the majority. This was the lesson Hayek took from Tocqueville: that democracy could only be preserved when democracies learn to leave the future open. The alternative is the tyranny of the majority.

But Hayek only saw one side of the problem and one side of Tocqueville. There were two sources of democratic fatalism for Tocqueville. One was the inexorable trend toward equality of conditions. The other was a blind faith that nothing is ever as bad as it seems. In 1947 Hayek did not see the second as a threat, certainly not for the battered, bowed-down people of Europe. His fear was the first: the democratic embrace of equality would be bought at the expense of faith in the future. He did not recognize the ways that an embrace of experimentalism can be a straitjacket too. Democracies that put their faith in the future close off their options in the present. They lose the ability to change their circumstances. Insisting on the long view is also a form of shortsightedness. Democracies that embrace it won't see what they are doing wrong until it is too late.

What Hayek was after was incredibly demanding, as he recognized—democratic self-control requires heroic restraint. Nevertheless, he made it sound too easy. All democracies had to do was put themselves beyond the reach of temptation. Knowing how hard self-control is should enable democracies to want to avoid the risk of having to exercise it. The image that sums up what Hayek was after—it is one he and his followers were to employ repeatedly—is the story of Ulysses and the Sirens. Hayek acknowledged that democracies had to be the captains of their own ship: if someone else was steering then these weren't really democracies. But the way ahead was extremely perilous. The sweet song of security was in the air; no more danger, no more risks, sang the planners, just come over to us. It would be all too easy to steer the ship onto the rocks. Hayek wanted democracy to learn how to bind itself to the mast in order to resist the siren song of socialism. This was the kind of self-knowledge he was after: the knowledge of our own susceptibility to temptation.

It is a seductive image. But it's also a misleading one. First, no one ever binds themselves to the mast; someone has to tie you up, and to untie you, if the method is going to work.[13] Any democracy that ties itself up can untie itself. A democracy that votes for constitutional restraint, or a balanced budget requirement, or limitations on public spending, can un-vote all these things. Second, Ulysses knew where the danger lay: it was those rocks over there. He could tell his crew to tie his hands so long as the temptation lasted, during which time they were not to listen to his desperate pleas to be released. Once the ship was out of earshot of the Sirens, then they could set him free and he would resume his command. When would democracy be out of earshot of temptation? When could it be set free?

One possible answer was never. This would mean democracies having to institute some permanent constraints limiting majority rule and protecting market freedoms. One way to do this was to go back to the traditional gold standard, which many (including Hayek) still perceived as the ultimate safeguard against democratic ill discipline. Alternatively, the new democracies of Europe could learn from the founding of the United States, where constitutional safeguards had been put in place in order to keep majority rule in check. Hayek wanted European democracies to follow the example of America—he shared the view of his other hero, Acton, who once wrote: "We have made securities for democracy but no securities against it—in that line of thought America is beyond us."[14] However, securing against democracy is not the same as teaching a democracy how to limit itself. Permanent safeguards imply a lack of faith in the capacity of any democracy to recognize the dangers up ahead.

The other possibility was that democracy only needs to be limited in crisis situations. Such a crisis was clearly visible in 1947. For now Europe's shell-shocked democracies were far too close to the rocks to be left to their own devices. But over time, if the immediate dangers could be seen off, the ties could be loosened. In his more optimistic moods, Hayek seemed to hold open this possibility: if European democracies could be kept afloat, they would eventually be able to decide for themselves when it was safe to steer their own course, and when they needed to be constrained. This is where Hayek fundamentally differed from Keynes. Hayek thought that a stable, well-functioning democracy would know not to loosen its constraints in times of difficulty, because it would be aware of the risks. Keynes thought the whole point of a stable democracy, bound by a set of rules, was that it could afford to loosen its constraints in a crisis, so as to be able to steer away from danger. Keynes believed the nearer the rocks, the more need for freedom of action. Hayek believed the opposite.

On balance, Keynes was right, because he recognized that crises are inherently surprising for democracies. That's what makes them crises. This is why the Siren image doesn't work. No one knows where the rocks are. Democracies can't bind themselves to the mast for as long as is takes and then get set free when the danger is past. Either they are going to be permanently tied up so they can't escape, in which case they are not in charge of the ship, or they have to be tied up loosely enough that they can escape, in which case they are liable to break free at the moment of danger. The Siren image remains a seductive one: self-aware democracy, able to deploy its experience of its past failings to regulate its own weaknesses. But it is a dangerous fantasy, as later crises would show. The music Hayek was sending down from Mont Pelerin in 1947, warning of the Siren temptations to democracy, was not much heard at the time. He was right that it would take a while to filter through. When people did start to listen to it, later in the century, it would turn out to be its own siren song. It leads back onto the rocks.

THE AFTERMATH

Kennan and Hayek, in their very different ways, thought the postwar world was too dangerous for democracy to muddle through. The democracies had to take charge of their destiny. On the other hand, neither of them had any illusions about democracy. They knew that muddle and confusion and fear and misplaced hope were its modus operandi. Democracies did not know what was best for them at any given moment. What Kennan and Hayek were after was some way to get the democracies to see this for themselves. They were looking to engender self-awareness on the part of democracy out of the crisis circumstances of 1947. The only way for the democracies to take charge of their fate was to understand the pitfalls of trying. The strength that comes from knowing your own weaknesses; that was the best you could hope for. It was what Churchill wanted too.

Still, it was hoping for too much. Their experience in 1947 and thereafter did not breed self-awareness on the part of the democracies. They did not acquire a sense of perspective. They muddled through.

In West Germany a public philosophy emerged that was close to what Hayek had been after. It was called "ordoliberalism" and it had ties to some of the leading members of the Mont Pelerin Society, including the German economist Walter Eucken and the first West German finance minister Ludwig Erhard, who joined the society in 1950.[15] Ordoliberals believed that a strong state was needed to provide the framework on top of which market forces could operate. The job of the state was to control and limit all those entities that might disrupt the operation of the market, including business cartels and impulsive democratic majorities.

This was democracy protected from its short-term weaknesses in an attempt to secure its long-term strengths. But it was not a recipe for democratic self-awareness. It was a top-down arrangement, designed to keep democracy safely under control.

It worked. West Germany, aided by the money that came from the Marshall Plan, guided by the wise hands of the ordoliberals, prospered, became stable, secure, and soon quite affluent. There was something almost magical about this. The magic was symbolized by one of Erhard's decisive early acts. In July 1948, as provisional finance minister he lifted price controls on some consumer goods, ending the miserable shortages of the postwar years in one fell swoop, swamping the shops with items that previously had been hoarded and creating a consumer economy almost overnight. Prices soared, then stabilized. After the initial shock, people began to believe in a more prosperous future and to put less faith in the socialist alternatives.

Yet this was not a moment of truth. It was an administrative act foisted on an unsuspecting public with the connivance of the occupying military authorities. It was not the action of a functioning state, since West Germany still had no separate constitutional identity in 1948. It was an inspired piece of improvisation designed to prop up an ad hoc system until it could be stabilized. It did not put a check on the illusions of West German democracy. It gave them room to breathe.

When West Germany finally got a constitution in 1949 it was also something of a contrivance. The constitution was a holding arrangement—or "basic law"—designed to set the ground rules for this improvised state until it could be properly reconstituted as part of a unified Germany. This was the idea that Lippmann had derided: that West Germans would be satisfied with something that called itself a democracy yet only mimicked its ability to make meaningful choices about the future. West Germans were being offered security in exchange for the ability to control their own destiny, which looked like it was being indefinitely deferred. Lippmann felt sure this arrangement could not last. If Germans were ever given a real choice, they would choose to grasp their democratic destiny now. If they were denied that choice, they would come to realize they were not a real democracy.

Lippmann was wrong. The arrangement lasted. The fact that it was built on a deferred promise did not make it unacceptable. It simply made it hard to fathom. The surface appearance of West German democracy—that it was a temporary fix—belied the underlying reality—that it was here to stay. Raymond Aron thought that Lippmann had fallen into the trap of thinking that the truth about politics must be written on the surface of events. His complete failure to understand what the Germans would and would not put up with was, Aron wrote, "a lesson in prudence to those who would accept the thankless task of reacting to events and discerning their meaning before their consequences become apparent."[16] Aron saw it as a warning to all journalists, himself included: never tempt fate. Or rather, because all journalists have to tempt fate all the time, never think you have gotten away with it.

For Aron, the survival of West German democracy simply showed the impossibility of making sense of democratic destiny. It was a mystery, which did not mean it was a fraud. The architects of West Germany's constitution, including its first chancellor, Konrad Adenauer, believed the division of Germany would be destabilized once it was officially recognized. So by rejecting it in principle they helped to maintain it in practice. "The only truth accessible to objective understanding," Aron wrote, "is the recognition of these contradictions. If there is Providence in this chaos, it escapes us."[17] Many, including Jean-Paul Sartre, accused Aron of fatalism. Aron thought the way to avoid fatalism was to have no illusions at all.

West German democracy was also folded into another improvised arrangement: a Franco-German alliance. The only way the French could feel safe with German democracy, after their experience last time around, was to keep it under wraps. Adenauer was happy to play along; his conception of the safest future for West Germany was as part of a Western European federation. But this alliance was not a clearly defined political project. It too was an ad hoc series of economic arrangements, designed to facilitate the working of the Marshall Plan, to keep the European economies growing, and to postpone major political decisions for as long as possible. Western European democracy was not being asked, or expected, to take control of its fate. It was simply being encouraged to feel its way into the future.[18] No one was looking for the moment of truth for fear of the damage it might do.

One reason for deferring the moment of truth was that French democracy in this period was nothing like German democracy. France had gone down the plebiscitary route in establishing a constitution for its new (its fourth) republic:

elected representatives in a constituent assembly whose proposals would be put to the people in a referendum. The resulting constitution was highly democratic, in the sense that it tried to accommodate as many different interests as possible. Under its auspices France would go through twenty different governments in the decade from 1948 to 1958, while West Germany would go through one. Ordoliberalism might be good for stabilizing democracy, but it's hard to get nascent democracies to choose ordoliberalism.

Italy went down the French route of a democratic constitutional assembly, with similar results. In 1948, the Italian general election raised the real possibility that the communists would win the vote and form a government, fulfilling some of Stalin's fondest hopes. In the end, American money and Vatican propaganda secured a victory for the Christian Democrats. Italian democracy was not stabilized; there would be seven different prime ministers from 1948 to 1958. But it was secured.

As the European case shows, there was no single pattern by which the postwar democracies stumbled into their shared future. Outside Europe, the differences were even greater. The three most significant new democracies—India, Japan, Israel—were constituted in very different ways. An indirectly elected constituent assembly spent three years debating the form India's new democracy should take, judiciously and somewhat ponderously considering the pros and cons, while violence and passion seethed outside. "There is such a thing as too much of a democratic procedure," Nehru told the delegates, trying to guide them in the way of self-control.[19] The democracy that emerged was not self-controlled, but it was confident of its own special destiny.

In Japan, a constitution was imposed by the American occupiers. It did everything it could to defang Japanese democracy of its most dangerous instincts. The new Japanese constitution included a clause renouncing war. This clause was to prove hugely popular with the Japanese people, whose experiences of war had not been good. Yet it could almost certainly not have been passed by an elected constitutional assembly, which would have felt constrained to answer to those same instincts it was trying to renounce.

Meanwhile, Israeli democracy was born in a condition of war, and its constitution was that of a fighting republic. It allowed considerable leeway for the military and the secret service by making sure their roles were not clearly defined. It provided a framework for the defense of Israeli democracy from its own weaknesses by making sure that Israeli democracy was never left knowingly undefended.

How could Germany, France, Italy, never mind India, Japan, Israel share a common democratic destiny? Yet they did: their constitutional variety was evidence of democratic adaptability, which is what gives democracy the edge. It remained an improvised, inadvertent form of politics. All these differences did not mean the new democracies would be in a position to learn from each other's mistakes, as Tocqueville might have hoped. Their separate mistakes merely led them to mistrust each other. Their shared destiny was to keep going regardless.

There was, however, one new factor in world politics that promised to erase the difference between the various democracies and give them a joint perspective on their common fate: the bomb. It was the threat of nuclear confrontation between the Soviets and the Americans that did most to persuade Kennan that an inflexible policy of standing up to the Russians was too dangerous. It would draw the United States into showdowns where the stakes were far too high. It would make reasonable discussions about disarmament practically impossible. Kennan joined Lippmann in arguing for the demilitarization of Germany in order to provide a buffer between the superpowers and give containment some breathing room. Rollback would have to be rolled back. Kennan's fear throughout his life was that the democracies would stumble into a nuclear showdown inadvertently, because they had taken insufficient care to guard against their own impulsiveness. Democratic muddle and nuclear arsenals seemed fundamentally incompatible.

If anything could put things in perspective for the democracies, it was surely the threat of the ultimate crisis: a nuclear holocaust. But in this, too, Kennan would be disappointed. The democracies did not gain insight into their own weaknesses under the shadow of the bomb. As we will see, they muddled through.

CHAPTER 4

1962

On the Brink

THE CRISIS

ON DECEMBER 29, IN ITS END OF YEAR REVIEW, THE *Economist* summed up the general feeling of relief. "Asked what it did in 1962," the newspaper wrote, "the world can reply curtly that it survived."[1] What it had survived was the most dangerous moment of the Cold War, perhaps the most dangerous moment in human history: the Cuban Missile Crisis, which for a few days in late October brought the Soviet Union and the United States to the brink of all-out war. The showdown between the two superpowers over Russian nuclear missile sites in Cuba is often remembered as *the* crisis point of modern politics. For a short time, almost everything was at stake. The fate of the world stood in the balance.

For that reason, it can be hard to see the Cuban Missile Crisis as a crisis of democracy. It looks both too big and too small for that. Too big because the stakes were so high: if the worst had happened, little else would have mattered. The advantages of democracy over other systems of government don't count for much in the face of Armageddon. Nuclear conflict between the United States and the Soviet Union in 1962 would not have spelled the end of politics, because it would not have spelled the end of the human race, and human beings are political animals. But it would have spelled the end of politics as we know it. God alone knows what would have come next.

It looks too small because of the scale of the event. The crisis took place over a very brief period—it was just a couple of weeks from the Americans' discovery of nuclear launch sites on Cuba to Khrushchev's announcement of his decision to dismantle them—and involved only a small group of people on either side. There was hardly the time or space for democracy to play a part. Two cloistered political elites, sweating it out in smoky rooms, groping in the dark for signals from the other side, stumbling with relief at the end of it all back out into the light—where was the room for democracy in that?

It's this juxtaposition between the tight confines of the decision-making process and the unfathomable consequences of a misstep that has given the Cuban Missile Crisis its totemic quality and made it a source of endless fascination, for filmmakers and novelists as much as historians and political scientists. It's where you go to breathe the pure air of decisionism, and also to get a whiff of the sulfurous odor of the abyss. It's not where you usually look for the clang and clatter of democracy in action.

However, as so often with democracy, appearances can be deceptive. The Cuban Missile Crisis was a quintessential democratic crisis, and it fits squarely into the story I am telling in this book. There are three reasons why. First, democracy did play a part in resolving the crisis, but only indirectly. The outcome was something more than luck, but less than design. It was, if anything, a victory for democratic inadvertence. Second, for that reason it was not much of a learning experience. The easiest lesson to draw from the successful resolution of the crisis was that democracy is a providential system of government. The crisis did more to foster democratic fatalism than to correct for it. Third, it was not the only threat to democracy to emerge in late October 1962. The existential drama of the Cuban Missile Crisis has tended to leave the impression that the world held its breath for a few days, waiting for permission to exhale. But the world kept turning.

In that same week in October, two other significant democratic crises were unfolding, one in India, one in West Germany. On October 22, the day President Kennedy went on television to warn the American people of the threat to their safety coming from Cuba, the Indian prime minister, Nehru, made a radio broadcast to inform his people that they were under attack from China, and that their very security as a democracy was at stake. On the night of October 26/27, when the Cuban Missile Crisis had reached its critical juncture and the protagonists were peering into the void, the West German defense minister, Franz Josef Strauss, authorized a raid on the offices of the magazine *Der Spie-gel*, prompting the biggest crisis in the brief history of West German democracy.

Neither the Sino-Indian war nor the *Spiegel* affair has quite the all-or-nothing quality of the big one, which explains why they are less well remembered today outside of their home countries. But both, in their different ways, revealed something fundamental about how democracies deal with crises, and how crises shape democracies. The world did more than simply survive in 1962. It also got a glimpse of its future.

This chapter is about three crises that erupted in the space of a few days in late 1962. The crises were interrelated but they were also very different. In each case democracy made it through the crisis intact. But in none of the three cases was it possible to draw much comfort from that fact. The crises of 1962 showed just what democracy can survive, and just how hard it is to learn from the experience.

CAN DEMOCRACIES BLUFF?

By the early 1960s Tocqueville's view that democracies are bad at foreign affairs had become the conventional wisdom, particularly among intellectuals who considered themselves "realists" about international politics. The doyen of the realists was the US-based German émigré Hans Morgenthau, who drew directly on Tocqueville for his analysis of the failings of democratic foreign policy. Democracies, Morgenthau argued, were not stupid, but they were unreflective. They did not pause to think about what they were doing. This made them blow hot and cold: hot, because crude popular ideas of good and evil breed crass and impulsive judgments; cold, because democracies change their minds with difficulty and find it hard to adapt to new circumstances. "For government to postpone action until after public opinion has spoken," Morgenthau wrote, "is tantamount to doing nothing."[2] Democracies needed to be educated about the reality of foreign affairs by their political leaders; they had to be guided in what to think. So far in the Cold War, despite all the propaganda, there was little sign of that happening. Instead, the conflict was producing remote and technocratic government, lacking in political vision. Public opinion was being kept in the dark, where it would never learn.

Others in the realist camp included Walter Lippmann and George Kennan, their differences by now largely forgotten. Kennan spent the second half of the 1950s researching and writing a monumental history of America's disastrous misreading of the Bolshevik revolution as it had unfolded from 1917 to 1918. It had been a personal failure on the part of Woodrow Wilson, but it was also a failure of democracy. Kennan concluded:

> The reasons for this failure of American statesmanship lay in such things as the deficiencies of the American political system from the standpoint of the conduct of foreign relations; the grievous distortion of vision brought to a democratic society by any self-abandonment to the hysteria of militancy; the congenital shallowness, philosophical and intellectual, of the approach to the world's problems that bubbled up from the fermentations of official Washington; the pervasive dilettantism in the execution of American policy.[3]

"How pleasing it would be," Kennan went on, "if one were able to record that these deficiencies had been left behind . . . to be contemplated, now, from a safe distance, as the components of a dead situation, only partially relevant to our own." He was being ironic.

The fear for the realists was that the democracies were being repeatedly outmaneuvered by the Soviets, who were unencumbered by the dead hand of public opinion. By 1962, the Russians were displaying their ruthlessness and taste for brinkmanship in Berlin, where the previous year a wall had gone up to prevent East Germans from voting with their feet and moving west. West Berlin was now cut off and vulnerable. Did the democracies have the wit to defend it without being sucked into a wider conflict? They appeared to lack either the stomach for war or the foresight for peace. They were caught between their indignation and their desire for an easy life. They were stuck.

Two images were popular in commentary and journalism at this period to capture what was wrong with democracy, borrowed from the national pastimes of the two sides in the Cold War. The reason the democracies were losing the contest was that they were no good at the American game, poker, or the Russian game, chess. They couldn't play poker because democracies can't bluff. They are not secretive enough—too much information is out in the open—but also not decisive enough—it is impossible to bluff your opponent if you are unable to pick a course and stick to it. A good bluffer needs a steady nerve, which democracies lacked. Meanwhile, democracies couldn't play chess because they couldn't think ahead. They take each move as it comes, preferring cheap gains to long attritional contests, and find it hard to make sacrifices. Without the occasional sacrifice, chess is a lost cause.

However, as one or two commentators were starting to point out, these analogies were missing something. A great deal depends not just on the game, but for what you are playing. The threat of nuclear war had raised the stakes immeasurably. Poker is not exactly poker if either side has a nuclear option, so that even the winner might lose everything. Chess is not exactly chess if neither side can afford to lose. The political philosopher Louis Halle, a close friend of Kennan's, made this point in an article he published in January 1962. Halle stuck to the conventional line that "countries in which popular opinion is supreme are unable to play chess."[4] But he added a rider: as well as not knowing how to win, this also meant democracies did not know how to lose. They did not resign simply because they had been outplayed. They kept going, refusing to admit defeat. In a conventional game of chess, this would result in defeat anyway. But the Cold War was not a conventional contest, because before defeat both sides had the option of unleashing their nuclear arsenal. They could kick over the board.

So not being able to play chess gave the democracies an unforeseen edge when pitted against the "chess-player's logic of Mr. Khrushchev": it left him unsure how far to push his advantage. "It is a new kind of weakness [Khrushchev] is experiencing," Halle wrote, "the weakness of the strong, the weakness of the superior power that, in spite of its superiority, cannot afford to risk the test of force. The essential lesson one must hope he is learning . . . is that we on our side cannot play chess."[5] Democratic weakness had become a perverse kind of strength, so long as the other side was smart enough to notice it.

Halle was touching on a new strand of political science, one that had recently come up with a sophisticated rationale for this way of thinking. In 1960 the economist Thomas Schelling had published his groundbreaking book *The Strategy of Conflict*, which analyzed all-or-nothing showdowns in terms of the best strategic options of the participants. One of his conclusions was that in games of chicken—where the loser is the one who blinks first—the rational strategy is to behave irrationally, so as to convince your opponent you are incapable of recognizing when it's time to blink. That way, he won't dare put you to the test. The difficulty for the rational actor is to put on a convincing show of irrationality: if your opponent knows it's just an act, designed for strategic purposes, it won't work. That's not a problem for actors who are genuinely irrational, however. Their threats are convincing because they are incapable of calculation. So perhaps unthinking, unreflective democracies, which don't know how to bluff and can't play chess, had the advantage.

The Cuban Missile Crisis put some of these theories to the test. Part of the frisson of fear, in retrospect, comes not simply from the fine line between success and failure but between rationality and irrationality in democratic politics. Something that still has the power to shock, given what was at stake, is the extent to which President Kennedy was worried about how his response to the crisis would play with the voters in the forthcoming midterm elections. When he first got news of the Russian deployment to Cuba, he bemoaned the unfortunate timing: couldn't the crisis be delayed for a month, until after the election? Once it was clear it could not be delayed, Kennedy realized he had to raise the stakes. He couldn't afford to appear weak in the eyes of the voters. The complaint is often made against democratic politicians that they are unable to see the wider picture because the relentlessness of the electoral cycle won't allow it. They can only see their way to the next round of voting. Here was the future of the world at risk, and Kennedy was anxious lest it cost his party seats in Congress. It looks grotesque.[6]

But in this case, the shortsightedness was an advantage. It helped to anchor Kennedy's response in a situation where the existential stakes might have left a politician with a freer hand paralyzed by indecision. Kennedy was driven during the crisis by what he took to be the two nonnegotiable requirements of democratic public opinion: first, that he should do everything in his power to avoid a conflict; second, that he should not be seen to back down. Democracies hate unnecessary wars, but they also hate making concessions. This is not a reasoned position and the twin imperatives can be contradictory: sometimes, to avoid war you have to back down; sometimes, to avoid backing down you have to go to war. But in this confrontation, the unreasonableness helped Kennedy. The knowledge that he was constrained by unthinking public opinion made him harder to outmaneuver.

As well as being a tactical advantage, the unthinking quality of democratic public opinion can also be a consolation. It is easy to ignore the extent to which democratic politicians are consoled by the relentless demands of electoral politics: it ensures that the choices they face have a manageable quality. Asking how it will play in Peoria seems bathetic when faced with decisions of far wider significance, but the bathos of democracy—its lack of proportion—helps keep the politicians sane. In one of the most famous exchanges of the crisis, the president and his brother comforted each other with the idea that they were boxed in. They were speaking in private on the evening of October 22, in a conversation that was captured on tape.

> JFK: It looks really mean, doesn't it? But on the other hand, there wasn't any choice. If he's going to get this mean on this one, in our part of the world, no choice. I don't think there was a choice.
> RFK: Well, there isn't any choice. I mean, you would have been impeached.
> JFK: Well, I think I would have been impeached.[7]

Khrushchev, of course, faced his own constraints. He too had to worry about what other people thought: his colleagues, his generals, his party, even his public. Autocrats are often highly sensitive to public opinion, which is why they go to such lengths to control it. But Khrushchev was freer to set his own timetable for the crisis: when to escalate it and when to diffuse it. This relative freedom of action may explain why he was the one much closer to the edge of sanity. The erratic, sometimes manic quality of Khrushchev's communications during the crisis are often taken as evidence of the extent to which he was a prisoner of competing factions in the Kremlin. But it is just as likely that they are evidence of his uncertainty. He was suffering from the tyranny of choice.

Military realists continue to insist that the reason Khrushchev backed down was that he was outmatched; the size of the American nuclear arsenal was four times that of the Soviets', which meant in any final showdown, however bad for everyone, it would go worse for the Russians. They would lose. In that sense, Khrushchev was the one who was bluffing. He may have been tempted by Kennedy's dithering over Berlin, and by his personal impression of him as a young and untested man, to push his luck. But it helped that democracies can't bluff, because in a game of poker, the ones who can't bluff are also the ones who can't be bluffed. They ignore the signals. Experienced poker players will always say these are the hardest people to play against, particularly in a one-off game for very high stakes.

One of Kennedy's crucial decisions during the two weeks of the crisis was to go public with satellite photographs of what the Soviets were up to. By broadcasting to the United States and the world the manner in which his administration had been duped, he reinforced his intention not to let them get away with it. The realists, including Lippmann, thought Kennedy was being naive and reckless: why risk dragging untutored public opinion into a hair-trigger negotiation that was best conducted by statesmen behind closed doors? But Kennedy understood that untutored public opinion was one of his weapons in that negotiation; it signaled to the Soviets that he could not afford to back down.

Kennedy's real challenge was to find some way to help Khrushchev back down without being seen to make any concessions. Here Lippmann provided accidental assistance. On October 25, Lippmann wrote an article suggesting that the Americans trade their nuclear weapons in Turkey for Russian weapons in Cuba. Khrushchev believed that Lippmann spoke for the administration and was signaling a willingness to compromise. In fact, Lippmann did not speak for

Kennedy; his influence in Washington was on the wane. A year earlier the president had complained: "I know Khrushchev reads him and thinks Walter Lippmann represents American policy. How do I get over that problem?"[8] Now, Khrushchev's misapprehension of Lippmann's importance—as an autocrat he could not understand how a journalist could say such things unless they were authorized—gave Kennedy a helping hand. It bolstered the private message Bobby Kennedy was conveying to the Russian ambassador in Washington, that his brother could only act on Turkey if it wasn't seen as a trade, since democratic public opinion wouldn't stand for it. Khrushchev had to be seen to act first, no conditions attached, which is what he did. He thought Lippmann had given him his cue. Five months later Kennedy withdrew the weapons from Turkey. It was a triumph for democratic inadvertence: Zelig's finest hour.

As in any crisis, luck played its part. American democracy was lucky in its leadership in 1962. Kennedy's temperament suited the crisis, both in his caution and in his resolve. It might have been very different if his vice president, the more belligerent but also more secretive Lyndon Johnson, had been in charge (though had Johnson been in charge perhaps Khrushchev would not have pushed his luck). However, the peaceful resolution of the crisis was down to more than just good fortune. The crisis also suited the temperament of a democracy that wanted peace but did not want to compromise, and that boxed its leaders in while giving them room to negotiate. The haphazard quality of democratic public life—its lack of proportion, its tendency to generate mixed messages—helped the leading actors to find their way through.

The outcome was not a clear-cut victory. It was merely a disaster averted. But avoiding disaster is what gives democracy its advantage: so long as nothing terrible happens, then democracy is the winner, because in the long run democracy has the edge. If the world doesn't end, then democracy marches on. This, in a sense, was Kennan's lesson. If Western democracy could hold itself in check and steer clear of crazy, mutually destructive confrontations then it would outperform and outlast its rival. However, the Cuban Missile Crisis was precisely the sort of crazy confrontation Kennan wanted the democracies to avoid. It horrified him (though he accepted that Kennedy's handling of it had been "masterful").[9] So the outcome also confounded the lesson he wanted to teach. American democracy had avoided catastrophe only by coming right up to the brink. It had not shown the qualities Kennan had wanted it to acquire: patience, foresight, vigilance, a willingness to take the long view and foreswear needless risks. It had been taken by surprise, felt itself outraged, shut its eyes to the risks, held its breath, and survived. It had lived in the moment.

Once it was clear the world would not be coming to an end, American voters soon resumed the regular round of democratic life. The midterms went on and the Democrats did better than they might have expected before the crisis gave Kennedy a boost, though not as well as might have been hoped given that he had just saved the world. As usual, local issues and short-term gripes trumped larger concerns. The crisis did not restore a sense of perspective to democracy. Tocqueville had hoped that brushes with disaster might wake up a democracy to the need to control its own fate. Not in this case. This near miss simply reminded people that some things were beyond their power to control. What else can you do, having peered into the abyss, except cross yourself and look away? It was not much of a learning experience. It was more of a providential event, and as such it was hard to see what nonfatalistic conclusions there were to be drawn. The Cuban Missile Crisis reinforced the idea that fate was on democracy's side.

It was another democratic crisis unfolding at the same time that fits somewhat better with the educative pattern Tocqueville described. While the United States was being taken by surprise by Soviet aggression in Cuba, India was being taken by surprise by Chinese aggression on its Himalayan border. The Indian government had less excuse for consternation, since the Chinese had done little to hide their intentions. Throughout 1961 the Chinese government had been threatening to seize back disputed Indian territory by force. In December of that year the Indian prime minister, Nehru, told parliament that the threats were not to be taken seriously, because war between India and China might drag the superpowers into a nuclear conflict. It was therefore unthinkable. The Chinese, he was convinced, were bluffing.

Nonetheless, Nehru had felt obliged to put up a show of resistance. In the spring of 1962 he faced a general election and, as he liked to say, "at election time the devil seems to take hold of the people."[10] Nationalist fervor and saber rattling by populist politicians persuaded him to move extra troops into the disputed region, promising to defend it against any threat. But it was Nehru who was bluffing. He intended this move as a sop to inflamed public opinion; he didn't think the soldiers would be needed to fight. As a result, they were unprepared and ill equipped for action. Nehru thought gestures of resolve were all that would be required.

He was wrong: democracies can't bluff. The Chinese were not fooled by Nehru's insistence that India would be ready to resist any attack. They understood that he was more concerned to appease domestic opinion than to confront the real prospect of war. His motives were transparent, which made them self-defeating. On October 20, Chinese troops invaded and overran Indian resistance. Within a couple of days, it was clear the Indian army was being routed. By this point the world had also discovered that the United States and the Soviet Union were involved in their potential dance of death over Cuba. Nehru's hopes that the prospect of international escalation would deter the Chinese turned out to be wishful thinking. International tensions had escalated to such a point that a Sino-Indian war was reduced to an afterthought. The world had other things to worry about, which is what allowed the Chinese to seize their moment. Indian democracy was on its own.

Nehru had always conceived of Indian democracy as different. He had been the country's only prime minister since independence, and he saw himself, as he told the American ambassador John Kenneth Galbraith, as its "schoolmaster . . . the last Englishman to govern India."[11] His temperament and bearing were aristocratic: he hoped to educate the Indian people in democracy, and to protect them from their own worst instincts. Nehru wanted India to steer a path between the two sides in the Cold War, identified with neither, offering an alternative to both. He sought to bridge the gap between Soviet-style socialism and Western democratic capitalism. Under his leadership India adopted a series of five-year plans, approved by parliament, and the Indian state imposed a plethora of controls on the economy as well as providing large subsidies to support ailing sectors. Nehru's intention was that Indian democracy would sacrifice breakneck growth for steady progress and replace the chaotic conditions of the free market with the guiding hand of state control. It would be nothing like democracy in America.

But the crisis of October 1962 suggested that Indian democracy was not so different after all. It suffered from the standard democratic weaknesses of inattention and over-reaction. It was taken by surprise by an event it had been ceaselessly fretting about. Indeed, the endless chatter regarding the Chinese threat was one of the things that had made it so hard to take it seriously. As Tocqueville wrote of the French political class on the brink of revolution in 1848, India's politicians "had asserted these things so often, without believing them very much, that in the end they came to believe them not at all, just at the moment when events were about to prove them right."[12] One reason democracies get taken by surprise is that they are forever crying wolf. The ruthlessness and decisiveness of the Chinese intervention seemed to highlight the difference between a democracy and an autocracy: while one was talking without doing much about it, the other was doing without talking much about it.

However, as well as illustrating some familiar weaknesses of democracy in action, the Indian response to the war also pointed to some of its underlying strengths. The country and its political elite woke up to their failings quite quickly and did not try to hide from them. In his broadcast of October

22, Nehru told the Indian people: "We were getting out of touch with reality in the modern world and we were living in an artificial atmosphere of our own creation; we have been shocked out of it, all of us, whether it is the government or the people."[13] Although there was some muted criticism of Nehru's personal unpreparedness, public opinion did not turn on the government. Instead, it rallied, and there were strong demonstrations of support across the country. The advancing Chinese did not have it all their own way; some Indian troops resisted strongly, and after four days of fighting the Chinese called a halt and declared a ceasefire. By now they were well inside Indian territory, though a long way from any major centers of population. To advance further would have meant encountering serious popular resistance. China had no desire to get embroiled in an open-ended conflict, which it might lose. Tocqueville was right: an autocracy that does not defeat a democracy quickly always runs the risk of being defeated by it. The war had been a humiliation for India. But it was not a catastrophe.

Indian democracy also had the advantages of its flexibility. This was not democratic flexibility as Nehru had previously conceived it: nonaligned India able to pick and choose its allies according to its own moral imperatives. Rather, it was the flexibility of the desperate. Democracies in a crisis do not cling on to their principles. They take help from wherever they can get it. Nehru was willing to accept military assistance from anyone. He started by approaching the Americans, from whom he had previously tried to keep his distance. Until the Cuban Missile Crisis was resolved the Americans were unresponsive. But once it was over they made it clear that support would be forthcoming, which helped to put the brakes on any further Chinese advances when fighting flared up again in November. In the meantime, Nehru took weapons from the Russians. He even approached the Israeli government in an attempt to source military supplies, until the Egyptians blocked him.

Democracies are not proud when it comes to facing up to their mistakes, largely because they make so many of them. They tend to be pragmatic. As Tocqueville said, more fires get started in a democracy, but more fires get put out as well. The problem for democracies is not admitting their mistakes, but noticing them, amid all the noise. Once it becomes clear that something has to be done, elected politicians have no choice but to act, even if it means pursuing options they had once denounced as unacceptable. Autocrats find it much harder to own up to their failings. They do not want to seek help from uncongenial sources, because that would represent a public admission of something having gone badly wrong. They prefer to suffer in silence (that is, to let their populations suffer in silence). The Chinese government in 1962 would never have gone begging to the Americans, no matter how badly things had gone. Indian democracy lost some of its self-perceived moral distinctiveness after the fright it received in October 1962. It showed itself to be more adaptable than principled. It also showed that it knew how to survive.

This points to the fundamental difference between Indian democracy and Chinese autocracy at this period. The Chinese state, centralized, highly coercive, and ideologically driven, was well suited to the sort of military conflict it engineered against the far less well prepared and well organized Indian regime. Nonetheless, the confrontation was a sideshow, and intended as a sideshow, from the fundamental crisis that had been gripping the Chinese nation: a famine that is now estimated to have caused the premature deaths of as many as forty million people during the four years from 1958 to 1962. In 1962 the world still had little knowledge of the disaster taking place inside China, because the regime did nothing to advertise it. Its policies of agricultural collectivization had helped to create the crisis; far worse, its refusal to face up to the extent of the problem or to seek outside help turned these policy failings into one of the greatest man-made calamities of the twentieth century. When the Chinese state made serious mistakes, the consequences were unfathomable. Indian democracy, for all its failings, did not fail like this.

Later in the century, the Nobel Prize–winning Indian economist Amartya Sen would make famous the dictum that famines do not happen in democracies, because free public opinion forces democratic politicians to face up to disaster before it is too late. It is scarcity of information, not scarcity of food, that causes people to starve to death. But in 1962 this idea lay in the future. For now, in the immediate crisis circumstances of military confrontation, India looked weak and vulnerable in the face of the Chinese assault. Rather than revealing the underlying advantages of democracy, the Sino-Indian war seemed to confirm some traditional fears. Democracy was chaotic, haphazard, and wishful. Autocracy was ruthless and decisive. The Indians had tried to bluff the Chinese and had been exposed. Yet in the end exposure was good for Indian democracy, because it stopped the worst from happening. It is only the systems that cannot be exposed that are capable of doing their very worst.

The truth is that democracies can't bluff. The events of late 1962 confirmed as much. They also indicated that there are worse things than not being able to bluff.

THE OLD MAN AND THE SCANDAL

Nehru was seventy-two at the time of the Chinese war, and he had been prime minister for more than fifteen years. His misjudgments in the run-up to the conflict made it easy to conclude that he had been around too long: the patrician schoolmaster looked ponderous and out of touch. Although only a decade older than his Chinese counterparts—the sleek Mao Zedong and his smiling, proficient sidekick Zhou Enlai—he appeared to belong to an earlier generation. He did come from another generation entirely than John F. Kennedy, who was young enough to be his son. Kennedy symbolized the capacity of democracies to renew themselves. Nehru appeared old-fashioned and set in his ways by comparison. He seemed to symbolize how democracies can get stuck.

Yet Nehru was far more typical of democracy in 1962 than Kennedy was. One of the misleading features of the Cuban Missile Crisis, when viewed in isolation, is the impression it gives that the Cold War had boiled down to a face-off between youthful democracy and battle-hardened autocracy: the fresh-faced, relatively untested Kennedy against the older, tougher Khrushchev; the older man underestimating the younger one and paying the price. We are used to thinking of the Soviet system as a gerontocracy, because of the

problem any autocratic regime has in replacing one leader
with another: absent a revolution, you usually have to wait
for them to die first. Democracies do not have this problem.
At least that's the theory. But in 1962, it was not the practice
in many countries. Gerontocracy did not look like it was the
Soviet problem. It looked more like the democratic one.

In "The Sources of Soviet Conduct," back in 1947, Kennan
had spelled out the time frame he had in mind if a long-term
policy of containment was to be given the chance to work:
ten to fifteen years. This was a long time for any democracy,
which is why it called for patience. It was longer than the
two world wars combined, the equivalent of three or more
presidential cycles, half a human generation. The democracies needed to wait for the fundamental inflexibility of the
Soviet system to catch up with it. Yet by 1962 the time frame
Kennan had envisaged was up. It turned out to be nowhere
near long enough.

The Soviet Union had survived the event that Kennan
had hoped might precipitate its downfall: the transfer of
power from one leader to the next. Stalin had died in 1953,
to be succeeded, after a bitter internal party struggle, by
Khrushchev. The new leader did make some attempt to
change the political culture of the Soviet Union, criticizing his predecessor and initiating haphazard reforms of
the state's most oppressive structures. But it did not last.
The experiment with openness was soon stifled, and the regime reasserted control. Kennan remained convinced it was
the inflexibility of the West that had killed off Khrushchev's reforms before they could eat into the underpinnings
of the Soviet system. By sticking to the crudest version of
containment—don't give an inch—the United States had

made it too easy for hardliners in Moscow to regain control. Mimicking the Russians had left the Russians mimicking themselves.

Still, the Soviets had managed a transfer of power between political generations without falling apart. By 1962, it was the democracies that looked like they were frightened of making a change. Most of them were being ruled by old men who appeared to be clinging on. These men were often, like Nehru, the founding fathers of their countries' political systems. The father of West German democracy, Adenauer, was still in office in 1962, so was the father of Israeli democracy, David Ben-Gurion. In France, the fifth republic was headed by its architect, Charles de Gaulle, who had conceived it as a vehicle for presidential power and his own personal prestige. None of these democracies had managed a successful handover at the top (Israel had tried in 1954, but a year later Ben-Gurion was called back to the helm; his country apparently couldn't cope without him). It was not clear what would bring about a changing of the guard. Did the old men have to die first?

Stability in many new democratic states seemed to have been bought at a high price. It raised the question of whether these countries were actually democracies at all. West Germany, France, India, Israel looked to some observers more like paternalistic regimes in which the children were frightened of what life might be like without a grown-up to tell them what to do. The alternative, however, looked no more attractive. The new democracies that did know how to change their leaders did not seem to know how to stop. Japan got through seven prime ministers in the decade before 1962. Italy got through ten. In France, there had been twenty changes of government between 1947 and 1958, which is what paved the way for de Gaulle's fifth republic to take over from the fourth. Too slow to change or too quick to change its mind: that was still the double trouble with democracy.

In 1962 the question of how to find a path between instability and political sclerosis was most acute in West Germany. Adenauer was now eighty-six, old enough to be Kennedy's grandfather. In 1917, the year Kennedy was born, Adenauer was already mayor of Cologne. He had lived through all the calamitous ups and downs of German democracy during the first half of the twentieth century. He saw his role as to ensure that nothing like it ever happened again. West Germany needed stability, security, and a steady hand on the tiller. In this task, Adenauer viewed himself as indispensable. In 1954 he had been overheard at a conference lamenting to the foreign ministers of Belgium and Luxemburg: "What will become of Germany when I am gone?" The arrival in power of de Gaulle, and the relatively good relations Adenauer established with him, only confirmed his sense that no one else was up to the job: great statesmen needed each other. In 1961 he had been persuaded to offer a pledge to stand down before the next federal election, but this was not due until 1965, when he would be eighty-nine. Who knew what might happen in the meantime?

West Germany was supposed to be a functioning democracy, which meant that no leader was indispensable. So how would this one be ushered off the stage? By 1962 it was the issue dominating West German politics, and causing consternation in Adenauer's own party, the center-right Christian Democratic Union (CDU). Successors were lining up and jockeying for position, which made Adenauer ever more determined to cling on. He viewed all his potential successors as unsuitable, and the favorite, his finance minister Ludwig Erhard, the architect of the West German economic "miracle," as more unsuitable than most. Adenauer considered Erhard a technician, not a statesman, and he thought West German democracy would not survive even a short bout of weak leadership. Yet Adenauer's refusal to budge was threatening to destabilize the democracy he was claiming to protect. Discipline was breaking down in his party. His authority was being openly questioned. West German democracy appeared caught in a bind: its inability to dislodge Adenauer was creating the fractious conditions that Adenauer believed made it essential that he remain in post.

In the end, what broke the deadlock was a scandal. Throughout 1962 the left-of-center magazine *Der Spiegel* had been involved in a war of words with Franz Josef Strauss, Adenauer's combative defense minister and the lightning rod for much of the criticism of his government. Strauss had sued *Der Spiegel* over an earlier article that accused him of being a putative dictator; the courts decided for Strauss, but only on technical grounds. Then the magazine accused the minister of having profited from US army contracts; again Strauss sued and again he won only a partial victory. Finally, on October 10, the magazine published details of secret NATO maneuvers that had taken place the previous month, which it claimed had revealed the incompetence and inadequacy of the West German defense program under Strauss. The article also claimed that Strauss wanted to replace conventional German forces with tactical nuclear weapons, which he would be willing to deploy in a preemptive strike. Strauss responded by accusing the magazine of treason.

On the night of October 26, with Adenauer's consent, Strauss authorized a raid on the offices of *Der Spiegel*. This was done without consulting more widely within the government; other ministers felt they had been kept deliberately in the dark. The following day Strauss ordered the arrest of the magazine's editor, Rudolf Augstein, and his deputy, Conrad Ahlers, who had written the offending article. The result was uproar. Public rallies in favor of the freedom of the press took place around the country. Other newspapers, from across the political spectrum, expressed outrage at the violation of their right to publish critical material and at the arbitrary nature of the arrests. On October 31, the justice minister, Wolfgang Stammberger, resigned, claiming he had not been informed about the decision to move against the magazine and its editors. Stammberger belonged to the coalition party in Adenauer's government, the Free Democratic Party (FDP), which withdrew its other ministers from the cabinet in solidarity. They would only agree to serve again if Strauss would resign. Faced with this threat to bring down the government, Strauss felt had no choice, and on November 30 he quit. Adenauer then set about repairing the damage. But he discovered that a condition being set by his potential partners in any new coalition was that he should set a firm date for his own retirement. On December 6 he acquiesced and agreed to step down the following year. He tried to retain some wriggle room to the end. Asked by an American television reporter what lay in store for the Federal Republic after he was gone, he responded: "That question cannot be answered at all. . . . The political situation—both the domestic situation here in our country and especially the international situation—is unclear, and we don't know what the year 1963 will bring."[14]

The *Spiegel* affair proved to be a defining moment in the history of West German democracy. It helped to break the paternalistic spell of the Adenauer era and to dispel the idea that democracy in Germany could only survive if it was kept under wraps. The 1950s—the miracle years of dramatic economic growth and swift recovery from the horrors of Nazism—had helped to create the impression that West German democracy was treading on eggshells. Something fragile and fundamentally mysterious had taken place, and it did not do to ask too many difficult questions about how it worked. It was better not to know what might be lurking in the shadows than to risk bringing the demons of German politics back into the light. West German democracy at this stage of its development could not afford a crisis; that had always been Adenauer's position and his justification for his particular style of rule. But it turned out that a crisis was precisely what West German democracy needed at this stage of its development. It helped to get things moving again. As well as breaking the deadlock at the top, the affair invigorated public debate and helped to create the space for much more direct criticisms of the failings of the West German state. It brought a new generation of intellectuals into German political life, and it gave them a platform. It made West Germany look much more like a modern democracy.

However, it is important to emphasize what the *Spiegel* affair did not do. It did not galvanize the West German voting public into demanding change. Adenauer's personal popularity rose after the scandal broke. The public rallied to his side, protective of a dignified old man at bay. For many Germans, the affair confirmed their view of him, which coincided with his own view of himself: that he ought to be treated as above the grubby machinations of ordinary politics. His rivals within his own party used the scandal to push him out, yet they had to be careful not to seem precipitate: he was allowed to delay his departure until later the following year so that it shouldn't seem as though he had been forced from office by scheming politicians in the face of public opinion. Nor did they want to give the press an inflated sense of its ability to make or break governments. Strauss also saw his popularity rise with the electorate as an immediate consequence of the scandal. On November 25, just five days before he was forced to resign, he had fought an election in his home state of Bavaria under the slogan "Security or Treason?" He won a resounding victory. Newspaper outrage, as so often in democracies, was an unreliable indicator of what might happen at the ballot box.

What brought Strauss down was not the substance of *Der Spiegel*'s allegations against him, but his response to them. The accusations could hardly have been more serious: not only was his administrative incompetence said to be putting national security at risk, but his fixation on getting West Germany its own nuclear deterrent, and his apparent readiness to use it, was a threat to the peace of the world. Strauss's defenders claimed the accusations were baseless and hinted darkly that the Soviets had given the source material to the magazine. That the scandal should have coincided with the denouement of the Cuban Missile Crisis might have been expected to focus attention on these hair-raising charges from both sides. But the opposite happened. The arguments that raged among press and politicians did not for the most part concern questions of national security, nuclear deterrence, and superpower rivalry. They were all about who had said what to whom and when they had said it. This is the way with scandals in democracies. Process takes precedence over substance.

Strauss's procedural failings were twofold: first, he did not consult widely enough before authorizing the arrests of the two journalists; and second, he lied about the extent of his personal involvement. When he discovered that Ahlers was holidaying in Spain on the day the warrant was issued for his arrest, Strauss had called the German military attaché in Madrid to insist that he be apprehended. He then denied to parliament that such a phone call had taken place. This denial cost him his job. As the cliché now has it: it's not the crime, it's the cover-up.

In these arguments about process, the government's critics made large claims. If Strauss were to get away with his arbitrary actions, wouldn't that prove that West German democracy was really a sham? Could a government minister be allowed to take personal revenge on his newspaper critics in this way? As one conservative commentator, previously sympathetic to Adenauer's government, put it: "The question is whether the Federal Republic of Germany is still a free and constitutional democracy, or whether it has become possible to transform it overnight by some sort of coup d'état based on fear and arbitrary power."[15] But if that was the question, the *Spiegel* affair did not provide a very satisfactory answer, because so many other questions of detail kept getting in the way. The minutiae of the scandal were what enabled it to claim Strauss as its primary political victim, even though his destruction was only temporary; he was back in government three years later. But the procedural details were also what made it easy to lose sight of the bigger picture. Scandals galvanize democracies, and they can obsess them. But they are rarely a means of resolving the fundamental questions about what a democracy is for.

Ultimately the *Spiegel* affair was a disappointment to the many German intellectuals who had hoped it might be the moment of truth for West German democracy and expose what lay behind the hastily constructed facade. In the heady days of late 1962 the precedent most often invoked was that of the Dreyfus affair, which had divided France at the turn of the century, revealed the hollowness at the heart of the republic, and reshaped the country's politics for a generation or more. Didn't the *Spiegel* affair promise to do the same for West Germany? Ultimately, the answer was no. The Dreyfus example has always inflated expectations of what a democratic scandal can achieve. It is the exception, not the rule, and it invariably leads intellectuals to get carried away with a sense of their own importance. The *Spiegel* affair was actually a much more typical democratic scandal. It recalibrated relations between politicians and the press; it helped to prize one group of politicians from power and opened the door to another; it gripped the country for weeks at a time. But it did not represent the moment of truth for democracy. Such moments remain elusive.

Scandals appear to take you to the heart of democratic politics, but in reality they take place at the surface of political life. We call them crises because of their capacity to consume political energies. "The crisis of the scandal" is akin to "the crisis of the election" Tocqueville described:

The entire nation falls into a feverish state; [the scandal] is the daily text of the public papers, the subject of particular conversations, the goal of all reasoning, the object of all thoughts, the sole interest of the present.

As soon as fortune has pronounced, it is true, this ardour is dissipated, everything becomes calm, and the river, one moment overflowed, returns peacefully to its bed. But should one not be astonished that the storm could have arisen?

Regular scandals are one of the distinctive features of democracy ("affairs, scandals, symbolic conflicts, magnificent crises that inflame the burgher in alternating dances, a new one every year," as Thomas Mann put it in 1918). Autocratic regimes do not operate like this, because a scandal for an autocracy is a genuine crisis, since it indicates a fundamental loss of control.[16] In democracies scandals often arise from politicians' attempts to exercise the sort of control for which democracy does not allow. That is what generates the passion, the sense that everything is at stake, the feeling that it is indeed a "crisis for the republic" and that the people must take this chance to regain control of their destiny. It does not last. Eventually the passion gets dissipated and democracy muddles on as before.

Scandals do not restore a sense of perspective to democracies, allowing them to see what really matters. They do not wake them up to their true circumstances. Instead, they exemplify the absence of perspective that is characteristic of all democracies. The issues at the heart of the *Spiegel* affair—the rule of law, national security, freedom of the press—were vital to West German democracy. But in a scandal the big issues get muddled up with the small ones:

substance with process, principles with personalities. That is how scandals work and why they tend to achieve only limited change. There are winners and losers in any democratic scandal: reputations are made and reputations are broken; individual careers hang in the balance. But democracy itself is rarely either the winner or the loser. It is the backdrop against which the drama takes place.

The *Spiegel* affair did mark West Germany's coming of age as a democracy, but not because it was a transformative moment. Rather, it showed how democracy renews itself without transforming itself. The scandal is all consuming and yet it is also something of a charade. The old man is ushered off the stage. Nobody dies.

THE AFTERMATH

The three democratic crises of late October 1962 operated on very different scales. The missile crisis was so dangerous there is almost nothing to compare it with. It was a success for democracy but it was hardly a teachable moment. You did not have to be of Kennan's temperament to think it would be tempting fate to try to recreate the conditions under which another such success might be achieved. The most sensible lesson was to try not to come so close again.

The Sino-Indian war was an event on a more familiar scale, seen in the broad sweep of modern history. It was an armed confrontation between a democracy and an autocracy that could have come out of the pages of Tocqueville. Democracy was the short-term loser. But democracy survived its loss.

Some pessimists wondered whether the defeat would destroy confidence in Indian democracy, whether, as one commentator put it, "the challenge of China would strengthen the hand of those who have long argued that totalitarian controls are necessary for rapid progress" and that "in losing confidence in Nehru, Indians would lose confidence in themselves."[17] It did not happen. For Indian democracy, 1963 was a difficult year, but it clung on, and Nehru clung on. Of the democratic father figures, he was the only one to die in office, impossible to budge until the bitter end even as his health failed, more like a dynastic ruler than a democratic prime minister. Nehru had hoped he might last long enough to enable power to pass to his daughter, Indira Gandhi. When he finally died in 1964 she turned down the opportunity to succeed him, but she took her chance before long.

Indian democracy was therefore both typical and atypical. The crisis of the war with China emphasized its similarities to other democracies and its differences. The military failure and the scandal of unpreparedness did not entirely break the paternalistic spell. But Indian democracy lost some of its innocence in defeat, and it learned its lesson: the Indian state was never again so militarily unprepared for conflict and never again did it try to bluff. It became, like other modern democracies, more prone to military overkill than to bluster. India has learned to pick the fights it thinks it can win (above all with Pakistan). The result is that there has been no renewal of armed conflict with China since 1962. That crisis was, if not a one-off, then the last in a line. The next war between India and China, if it comes, will be very different. The Soviet-American confrontation of 1962 may provide a closer precedent.

The crisis that operated on the most familiar scale was the *Spiegel* affair. Scandals matter, though not as much as they appear to matter at the time. Once the dust has settled and the smoke has cleared, the scene doesn't look so different. But the leading actors find out they are not so indispensable as they once thought. Adenauer was not the only patriarch to discover this. He tried to cling on during 1963, putting barriers in the way of Erhard's succession, but his authority had been fatally weakened, and in the end he was powerless to resist the clamor for change within his own party. He resigned on October 16 and Erhard took over. A few months earlier Ben-Gurion had quit as prime minister of Israel. His authority had also been undermined by a scandal, the "Lavon affair," which is often described as "Israel's Dreyfus affair." The substance of the scandal concerned a covert Israeli terrorist campaign in Egypt in 1954, which had done serious damage to Israel's international standing when it was exposed. But over the following decade the affair had devolved into a series of accusations and counteraccusations, inquiries and counterinquiries, into who had known what and when. Lavon, the defense minister, was fingered by Ben-Gurion's supporters as having authorized the fiasco. Lavon's supporters claimed he was being framed, and that the old man himself was behind it. Sides were taken, both by politicians and the public, and although Israel's strict military censorship rules made it difficult to report on the details of the events, the affair galvanized the country's newspapers to assert themselves. By 1963 Ben-Gurion's support inside the government had eroded, and on June 16 he quit, apparently sick of all the infighting. He may have hoped that he would get the call back, as he had been called back before, once the country discovered how hard it was to cope without him. If so, he was to be disappointed. The call never came.

On October 18, two days after Adenauer stepped down, another prime minister left office in the aftermath of a scandal. Britain's "Profumo affair," with its mix of call girls and Russian spies, state secrets and lies to parliament, is often seen as the template for a modern democratic scandal. Harold Macmillan, the British prime minister, was another old man, though not quite as old as he looked; despite giving ill health as the reason for his departure (as did Ben-Gurion), he had more than twenty years still to live. Macmillan had cultivated a fatherly, or even grandfatherly air in office, and during Kennedy's presidency he deliberately portrayed himself as the wise old head for the younger man to turn to. During the Cuban Missile Crisis Kennedy had consulted him regularly, and the older man's calm reassurance had suited the gravity of the occasion. But it had not suited the levity of a sex and spies scandal, when Macmillan's statesmanlike demeanor was fatally punctured by the sense that he was a relic from another age.

Macmillan schemed from his sickbed to prevent the man expected to succeed him, Rab Butler, from getting the top job. Butler was a pragmatist and a political technician who had held most of the leading cabinet positions, including chancellor of the exchequer; Macmillan thought he was fundamentally weak and unsuited to leadership. Ben-Gurion had also tried to prevent his obvious successor and long-time finance minister, Levi Eshkol, from succeeding him; he thought Eshkol was incapable of making the really tough decisions required of a national leader. This is how Adenauer felt about Erhard as well. One of Nehru's reasons for clinging on to the bitter end was to prevent his finance minister, Morarji Desai, from replacing him. Prime ministers invariably distrust their finance ministers, whom they suspect of being number crunchers rather than statesmen. They insist that democracy needs something more than bloodless technical expertise at the top.

Just as intellectuals overrate the importance of intellectuals to democratic life, so statesmen overrate the importance of statesmanship. Macmillan and Nehru got their way in the short run, though Desai would eventually become prime minister, as the successor to Indira Gandhi; and Macmillan's chosen successor, Alec Douglas-Home, would lead his party to election defeat the following year, losing to the political technician Harold Wilson. Adenauer and Ben-Gurion failed in their scheming and had to watch as the man they had tried to block replaced them. In the eyes of the retiring leaders, everything was now out of scale. The fathers of their nations had been undermined by the pettiness of political scandal mongering; they had been succeeded by bean counters; their respective democracies had lost all sense of proportion. Big decisions required big men and big men required something more than mockery and carping from the sidelines.

Hans Morgenthau, the "realist" advocate of educative statesmanship, shared this feeling that the democracies increasingly lacked any sense of perspective. Democratic politics was in danger of becoming a joke. When he traveled to West Germany in 1963, Morgenthau was unnerved by what he saw as the lingering effects of the *Spiegel* affair. Scandal had not promoted seriousness nor had it created a better-informed public; instead, it had encouraged triviality and contempt. "There is a cynicism about democracy, politicians and the Bonn regime," Morgenthau wrote, "which expresses itself as thunderous applause whenever a nightclub comic makes a crack about them."[18] The Profumo affair had the same effect in Britain: it created a satire boom. People were taking politics less, not more seriously. The world was still an intensely dangerous place in 1963, and here were the democracies, laughing at themselves. How would they ever learn? Yet mockery and carping are one of the ways that democracies learn to cope with danger. It is how they make molehills out of mountains. These are among the resources that autocracies lack.

Not every democracy followed the same pattern of scandal and renewal. Britain, West Germany, India, and Israel were parliamentary systems, in which prime ministers (or their equivalent) are vulnerable to being unseated from within their own cabinets. Presidents do not face similar threats. France had moved from a parliamentary to a presidential system under de Gaulle precisely to foreclose this sort of ongoing instability within the government. De Gaulle was a statesman with an epic sense of seriousness. He believed in keeping things in proportion: France, as a great nation, needed a great man at the helm. In 1963 he was the only one of the democratic patriarchs left in office, and his position was still secure. American presidents do not have to worry about being usurped by their secretaries of the treasury (none of the seventy-five holders of that office has ever gone on to become president). It does not follow, of course, that American presidents are therefore great statesmen. But they tend not to be bean counters.

Yet in 1963 American democracy was gripped by its own sense of domestic crisis. His success over Cuba had restored the gloss to Kennedy's presidency, but it had done nothing to overcome the basic difficulty he faced, which was his administration's inability to get its legislative program past the US Senate. The American constitutional system of checks and balances had produced deadlock, and some commentators were beginning to fear that deadlock might be a permanent feature of American democracy.[19] The primary barrier to change lay with the bloc of southern Democratic senators. Many of these senators were very old men who had seemingly been around forever. Despite its youthful president, American democracy was also a gerontocracy. The old men in the Senate were more or less impervious to electoral challenge. What would shift them? Did they have to die first?

It is one of the supreme ironies in the history of American democracy that it did take a death to get things moving again, but it was not the death of an old man, it was the death of a young one. Kennedy's assassination on November 22, 1963, was the defining event of the age, the one moment everyone remembers, when for an instant the world was frozen in time. The assassination created a pervasive sense of shock, but not one of crisis. The resilience of American democracy, its ability to withstand even the most extreme shocks, was what stood out for many observers, both those close to the event and those far removed from it. Kennedy was succeeded by Lyndon Johnson, who appeared an old man by comparison (though he too was not as old as he looked). Johnson had previously been part of the southern bloc in the Senate, and he understood it inside out. He knew what could be done with it, and what could be done without it. Over the next few years he succeeded not only in pushing through Kennedy's legislative program but also in going further to create the most radical and far-reaching reform agenda that American democracy had seen since the civil war. It was the old man, not the young man, who ended up as the agent of change.

There was another side to Johnson. During the Cuban Missile Crisis Kennedy had been horrified by the thought of his vice president succeeding him as president, after what he had seen of his behavior during those two harrowing weeks. Johnson had seemed to embody all the crudest elements of democratic public opinion, its belligerence, its intransigence, its lack of foresight. Johnson was a hawk who wanted to tackle the Russian threat head-on. At one meeting of ExComm, the top-level group assembled to advise the president during the crisis, the vice president took advantage of the fact that both Kennedy brothers were out of the room to let the assembled company know what he thought. "All I know is that when I was a boy in Texas, and you were walking down the road, when a rattlesnake reared up ready to strike, the only thing to do was take a stick and chop its head off." As Johnson's biographer records, "there was a little chill in the room after that statement."[20] When the president and his closest advisors hatched their final scheme to help Khrushchev find a way out of the crisis, they did not even tell Johnson what they were up to, for fear he wouldn't understand. The unreasonableness of democratic public opinion was a weapon they felt they could use. But that was because they were reasonable men. Johnson, as the embodiment of unreason in their eyes, would have no idea what they were up to.

The lesson Johnson took from the Cuban Missile Crisis was that democracies should never back down. Containment, as he understood it, meant refusing to shirk any fight. If democratic public opinion wouldn't stand for it, then he would keep the public in the dark about what was going on. "I am not going to lose Vietnam," he insisted to members of Kennedy's foreign affairs team two days after the assassination. "I am not going to be the President who saw South-East Asia go the way China went."[21] He told them to keep the men and money flowing into the conflict but to do it with the minimum of publicity. The man who got American democracy moving again was also the man who got it bogged down in the most disastrous war in its history.

It is asking too much to expect democracies to learn the right lesson from each crisis they survive. Some lessons are learned—India learned from its experiences in 1962—but some are not. What is true is that they survive the crisis and move on, which means they move on to the next one.

CHAPTER 5

1974

Crisis of Confidence

THE CRISIS

BY THE MID-1970S THE PROBLEMS FOR DEMOCRACY were mounting up: there was trouble from rising prices, from diminishing energy supplies, from stagnant growth, from endless scandals; the problems were felt in the United States, Latin America, in Europe, the Middle East, the Far East; nowhere was immune. A perfect storm appeared to be brewing, which was all the more alarming because no one could be sure when or where it would break. Multiple crises demanded attention, but they also fractured attention, making it hard to fix on a decisive course of action. The year 1974 began with a sense of foreboding, and it closed with a growing feeling of despair.

On March 2 James Reston of the *New York Times* published a widely syndicated column that was headlined "The Crisis of Democracy." Reston, who had supplanted Walter Lippmann as American journalism's number one confidant of presidents and prime ministers, was in London to report on the aftermath of the British general election, which had taken place three days earlier. Prime Minister Edward Heath had called the election in an attempt to break the deadlock in his debilitating struggle with the National Union of Mineworkers. The ruling Conservative Party campaigned under the portentous slogan "Who Governs Britain?" Was it popularly elected governments or was it sectional and unaccountable unions? The answer the voters returned was not the one Heath had been hoping for. His party won the popular vote by a small margin but lost seats to the Labour opposition. On March 3, Heath tried and failed to form a coalition government. The following day he resigned, allowing Harold Wilson to return at the head of a minority administration.

The British election of February 1974 was not an obvious calamity. The campaign had been strident, ugly, and inconclusive, played out against a backdrop of increasing economic hardship, but the result did not indicate a country on the verge of falling apart. Instead, it signaled a country that was deeply unsure what to do next. This gave Reston his cue. The crisis of democracy he diagnosed was not one marked by immediate and pressing danger but by a pervasive sense of drift. The Western democracies lacked conviction. "The world," Reston wrote, "is now being run by Communist governments that rule by fear and force and by non-Communist governments that do not have the confidence of their peoples." What was happening in Britain was symptomatic of a wider malaise: things were bad, but not so bad as to force the politicians to get a grip on them.

In place of "the men of eloquent idealism," Reston said, the democracies were being ruled by "political technicians," who met each challenge with compromise and fudge. The democracies were on an unsustainable path, pandering to the whims of their electorates while failing to address the long-term challenges posed by "stagflation" (rising prices with minimal growth) and an insecure energy supply. The situation, in Reston's words, was "awkward, disturbing, alarming even, but not 'disastrous.'" As a result, "Mr. Heath and Mr. Wilson stick with the paradox that the country is in grave danger but not so grave as to require their combining to save it. So they will muddle along repeatedly." This couldn't carry on indefinitely: perpetual muddle would catch up with democracy in the end. "The political 'decline of the West,'" Reston concluded, "is no longer a subject for theoretical debate but an ominous reality."

In Britain the muddle continued throughout 1974. The new Wilson government did not last. Amid worsening economic conditions, a second election was called in October. This one was barely more conclusive than its predecessor, and Wilson was forced to stumble on with a tiny majority in parliament. In the meantime, democracies around the world were following a similar pattern. Governments fell, to be replaced by new ones with no more apparent power or sense of purpose. Often what brought them down was scandal, which undid elected leaders in Germany, Japan, Israel, Italy, and America. Watergate, the biggest scandal of them all, consumed vast political energies in the United States, at a time when economic and geopolitical tensions seemed to be reaching a peak. American democracy, struggling to come to terms with its failure in Vietnam, was now turning in on itself. It added to the feeling that Western democracy was rudderless.

In its end of year review, the *Economist* described 1974 as a "memorably awful year." It had been marked, the newspaper said, by "the politics of putting-off-the-evil-day."[1] Fundamental problems remained unaddressed while passing concerns were allowed to become all-consuming. The *Economist* retained its habitual confidence that democracy would pull through. But lurking in the background were serious threats. Beneath the distractions of democratic life were rumblings of something much nastier. It had become a truism of political debate in many western countries that no democracy could survive a sustained bout of high inflation: the social dislocation would be too great and autocratic measures would be required to keep the peace. The cut-off point for a democratically unsustainable inflation rate was usually put at around 20 percent. By the end of 1974 the rate in Britain had reached 19 percent and was still rising; in Italy, Israel, and Japan it was even higher. The baleful example of Latin America was often invoked.

The previous year in Chile, the elected socialist government of Salvador Allende had been overthrown in a military coup, and in 1974 General Augusto Pinochet had himself declared the country's head of state. Argentina saw the return of the faded music-hall autocrat Juan Perón, who died in July to be succeeded by his third wife. At the same time, leftist terrorism was on the rise, not just in Latin America, but also in Europe, where the Red Army Brigades in Italy and the Red Army Faction in West Germany were responsible for regular acts of violence. In Northern Ireland, the British state was struggling to keep a lid on sectarian conflict, which had spilled over into terrorist outrages on the mainland. Soldiers were regularly to be seen on the streets of many Western European capitals. In 1974, amid dark warnings about the need for emergency measures, the fabric of democracy looked frayed. What would happen if it ripped?

Yet the political conditions of 1974 did not simply represent a crisis for democracy. It was a bad year all round: this was a genuinely global crisis. Inflation, economic uncertainty, political unrest were problems for every type of regime (with the possible exception of the oil-rich autocracies of the Middle East). It looked worse for democracy because the dislocations of democratic life were written on the surface: the scandals were more visible, the acts of violence more widely reported, the sense of impending upheaval more keenly felt. This surface activity, as well as being a distraction from more serious concerns was an outlet for discontent. Autocratic regimes did not have a similar outlet. Dissatisfaction with the regime had to be buried if it was not to prove overwhelming. In 1974 the stronger autocratic regimes, particularly in Eastern Europe, suppressed the conditions of the crisis, with disastrous long-term results. Other, weaker autocracies, particularly in southern Europe, succumbed to them.

In retrospect, 1974 was a good bad year for democracy. The bad things that happened were often in lieu of something worse. It was the nondemocratic states that could not face up to bad things happening that suffered the most serious consequences. Very few people living in the democracies saw this at the time. Most, like Reston, felt that democracy would be the loser in the long run if it could not get its act together. But the crisis of 1974 did not herald the decline of the West. If anything, it helped to put off the evil day.

This chapter is about the crisis-that-wasn't for Western democracy. The perfect storm never broke, and democracy survived. How it survived is instructive: the feeling of impending disaster proved an asset, because it enabled the democracies to let off steam. Nonetheless, it meant they did not really know what they were doing. A sense of distraction, not of determination, is what saved democracy in the 1970s.

War and Détente

In 1972, on the twenty-fifth anniversary of Lippmann's inauguration of the Cold War, his original book of that title was republished in the United States, alongside the essay by Kennan that had provoked it. The editor of the new volume suggested that these works were worth rereading because, in his words, "the Cold War is dead and the autopsies have begun."[2] The war had not resulted in victory for either side. Instead there had been a tailing off, as confrontation came to be replaced by accommodation, and superpower tension gave way to détente. The two sides were now looking for ways to coexist. It was clear from which side the impetus to wind things down had come: the democracies had wearied first. They no longer had the stomach for the fight. It had been too drawn out, too costly, and too frustrating. Once

Kennan's ten- to fifteen-year timescale had been stretched out to a quarter of a century, containment proved unsustainable. This explained the need for a new edition of Lippmann's book: his argument with Kennan from 1947 was worth rereading a generation later because of the ways in which Lippmann had turned out to be right.

The step too far for American democracy was the Vietnam War. Lippmann believed the conflict confirmed all his worst fears about the ongoing attempt to defend the indefensible around the globe. The project was unsustainable because it was uncontrollable: "threats to democracy" were a fire that would never get put out. Lippmann criticized Johnson's pursuit of victory in this crusade in just the terms he had criticized Truman, the man who initiated it: "The fact is that his war aims are unlimited: they pursue the pacification of all Asia. For such unlimited ends it is not possible to win a war with limited means. Because our ends are limitless, we are sure to be 'defeated.'"[3] The limits to the resources of American democracy were moral as much as material; Americans could not endure the brutal methods and careless disregard for human suffering (both their own and that of their enemies) the conflict entailed. They were too impatient for good news and too squeamish for bad, particularly since in a democracy journalists will compete with each other to let the public know the worst of what is happening.

If the war was a "defeat," was it also a learning experience? After all, it had not been a defeat in the absolute sense (hence Lippmann's scare quotes); for all the damage to its prestige, America remained the richest and most powerful nation on earth. Instead, this had been a defeat for illusions, which is one of the preconditions of self-knowledge. Raymond Aron, the European intellectual who remained closest to Lippmann and the American realists, saw hopeful signs. Writing in 1974, he declared containment a failed experiment but one from which it was possible to learn. Echoing Lippmann, he argued that "imperial logic makes ubiquity imperative and cannot tolerate defeat." It is the states that cannot tolerate defeat that are unable avoid it. However, "after twenty-five years, containment has not led to the victory of one side or the other but to accommodation. . . . Failure becomes success because it induces withdrawal, teaches moderation and prepares the way for an equilibrium between states."[4] Western democracy in general, and American democracy in particular, was coming to understand its own limits.

Some of the other realists were not so sure. They saw in the debacle of Vietnam evidence that democracy was reaching the end of the road. Public opinion could not stomach war but lacked the wit for intelligent compromise. It made impossible demands of politicians, which encouraged the politicians to ignore the public. This is how democracies fall apart. Louis Halle, the man who had previously warned that democracies cannot play chess, contrasted the situation barely a decade on from what had happened at the time of the Cuban Missile Crisis. Then the irrational intransigence of democratic opinion had induced a Russian retreat, because the Russians had "accepted the consequent humiliation, as perhaps the government of the United States could not have."[5] Now it was the Americans who did not know how to retreat from a war they could not win. They were being humiliated, yet they could not even discuss their options intelligibly. Halle invoked Tocqueville, who had been "the first to observe that authoritarian government is better able than that of a liberal democracy to keep the conduct of its foreign relations, however cynical, under control."[6] He went even further back. The liberal societies of the West were approaching a "termination" that has awaited every democracy, from ancient Athens on. The toxic combination of imprudence overseas and disorder at home led democracies into a condition of "moral and political bankruptcy." Once this state has been reached, "an authoritarian receivership is the only workable alternative."[7]

Lippmann was equally gloomy, though more detached. Now eighty-four, and very near the end of his life, he gave an interview in April 1973 in which he declared Western democracy "a doubtful experiment." Modern states had reached a size and scale that rendered democracy "increasingly unworkable."[8] It was simply too cumbersome to know how to rescue itself from difficulties of its own making. The original realist Hans Morgenthau identified an element of tragedy in the situation. Like Aron, he wanted democracies to learn from their failings and reconstruct themselves on more realistic lines. But the timing was never right. Democracies that see the need for restraint are usually past the point where they know how to exercise it. This is the tragedy: "When [a democratic society] could still be saved by democratic measures of reconstruction there appears to be no need for them, and when the need has become obvious it is too late for them."[9] The space for democracies to learn from their mistakes was vanishingly small. When the mistakes are bad enough to learn from, they tend to be too bad to recover from.

This view was shared by the most important public policy intellectual of the era, Henry Kissinger. A man of formidable intellectual self-confidence and political ruthlessness, Kissinger came to dominate foreign policy during the Nixon administration. He saw his role as to recalibrate the projection of American power on more realistic lines. Gone would be the all-or-nothing defense of democracy, to be replaced by a flexible strategy of adapting to what was possible. Kissinger did not want to amalgamate either the friends or the enemies of democracy into fixed entities; he wanted to play them off against each other. As one commentator has written, he was not so much a realist as an "opportunist." He believed in exploiting situations; he sought, in his own words, "to rescue an element of choice from the pressure of circumstance."[10]

Kissinger also liked to quote Tocqueville on the pathologies of public opinion in the conduct of foreign affairs. Democracies, he felt, were always doing too much or too little. It took a statesman to get it just right. Nor did he believe that democracies were suited to learning from their mistakes; whenever a democracy tried to confront its failings it threatened to implode. Democracies do not go from overconfidence to a sensible or reasonable level of confidence in what they can achieve. They lurch from overconfidence to a crisis of confidence. There is no stable equilibrium between these two states, just an endless back and forth. Later, Kissinger reflected on what he thought the Vietnam experience said about American democracy. "Surely no other society would have had comparable confidence in its ultimate robustness to thus rip itself apart, certain that it would put itself back together. No other people would have been so cavalier about risking breakdown in order to spark renewal."[11] There was something admirable about this but also something deeply disturbing. Americans were reckless even in the ways they tried to correct for their own recklessness.

If the lesson of Vietnam was that American democracy needed to be more measured in the conduct of its foreign policy, Kissinger did not think it was a lesson American democracy was capable of drawing for itself. Then there was another problem. A democracy that wanted to cut loose from its past failings could not admit what it was up to. It had to suck up its mistakes so as not to look vulnerable. Kissinger was convinced that America could only be rescued from the mess of the Vietnam War by refusing to acknowledge defeat. The country needed to continue to project strength as it sought a way out. An admission of weakness would simply embolden its enemies and allow them to exploit the fragile state of domestic opinion. They would demand ever-greater concessions, sowing ever-greater discord. Kissinger thought the way to protect American democracy from its inability to fight this war was to behave as though it hadn't been fighting hard enough. It was a confidence trick.

The result was that he and Nixon pursued a self-rescue project for American democracy that was secretive, deceptive, and ultimately corrupt. They sought to end the Vietnam War by escalating it, extending the conflict into Cambodia and greatly expanding the scope of American bombing. These decisions were made with minimal consultation inside the administration and almost no public discussion outside it. Against this backdrop of apparent intransigence, Kissinger pursued secret negotiations with the Vietnamese with a view to securing a workable peace. He wanted to present this peace to the American public as a fait accompli, something in which they could acquiesce because they had not been involved in the messy details. What he gave them in the end was a peace that looked like a defeat, secured by means they had not sanctioned. In 1974 the last American combat troops were home from Vietnam, leaving the country to its fate. Within a year the communists had taken over. In Cambodia a brutal war turned into something far worse under the Khmer Rouge. American democracy was deeply scarred by the conflict. But it was not obviously the wiser for the experience. Failure in this case did not lead to self-knowledge. It led to bitterness, confusion, and a desire to forget.

The Nixon administration had hoped to treat the conclusion of the war as a piece in a bigger puzzle that might unlock a series of concessions and reconfigurations across the communist world. Nixon's trip to China in 1972 was the most visible part of this strategy, and it certainly unnerved the Russians. Kissinger had not given up on the ultimate goal of containment, which was to play the Soviets at their own game, only play it better. Nor did he disagree with Kennan's original view that this was best done by being shrewder, rather than simply tougher, than they. Where he disagreed with Kennan was in the idea that this project could form part of a democratic education. Democracies could not cope with the moral compromises involved in trying to outsmart the Russians. They would, in Kissinger's terms, be too "unsettled" by it. If you wanted to keep democratic public opinion inside the loop, you had to make things simple enough for the public to understand. Kissinger wanted something more complicated, which is why the public had to be kept outside the loop. If you were successful, then you could feed the good news back in palatable chunks. And if you weren't successful, then nobody needed to know.

Kissinger was playing a double game, but it was not the only double game in town. The West German chancellor, Willy Brandt, who came to power in 1969, had been pursuing his own strategy of détente known as *Ostpolitik*, which sought to work with and through the idea of a divided Germany. Brandt initiated the official recognition of East Germany as a separate political entity, and from there he opened up a series of dialogues with Moscow about the future shape of Europe. As Aron had noted at the outset of the Cold War, the refusal of the founders of West Germany to recognize the partition of their country was a means of enshrining it in practice. Nonengagement was a form of acquiescence. Now Brandt was trying the opposite approach. By acknowledging the status quo, and the historical circumstances that had produced it, he hoped to move things on. He wanted to use the flexibility of the Western democracies to prevent the Eastern bloc from becoming completely set in its ways. Engagement required communist leaders to make some real choices, which would ultimately make it much harder for them to hold the line. Ideologies do not crumble when faced with intransigence; they crumble when faced with a world of myriad possibilities. This was not containment as it had come to be understood—the Nixon administration was initially appalled by Brandt's proposals—but it was consistent with Kennan's original idea: the way to get the Soviet system to unwind was to compel it to confront the world on terms other than its own. Making friendly overtures was one way to do this.

For a while, *Ostpolitik* looked like a success story. Moscow played along and so did Washington, once Kissinger saw that Brandt's search for common ground could help to box in the Soviets. East-West tensions declined and a new era of tentative coexistence looked to have begun. Berlin ceased to be a global hotspot and trade links opened between the two halves of Europe. Brandt became hugely popular, both outside Germany, where he was awarded the Nobel Peace Prize in 1971, and inside, where he won a decisive reelection victory in 1972. Yet by the following year Brandt was thoroughly disillusioned. A naturally gloomy man, prone to bouts of depression that his heavy drinking and womanizing did nothing to assuage (they most likely contributed), he found that a long-term strategy of constructive engagement could not survive the temperamental skittishness of democratic life.

His personal popularity slumped during 1973 in the face of a series of domestic scandals and a growing sense of economic crisis, fueled by rising inflation. In June of that year 76 percent of Germans had said they approved of Brandt's policies; by December the number had more than halved. Late in the year Brandt gave a notorious interview in which he intimated that European democracy might only have twenty or thirty more years of life left to it, before it "disappeared under the surrounding sea of dictatorship."[12] If it lacked the resolve and moral courage to hold itself together during the difficult times, then its long-term advantages were moot. Brandt suspected that the changeability of the democracies would destroy them sooner than it would save them. Before *Ostpolitik* could work its magic, the West would have thrown in the towel.

Kissinger, a more unpleasant and more robust man, never succumbed to this sort of pessimism. He always believed that the West could adapt and pull through. But that was, first, because he never had much faith in democracy anyway, and, second, because he never had to stand for election. Brandt was suffering from the disillusionment of the popularly elected politician who discovers that popularity is evanescent in a democracy. It is an occupational hazard. Kissinger was never popular, so he was never disillusioned. When he won the Nobel Peace Prize in 1973, an award he accepted "in all due humility," it already looked like a joke. By 1974, Brandt's world was unraveling. Kissinger's was turning the way it always did, from crisis to crisis, and opportunity to opportunity.

OIL AND INFLATION

If American democracy lacked the resolve to fight the Vietnam War, it also lacked the resolve to pay for it. The United States did not lack the material resources to finance a conflict on this scale, costly as it was. The Vietnam War, at its peak, cost a little over 2 percent of the annual GDP (though defense spending in total reached nearly 10 percent), around half the comparable cost of the Korean War and less than a tenth of the cost of the Second World War.[13] America could afford it. But America did not want to pay the price of affording it. This was not an absolute judgment any more than Vietnam was an absolute defeat. It was a relative one.

Financing the war went alongside a raft of other commitments and objectives. Some of these related to the ongoing
program of social reform initiated by the Johnson administration and largely continued under Nixon, which was proving very expensive. Others concerned the need to preserve
the dollar as a global reserve currency under the terms of the
Bretton Woods system. This meant maintaining the value of
the dollar against gold. High public spending on war and social security made this increasingly difficult: rising inflation
threatened a loss of confidence in the entire system. This
challenge could be met in one of two ways. Either the American government could embark on a program of austerity
and cutbacks to satisfy its growing number of international
creditors, or it could cut the dollar loose from gold. Nixon
chose the latter.

The so-called Nixon shock of August 15, 1971, involved a
series of measures designed to free the United States from
the constraints of Bretton Woods without signaling a complete abdication of monetary and fiscal discipline. Nixon
broke the link between the dollar and gold, allowing the currency to be devalued, but he also imposed wage and price
controls by presidential fiat and insisted on budget cuts.
These executive decisions looked like a relapse into mild
autocracy. But Nixon told the American public he was effectively putting his trust in American democracy, by free-
ing it from the need to satisfy the arbitrary demands of the
money markets under the terms of Bretton Woods. Now the
American people would have to prove their resolve to themselves. "A nation," he exhorted them in a televised address
on the evening he announced his decision, "has to have a

certain inner drive in order to succeed." Every action he had taken was designed "to help us snap out of the self-doubt, the self-disparagement that saps our energy and erodes our confidence in ourselves." He went on:

> Whether this Nation stays number one in the world's economy or resigns itself to second, third, or fourth place; whether we as a people have faith in ourselves, or lose that faith; whether we hold fast to the strength that makes peace and freedom possible in this world, or lose our grip—all that depends on you, on your competitive spirit, your sense of personal destiny, your pride in your country and in yourself.[14]

At the same time, he was effectively sending out a message to all the other democracies whose currencies had been tied to the dollar, and whose politicians had sometimes complained bitterly about their dependence on decisions taken in Washington: Now is the time for hard choices. You too have a chance to set your own course, if you are willing to bear the unpleasant consequences. It is up to you.

This was a shocking development because it appeared to replace the solidarity of the Bretton Woods system with a competitive order in which individual democracies would stand or fall by their own devices. What guarantees were there that enhanced freedom of action would promote self-discipline instead of ever-greater ill discipline? What guarantees were there that the United States would maintain its role as the linchpin of military order around the globe if it had abandoned its role as linchpin of financial order? The answer is that there were no guarantees: it was, as Nixon implied, a leap of faith.

The shock was then compounded two years later by another one. In October 1973 the Yom Kippur War between Israel and the Arab states threw the world off balance. The Israelis were caught by surprise, having failed to anticipate an attack by Egyptian and Syrian forces. For a long time Israel had been the one democracy whose inner resolve was seemingly impossible to doubt. The 1967 Arab-Israeli War, in which Israel had routed her enemies, had shown that a democracy could be as disciplined, ruthless, and militarily decisive as any autocracy. But like any successful democracy, Israel was also prone to bouts of complacency. By the early 1970s dynamic Israel seemed increasingly to be living on past glories, confident it could withstand any challenge. The country had begun to believe its own publicity, which meant the initial reverses it suffered in the Yom Kippur War came as a rude shock. The regime soon snapped out of its torpor and fought back, preventing a disaster and ultimately advancing into enemy territory. Kissinger helped to broker a ceasefire and to defuse Soviet-American tensions over the conflict. Détente, which came close to being derailed, survived intact. Nonetheless, the conflict shook all the participants: it did little to enhance anyone's sense of security.

The real shock came when the Arab states, acting through the oil-producers cartel OPEC, imposed a series of embargoes and price hikes that had the effect of quadrupling the cost of oil by the start of 1974. This was in part retaliation against the United States and her allies for arming and supporting Israel during the war. It was also a response to Nixon's devaluation of the dollar, which, since oil was priced in dollars on the international markets, had lowered the value of oil as well. The result of OPEC's decision was an economic contraction experienced around the world. Fuel consumption fell in all developed nations, particularly the United States, where it was down 20 percent by early 1974. Global trade declined and a recession spread across most western countries, bringing rising unemployment, plummeting stock markets, and the ever-present threat of inflation.

These two shocks—the Nixon shock and the oil shock—combined to revive some familiar fears about democracy. Together they offered an apparent contrast between democratic divisions and autocratic solidarity. In dismantling the Bretton Woods system, the Americans had gone their own way, preaching competitiveness and self-reliance (as Nixon saw it), or selfishness and short-termism (in the view of many of America's allies). The oil-producing states had come together in retaliation. The members of OPEC, led by Saudi Arabia and Iran, were all autocracies, many of them highly authoritarian ones. They had done something the democracies seemed incapable of in a crisis: they had agreed on a joint course of action and then stuck to it. These regimes did not have to worry about elections and fickle public opinion and constitutional proprieties; they could reach price-fixing agreements at the top that would hold all the way down. The democracies looked fissile and vulnerable by comparison. Both sides were aware of it. In an exchange in late 1973 with the Italian interviewer Oriana Fallaci, the Shah of Iran gave this response to the suggestion that his country would need to democratize to become more like the West: "But I don't want that kind of democracy! Haven't you understood that! I don't want any part of it. It's all yours, you can keep it, don't you see? Your wonderful democracy. You'll see, in a few years, what your wonderful democracy leads to."[15]

Nixon tried to address the growing sense of democratic vulnerability by advocating the need for national self-sufficiency in energy. On November 25, 1973, he made another televised address in which he picked up on the theme of his early declaration of faith in American self-reliance. Now that would have to extend to the energy supply. "America has made great sacrifices of blood and treasure to achieve and maintain its independence," he declared. "In the last third of this century, our independence will depend on maintaining and achieving self-sufficiency in energy."[16] No democracy could afford to be at the mercy of oil-rich autocrats. To wean itself off Arab oil a democracy could not simply rely on its aptitude for innovation. It would also have to display a capacity for restraint, discipline, and coordinated action. Yet these were precisely the qualities that democracies appeared to lack. Was national self-sufficiency in energy anything more than a pipe dream? Nixon made a start by reducing the national speed limit to 55 mph. It looked like a drop in the ocean.

Oil dependency was a long-term concern. By 1974 it had given way to a more immediate anxiety. How would the democracies wean themselves off their fatal propensity for inflation? The two shocks had combined to stoke the fear of inflation across the Western world. Nixon's break with gold seemed to fit the classic democratic tendency to take the path of least resistance: faced with domestic pressure to abandon a fixed monetary standard, a politician with an eye on the next election had buckled. The dramatic rise in oil prices showed how exposed the democracies were to external shocks: their appetite for consumption left them at the mercy of sudden breaks in supply. These were the two sides of democratic ill discipline. Short-term pressures on wages, a commitment to full employment, and the seeming intolerance of the voters for cuts to social security programs were making it hard for governments to maintain fiscal standards; meanwhile, the relentless demands of consumer societies and their continuing expectation of rising standards of living were making it hard to escape a reliance on potentially scarce natural resources. Could any democratic politician be expected to point out the limits of growth and to dampen expectations of continued expansion in living standards? Democracies need to believe in a better future in order to function; politicians need to champion a better future in order to get elected. Yet the promise of continued progress was making the present impossible to manage. With prices on an apparently inexorable upward path in 1974, the fear was that if democratic politicians did not get a grip, someone or something else would do it for them.

This is how the London *Times* summed up the domestic situation in June:

> The truth is that, if the full employment commitment is not voluntarily modified under democratic processes, it will be much more savagely breached by the sheer forces of hyperinflation, with much graver social and political consequences. If democrats do not do the job events will do it and will do it with much less concern for tempering the distress which will be caused . . .
>
> It will be said that such a programme is quite outside the tolerances of our political system. If that is so—and it has certainly been assumed to be so ever since the war—then there appears to be no way a democratic government can prevent

inflation accelerating to the point at which it would threaten democracy itself. Is there really no political leader who prefers to risk personal repudiation for outraging conventional notions of political possibility to seeing his country and his countrymen go down passively and helplessly in the face of forces which with sufficient courage may yet be overcome?[17]

Panic! Don't panic! seemed to be the message. The inflationary "crisis" of 1974 was threatening to become self-fulfilling. Newspapers and politicians regularly invoked the idea that continuing inflation would produce intolerable levels of social and political tension. The US treasury secretary, William Simon, told the German newspaper *Die Zeit* in October that "history is covered with the rubble of political systems that have failed from inflation," as if a German audience needed reminding.[18] The problem was that the symptoms of political instability were so hard to distinguish from the cause. Standing up to excessive wage demands seemed like an essential precondition of keeping prices under control. Yet democratic politicians who did this threatened to raise social tensions at a time when democracy itself was said to be under threat. They were caught in a bind. Fear of provoking instability led to concessions and temporizing measures, which fueled the inflation that was said to be the cause of instability. Refusing to make concessions looked highhanded and autocratic. Where was the room to stand up to the short-termism of popular politics without trampling democracy underfoot? Increasing numbers of commentators were beginning to fear it did not exist.

Tocqueville had hoped that occasional shocks would be good for democracies, by giving them a sense of responsibility for their own fate. The shocks of the early 1970s had not had that effect. They had created a pervasive sense of powerlessness and a creeping despondency. The call continued to go out for politicians of courage and vision to stand outside the limitations of the system and save it from itself. But where were these politicians? And how were they to be distinguished from the politicians who had come to destroy it?

REGIME CHANGE

Through 1974 the most visible sign of political instability was the difficulty governments had in holding on to office. Many saw inflation as the root cause. Milton Friedman, by now one of the leading lights in the Mont Pelerin Society, put it bluntly: "Inflation surely helped to make Mr Edward Heath Prime Minister in 1970 and, even more surely, ex-Prime Minister in 1974 . . . President Allende of Chile lost his life at least partly because of inflation. Throughout the world, inflation is a major source of political unrest."[19] However, despite Friedman's attempt to link them, there was a big difference between these two cases. It was not simply that one man lost his job while another lost his life. Heath's ups and downs represented routine change within a democratic system. Allende's demise represented change from a democratic system to something else entirely: military rule.

In this difference there was a warning and also a temptation. The back and forth between Heath and Wilson appeared to typify the inability of a democracy to make adjustments commensurate with the scale of the problem: as the ship went down, the voters simply rearranged the deck chairs. Regime change in Chile at least reflected the seriousness of the situation. The transition was violent and unpleasant. It was not for the squeamish (Kissinger, who was anything but squeamish, had no problem with it). But for anyone willing either to stomach or to turn a blind eye to the brutality on the ground, regime change could be presented as an opportunity for a fresh start. The problems of the Chilean economy far exceeded those in Europe (inflation in 1974 was running at close to 1,000 percent). Rearranging the deck chairs wouldn't do. When Pinochet began a series of radical free market reforms in 1974, largely inspired by a group of Chilean economists who had studied under Friedman in Chicago, it was tempting to think a clean break with the past might be the price to be paid for avoiding an even more unpleasant future.

To his credit, Friedman resisted that temptation. He never claimed that a Pinochet-style strongman was a price worth paying for anything (as opposed to the view, which he certainly endorsed and exported through his students, that if a strongman takes over anyway, you should encourage him to embrace the discipline of the market). Hayek was much more equivocal. He became something of an apologist for the new regime, arguing that it was better to have a dictator who preserved the rule of law than a democracy that ignored it. By the rule of law, Hayek meant above all the preservation of private property against the depredations of inflation. He viewed the socialist reforms of the Allende years as a way station on the road to serfdom. A dictatorial interlude offered a chance to get the country back on a path where democratic freedom was at least a future possibility.

In his own mind, Hayek had not given up on democracy. This was a point he often made during the 1970s, when he claimed he was one of the few intellectuals who still believed in it. He continued to argue that the only way for democracy to save itself was for it to learn to exercise self-control. When he won the Nobel Prize in Economics in 1974, Hayek said in his acceptance speech that it was time for economists to show "humility" about what they could achieve. They had overestimated their powers and ended up making a mess of things (particularly the control of inflation). The same lesson applied to democracies. They had to acknowledge all the things they could not do or they would destroy themselves. There was no middle ground between restraint and failure. That was the attraction of what was happening in Chile. It put the choice in stark terms: either an impossible democracy or an autocracy with the possibility of a democratic future. Hayek's intolerance for democratic muddle enticed him to plump for the latter.

Hayek was not the only leading member of the Mont Pelerin Society to think that some stark choices had to be faced. The American economist James Buchanan (like Friedman a future winner of the Nobel Prize) completed a book in 1974 called *The Limits of Liberty*, which described Western democracy as precariously poised between what he called "anarchy and the Leviathan [the all-powerful state]." Buchanan believed there still existed some middle ground between these two conditions, but it was narrow and getting narrower all the time. A decade earlier, along with Gordon Tullock, he had published a groundbreaking book called *The Calculus of Consent* (1962), which had used rational choice theory to make the case for democratic restraint. The authors believed it was possible to demonstrate from a democratic perspective that democracies need to curb majority rule if they are to function successfully. All it took was for people to think rationally. Now Buchanan felt he had taken too much for granted. He was no longer confident that rationality could get itself heard above the noise of democratic life, with all its bleating and hysterical self-assertion.

Buchanan felt he was living through an "era of intellectual bankruptcy," which is why it was time for some fresh thinking. Democratic states were out of control, spending more than they could afford, fostering inflation, pandering to interest groups, expanding their bureaucracies, and indulging the whims of the voters, who were rarely confronted with any hard truths. The only thing that could preserve democracy was recognition of the need for constitutionally imposed limits on public spending. Since this was democracy, the constitutional limits would have to be agreed on by the people. Like Friedman, Buchanan had no appetite for a dictator. The future of democracy depended on whether the voters could actually find it in themselves to tell their governments to stop. Buchanan wrote: "Can modern man in Western democratic society invent or capture sufficient control over his own destiny so as to impose constraints on his own government, constraints that will prevent its transformation into the genuine Hobbesian sovereign?"[20] The answer, probably, was no. But that, for Buchanan, was the only question.

Hayek and Buchanan, in their different ways, wanted to get beneath the surface and behind the noise of democratic life to uncover what they saw as the fundamental choice between restraint and excess. Yet during 1974, the fight against political excess was taking place at the surface. The loudest noise was the deafening screech of scandal. Watergate, which had been rumbling on for nearly two years, reached its crescendo in 1974, culminating in criminal convictions, impeachment, and ultimately, in August, the resignation of the president. Many saw Watergate as a tragedy. Kissinger viewed Nixon's demise as a miserable waste of the talents of a good man who had been brought down by his private demons. He also saw it as a dreadful waste of the opportunities his own geopolitical scheming had opened up. These opportunities needed a president of secure personal authority to exploit them, and by 1974 Nixon's authority was shot. For others, though, Watergate was entirely in keeping with the secrecy and lies of the Nixon-Kissinger years. An administration that mistrusted democracy had inevitably begun to abuse it. Now democracy was fighting back.

Watergate was in some ways a "pure" scandal. In the words of one commentator, "that is why [it] is more disturbing and dangerous. No sex. No dollars. Just power. It does not strike at oil leases; it strikes at democracy."[21] Inevitably, as with any scandal, it provoked talk of crisis. The revelations of presidential duplicity and paranoia seemed to be stripping democracy bare, exposing something rotten underneath. There were, as with any scandal, hopes expressed that exposure might prove cathartic, and that American democracy would seize the opportunity to refashion itself on more truthful lines. Those hopes were effectively dashed when President Gerald Ford pardoned his predecessor within a month of assuming office and encouraged the country to move on. American democracy had been distracted by Watergate, entertained by it, and also, at times, outraged by it. But it had not been purged.

Watergate was not the only scandal to grip the democracies in 1974. In May, Brandt resigned as West German
chancellor in the wake of the Guillaume affair, when it
was revealed that one of his closest personal assistants
had been working as an East German spy. A month earlier,
Golda Meir, the Israeli prime minister, had stepped down,
following the steady drip-drip of accusation and counter-
accusation that had plagued her government concerning
the country's unpreparedness for the Yom Kippur War. In
November the Italian prime minister, Mariano Rumor, left
office, dogged by accusations of bribery and corruption. In
December scandal brought down the Japanese prime minister, Kakuei Tanaka, who had been charged with nefarious
business practices and quit rather than expose his lover to
public humiliation. This one was all about sex and money:
stuffed envelopes and geisha girls.

These scandals were inevitably very different in their national circumstances and impact. In Italy, a democracy almost inured to corruption, there was talk of scandal fatigue.
Italians were so familiar with the foibles of their leaders that
they appeared, in the words of one observer, to have reached
a state of "cynical ungovernability."[22] Italian democracy was
regarded, as it has been for much of history, as the stalking
horse for Western European democracy: if the game was up,
this is where the news would arrive first. In Japan the public was also quite used to the idea of political corruption.
The shock came with the unfamiliarity of exposure; a society that was built on the maintenance of outward propri-
ety found the revelations of prime ministerial misbehavior
both titillating and disturbing. There was much talk of the
need to restore standards to Japanese public life, if only to

prevent its young democracy from going the way of Italy. But there was also a feeling that by facing up to the failings of its leaders, Japanese democracy had finally come of age. This was an illusion. Democracies do not grow up through scandals. An appetite for exposure and confrontation is a sign that a democracy has reached that condition of adolescent churlishness that is characteristic of all long-standing democracies.

In West Germany Brandt's fall provoked a fresh round of soul-searching. Was he the villain or the victim? Did a failure of judgment in his personal relationships invalidate his political judgment about the future relationship between the two Germanys? Brandt's demise, when it came, was swift: he was gone within two weeks of Guillaume's being arrested as a spy. Had it been too swift? One of the features of parliamentary systems like West Germany, Israel, Italy, and Japan is that scandals, when they acquire sufficient momentum, tend to rip apart a government quite quickly; parliamentary leaders, once their authority is sufficiently weakened, can be summarily dispatched. By contrast, part of the agony of Watergate was that it took so long. Presidents are very hard to budge. "With a parliamentary system like Canada's," one commentator wrote in the month before Nixon finally resigned, "the United States could have dealt with Watergate two months after it was discovered. With our rigid government we have instead reached a point of public helplessness that is demeaning to a great nation. Demeaning and dangerous." Other comparisons were even less flattering. "No other country on earth, save a dictatorship, could permit this discredited man to stay in office until now."[23]

Too hasty or too slow: that was still the problem with democracy. As always, the difficulty was achieving a sense of proportion. In the United States Nixon's clinging to power seemed to be a barrier preventing anyone else from getting a grip. But the rapid shuffling of leaders elsewhere seemed no better. Who would have time to get a grip if no one was able to stick around long enough to make a difference? Some of Brandt's advisers did what they could to persuade him to stay on, arguing that a democracy could not afford to toss over an experienced leader on a whim, simply because of some personal indiscretion. What mattered were the long-term challenges facing the country as a whole. Later on Brandt felt he had been hurried out of power.[24] But at the time he decided that resistance was futile. In a democracy leaders don't get to decide whether or not they are indispensible. Everyone is dispensable. That is how democracies work: a loss of confidence can strike the powerful at any time. It's only in autocracies that leaders get away with insisting the times are too dangerous to make a change.

What the democracies that ditched their leaders had in common is that they did not ditch their systems of government: no established democracy fell during 1974. Change took place according to the rules of the game. The rules themselves did not change. These rules looked incidental to the real dangers the democracies faced from stagflation and social unrest. Here were the democracies focusing on process—in each scandal, the question as always was who said what to whom—when the situation required substantive action. Yet it was the focus on process that helped to save the democracies. It provided an outlet for public anxiety and discontent without calling democracy itself into question. Meeting the "crisis" of 1974 on its own terms would have put democracy at risk; it opened the door to talk of emergency measures and military solutions. A system that tallies its response to the scale of the threat it faces will, when under serious threat, have to contemplate systemic change. The democracies never got that far. They were rescued by their inability to get things in proportion.

Regime change, when it occurred during 1974, brought down Europe's tin pot autocracies instead, which could not cope with the threats they faced. Inflation, routinely described as the curse of the democracies, was actually worse in the nondemocratic parts of Europe: it was above 30 percent in both Greece and Portugal, two countries then under military rule. In both places autocracy entered its death throes in 1974. The circumstances of regime change were haphazard and chaotic: in Portugal the António de Oliveira Salazar regime was overthrown in a coup by leftist junior officers, and the country teetered on the brink of civil war before emerging as a democracy; in Greece the colonels who were meant to be running the country fell out hopelessly among themselves, leaving the way clear for a restoration of democracy. Failed wars—in Africa for Portugal, in Cyprus for Greece—played their part in destabilizing these regimes, along with mounting economic chaos. Yet what was most striking was how brittle and inflexible they were under pressure: supposedly decisive autocrats did not know how to deal with the consequences of their own mistakes. The crisis of 1974, in Greece and Portugal, produced change commensurate with the scale of the problem because the regimes in question could not adapt to diminish its impact.

All they could do was raise the stakes, which is how you lose in the end.

In Eastern Europe inflation was also a serious problem. These, though, were not tin pot autocracies but ideologically founded regimes backed up by the military might of the Soviet Union. They were able to suppress the inflationary effects of the oil shock by means of extensive state subsidies and with help from the Soviets, who as oil exporters had benefited from the price rise. However, suppressing inflation is by no means the same as tackling it. Inefficiency and waste were entrenched by the reluctance of Eastern European governments to let their populations experience the full shock of rising prices and stalling growth. Part of this reluctance stemmed from their awareness that they were failing behind the consumer societies of the West. Détente had opened the eyes of many Eastern Europeans to what they were missing: cars that worked, TV that was worth watching, politicians who could be thrown out of office on a whim. It made their rulers increasingly nervous about admitting the scale of the challenge they faced, and the price that might have to be paid if they didn't keep up.

So they adopted a different strategy. The oil shock had created new sources of wealth in the Middle East: petrodollars that needed somewhere to go. The Nixon shock had accelerated the growth of offshore markets designed to take advantage of growing deregulation (the most liquid of these markets was in the City of London; it was "offshore" in the sense that it was not subject to national jurisdiction).[25] Petrodollars were recycled through offshore markets by Western bankers to Eastern European governments in the form of hard currency loans, allowing them to continue to subsidize the rising expectations of their increasingly demanding populations. It was a fatal compact. The communist leaders of the more "advanced" Eastern European states—East Germany, Hungary, Poland—hoped they could exploit the "adaptability" (meaning the greed) of Western capitalism to siphon off funds for their own ends. All they succeeded in doing was burying themselves in debt. Of course, it wouldn't matter if Western capitalism collapsed in chaos as it was meant to. But if that didn't happen, the communist states were caught. Borrowing to cover up for their weaknesses left them with nowhere to go when threatened with exposure except back to the bankers to ask for more. Eventually the bankers would say no, if only to preserve themselves from ruin. The Eastern bloc was in the process of becoming, in the words of one historian, "a Ponzi scheme."[26] But almost no one saw it at the time.

In 1974 all the talk of crisis and looming disaster was on the Western side, where such talk was cheap. Meanwhile, the real long-term crisis was brewing among the regimes of Eastern Europe and the Soviet Union. These were the states that lacked the ability to adapt but retained the power to soldier on. In the West the search continued in vain for politicians of selfless courage. Democratic leaders were said to be too afraid of their electorates to take the action needed to protect them. But the really debilitating fear was at work among the communist regimes that did not dare own up to their failings. Instead, they pressed on in that mixed and middle state between self-illusion and voluntary fraud, hoping that something would turn up to rescue them. The democracies were not tougher than the autocracies when confronted with a crisis. Nor were they more purposeful. Instead, they were more erratic, more jittery, and more easily distracted. This made them harder to control. In 1974 these qualities helped save them from a worse fate.

AFTERMATH

In 1975 a body calling itself the Trilateral Commission published a widely noticed report titled "The Crisis of Democracy." The commission had been set up in 1973 to bring together perspectives from the United States, Western Europe, and Japan on the joint threats facing the West (democratic Japan was by now considered part of "the West"). In the final report, its three authors—Michel Crozier writing about Europe, Samuel Huntington writing about the United States, Joji Watanuki writing about Japan—bemoaned the conjunction over the previous few years of external and internal threats to democracy. It might have been possible for democracy to cope with one or the other, but not both. "A system which did not have such significant demands placed on it by its external environment might be able to correct the deficiencies which arise out of its own operations," the coauthors wrote in their introduction.[27] The oil shock might have been manageable without the build-up of irresponsible public finance; democratic public finance might have been manageable without the sudden impact of the oil shock. It was the combination of immediate events and long-term trends that was proving deadly.

Crozier, a French sociologist, was the gloomiest of the three. He blamed all the usual suspects for democracy's plight: inflation, alienated youth, trivializing scandals, irresponsible intellectuals. The democracies of Europe were caught in "a vicious circle, which is very difficult for them to break without entering a deeper recession whose risks seem impossible to accept in view of the fragility of the social fabric." The EC (the forerunner of the European Union) was too weak at the center to coordinate a collective response. Instead, different countries groped their way forward from one temporizing measure to the next. This might work in time, but time was not on democracy's side. "Experimentation," Crozier lamented, "which is bound to succeed in the long run, looks very dangerous in the present vulnerable situation."[28]

Huntington, one of the world's leading political scientists, tried to resist existential despair. The game was not yet up. Any advantages of democracy were, however, close to being squandered. Huntington felt American democracy had done more than enough experimenting during the 1960s, with social as well as political institutions, and now was paying the price. Public spending was out of control at a moment when political alienation made remedial action extremely difficult. The voters wanted too much from government at the same time as having lost their faith in it: politicians were faced with an impossible mix of neediness and cynicism from their electorates. The best hope lay with public contempt for politics turning to resignation and apathy. Huntington had little confidence the voters would work out for themselves what needed to be done. But if they lost interest they would at least stop making their impossible demands, which might give the politicians room to act. The democracies needed more distraction, not less, if they were going to survive.

Watanuki was a little more sanguine. Japan was still some way from going down the American route. Despite the Tanaka scandal, public contempt for politicians was not yet pervasive. Many Japanese social and political institutions had survived the turbulence of the 1960s relatively unscathed. Japanese democracy certainly looked more stable than its counterparts. But Japan was a young democracy with plenty of catching up to do. Its turbulent years almost certainly lay ahead of it. If the crisis was not yet acute for Japan, it was probably just a matter of time. Watanuki concluded that the 1980s might well turn out to be Japan's 1970s: the point of breakdown.

The commission presented its report at a meeting in Kyoto in May 1975. One of those invited to respond was the Anglo-German sociologist Ralf Dahrendorf, who had recently been appointed head of the London School of Economics. Dahrendorf was a centrist and a pragmatist who distrusted grandiose, overarching ideas. He told the authors of "The Crisis of Democracy" that he didn't buy what they were selling. They had gone too far and lost their sense of perspective. They wanted the democracies to regain control of events, which meant they were judging democracy by the wrong standards: the standards of its rivals. "Could it not be argued," Dahrendorf suggested, "that one of the traditional characteristics of democracies is that we do not ask governments to give direction to their economies, societies and political communities, at least not to the extent that nondemocratic societies are doing this?"[29] It was the states that were unable to relinquish control that were in real trouble. "I am not," Dahrendorf went on, "contrary to many others, pessimistic about democracy today. It seems to me [that] recent social developments are likely to make life much more difficult for the dictatorships of this world." That made it crucial not to overreact. Talk of crisis always prompted calls for "deliberate retrenchment": a reassertion of control, a minimizing of risk. That would be a mistake. "What we have to do above all is to maintain that flexibility of democratic institutions which is in some ways their greatest virtue."[30]

Dahrendorf was in a minority among public intellectuals in refusing to overreact to the democratic crisis of the 1970s, but he was right. The flexibility of democratic institutions turned out to be their salvation. Yet it took time to reveal that the crisis of democracy was not what it seemed. Another pretty bleak year was 1975. "I must say to you that the state of our Union is not good," President Ford told the American people at its outset.[31] Both unemployment and inflation peaked in many countries as the recession ground on. In India, Indira Gandhi suspended the country's democracy in June, under the combined pressure of scandal (she had been convicted of charges of electoral fraud) and social unrest. The period of "emergency" she inaugurated was to last for twenty-one months. In November the long-time Spanish dictator, Franco, finally died, to be replaced by the young king, Juan Carlos, his chosen successor. It was not until the following year that Juan Carlos began the transition to democracy. To start with it was very unclear which way Spain would go. At a time of rapid political turnover in many countries, no one could be sure what was a passing phase and what was a permanent shift. India had lurched from democracy to semi-autocracy. Spain was stumbling from autocracy to tentative democracy. Who could know which state of affairs would last?

Only later did the pattern of these years become clear. For the new democracies it was two steps forward, one step back; for the new autocracies one step forward, two steps back. The transitions from autocracy to democracy were much more likely to endure than the moves the other way. The Indian emergency turned out to be a blip; Spanish democracy turned out to be a lasting phenomenon. The person who did most to identify this pattern, and who gave it a name, was Samuel Huntington. Writing a decade and a half after he had identified a crisis of democracy, Huntington labeled the period from 1974 to 1990 the "Third Wave" of democratic advance, following earlier shifts during the first part of the twentieth century and then after the Second World War.[32] For Huntington the causes of this new wave were complicated and multiple, which excused his failure to have spotted it as it was getting underway. Nor was the pattern in any way smooth. In some countries, notably in Latin America and Southeast Asia, the back and forth between democracy and autocracy continued for years. In other places, above all Africa, democracy still seemed unable to get a secure foothold. Nonetheless, the overall direction of travel was clear. Seen with the benefit of hindsight, 1974 now looked very different. The crisis of democracy had really been a turning point in democracy's favor.

Dahrendorf had glimpsed this at the time. Huntington had not. Yet in one respect, Huntington's view of the "crisis of democracy" turned out to be prescient. He foresaw that the established democracies might require further distractions. The crisis would only dissipate if democratic politics lost its sense of urgency. It would be better if people simply tired of it. As the 1970s ground on, there was a growing feeling of crisis fatigue. The idea that something was seriously awry never went away, yet the promised cataclysm never arrived either. Under these limbo conditions, it became easier for the democracies to experiment with new solutions. Toward the end of the decade, starting in the United States, elected politicians gave the task of taming inflation to central bankers (that is, the elected politicians chose not to stand in their way). The measures required—high interest rates, high unemployment—were the ones it had been feared earlier in the decade that no democracy would tolerate. Again starting in the United States, the democracies did tolerate it. However, the important thing to emphasize is that they did no more than tolerate it. They did not insist on it. The second half of the 1970s saw elected politicians take advantage of the tired, distracted state of public opinion to try something different. These were not, to begin with anyway, right-wing politicians elected on a promise of radical change. In the United States the experiment began during the Carter administration; in Britain it began during the Labour administration of James Callaghan. Their successors—Ronald Reagan, Margaret Thatcher—took it further only because they had been given an indication of what the public would put up with.[33]

The democracies effectively stumbled on the solution to their economic "malaise," more by accident than design.[34] At the same time, they acquiesced in their increasing lack of control over their own fate. The Nixon shock did not produce democracies that toughened up to embrace self-sufficiency. Instead, it produced democracies that acclimatized themselves to their growing dependence on outside forces. Their flexibility allowed them to adapt to the conditions of an increasingly interdependent world, without either having chosen to inhabit that world or having much understanding of how it operated. The publics of the democracies did not really know what they were doing at the end of the 1970s, as they inched their way into a globalized market economy. Things were being done to them, and for them, and tired of what they had been putting up with for most of the decade, they put up with this instead.

Their flexibility, then, was not quite as Dahrendorf had conceived it. He shared with other intellectuals a belief that democracies need to understand their own strengths and weaknesses. In this respect, he was not so different from the crisis mongers and pessimists he had been criticizing. Dahrendorf saw flexibility as an advantage the democracies could and should recognize in themselves. That way, they would be able to protect and enhance it. But democratic flexibility doesn't work like this. It is haphazard and inadvertent. The advantages of democracy remain easier to recognize in retrospect than in the moment, when they are always somewhere out of reach. The same is true of the disadvantages. The realists had thought that democracy could only survive if its weaknesses were properly acknowledged and catered for. But there was no satisfactory way to do this. Democracies will not acknowledge their own weaknesses. Yet if you try to manage their weaknesses for them—as Kissinger did—you end up with something less than democracy.

Democracy cannot escape its own inadvertence: it can't master it and it can't avoid it. In time, the outward failures of the 1970s turned out to be a success story for democracy. The success became fully visible in the triumph of 1989. But that triumph, like the crisis of democracy that preceded it, was not what it seemed.

CHAPTER 6

1989

The End of History

THE CRISIS

IT MIGHT SEEM ODD TO DESCRIBE 1989 AS A CRISIS FOR democracy. Nothing bad happened that year (if you discount what took place in China). A lot of what happened was wonderful, almost miraculous. Nonetheless, a crisis is a point of rupture, the moment when the present asserts itself in the face of the past. What makes it such an unnerving experience to live through is that so much can be at stake with so little warning. Suddenly the future is on the line. The dramatic events that surrounded the collapse of Soviet power in Eastern Europe constituted a genuine crisis for democracy.

The end of the Cold War was a lot like the end of the First World War: victory took the victors by surprise. We tend to think of the 1980s as an era of democratic triumphalism, because we know how the decade ended. That was not how it was experienced at the time. The prevailing mood, as so often in democracies, was one of anxiety and uncertainty. The 1980s were an extension of the 1970s rather than a preview of the 1990s. This is not surprising, given how little time had passed since Western democracy had undergone its most recent crisis of confidence. A decade was hardly long enough for such a complete turnaround. Bad news turned into good news so fast it was hard to get into focus what was happening. The sudden triumph of democracy over its enemies was disorientating.

As in 1918, there existed a strong temptation to deal with the confusion by rewriting history as it unfolded. Victory has many fathers. On November 10, the morning after the Berlin Wall had been breached the night before, Willy Brandt went to the city and told the cheering crowds they had taken charge of their destiny. "This is a beautiful day," he declared, "at the end of a long journey." Yet only five years earlier Brandt had conceded that the Cold War division of Germany was now permanent and reunification off the table for good. What happened in 1989 vindicated many different people. But that did not mean they had seen it coming.

For some, vindication seemed premature. One way to deal with the disorientating effects of victory was to deny that democracy had come out on top. Events in 1989 appeared far too good to be true, and therefore could not be what they seemed. Kennan was one of those who warned against treating the events of 1989 as a vindication of Western democracy. He was adamant that defeat for one side should not be seen as victory for the other. The fact that the

Soviets had lost the Cold War did not mean the democracies had won it.

This way of thinking was fairly widespread in 1989. Plenty of commentators warned against jumping to conclusions, overinterpreting what was going on, taking credit where credit was not due. Some worried that 1989 was liable to turn out to be a trap for democracy, because the wrong lessons would be learned. Democracies would become more profligate, not less, since they would no longer think they had anything to worry about. They would mistake the failings of their rivals for a confirmation of their own merits. They would indulge in the old democratic trick of giving way to their vices and calling it virtue.

Inevitably there were also those who saw 1989 as vindication. The Cold War had been a long, messy, compromised and compromising struggle, but its decisive outcome made things simple again. Democracy had won. The victory was not only real; it was complete. The most famous statement of the idea that liberal democracy was the clear winner from the drawn-out struggles of the twentieth century came from Francis Fukuyama, in the article he published in the summer of 1989 called "The End of History." Fukuyama's claim gave the triumphalists plenty of ammunition. But Fukuyama was not one of the triumphalists himself. His tone was more admonitory than celebratory. Like Tocqueville, he was worried that democracy would fail to understand the nature of its success. Fukuyama's reputation as the public intellectual face of blithe democratic optimism in 1989 is undeserved. His analysis was little help in understanding the events of the year as they were unfolding. But he did provide an inadvertent glimpse of the troubles ahead.

For anyone who lived through it, 1989 was a difficult year to understand. It was evident that something momentous was happening. But it was hard to know what lessons to draw. The democracies had shown their resilience in the long run. How they had done it, and what it meant for the future, was much less clear. The knowledge of their hidden strengths the democracies had been given did not translate into greater self-knowledge or self-control. Democracy was emerging victorious from the travails of the twentieth century. But it was little wiser for the experience.

THE PROPHETS

Who saw it coming? When trawling through the political prognostications of the 1980s, it is hard to find anyone who did. That does not mean people were blind to what was happening around them. It was quite clear to just about everyone, both inside and outside the system, that the Soviet Union was in big trouble long before it fell apart. During the 1980s, Western intellectuals did not come back from Russia with tales of having seen the future. Those who went tended to come back vaguely depressed: the country was a gloomy place to visit, shabby, uncomfortable, and oppressive.

Yet few in the West felt confident about the demise of Soviet power. During the 1980s there was a strong appetite in Western democracies for books that foretold doom, not victory. This is partly because there is always an appetite in democracies for books like that: doom sells. But it also reflected a widespread sense that the real crisis was yet to come. In 1984 the French intellectual Jean-François Revel published a book called *How Democracies Perish*, which was taken very seriously on both sides of the Atlantic (Peggy Noonan later described it as the one book "everyone" inside the Reagan White House read). Revel argued that although the Soviet Union was in its death throes, it was likely to drag Western democracy down into the grave with it. He wrote: "Democracy may after all turn out to have been an historical accident, a brief parenthesis that is closing before our eyes."[1] When it came to the crunch, the democracies were not resolute enough for the final crisis: they would temporize, they would indulge their enemies, they would pander to their electorates. The Soviets were better equipped for the politics of the end game. Almost nothing Revel said was new: his underlying thesis about democratic failings was a hodgepodge of familiar ideas drawn from the usual suspects (Plato, Tocqueville, Nietzsche). He found a ready audience because it is as easy to make this argument in good times as in bad. The West looked like it was finally winning the Cold War. Aha, Revel said, that's why we should be worried. Good news for democracy is always bad news in disguise.

In the United States, the late 1980s saw two other books capture the public imagination with stories of why things were much worse than they appeared. In 1987 the must-read was *The Closing of the American Mind* by Allan Bloom, a truly improbable best seller, which explained how promiscuity and postmodernism were turning American universities into morally empty pleasure palaces. Bloom was an intellectual historian whose pupils had included Fukuyama. He argued that creeping relativism was eating democracy alive. It had left it unable to defend itself in meaningful terms.

Like Revel, Bloom drew on the usual suspects to make his case (Plato, Tocqueville, Nietzsche), though he had a fresh cast of villains (Mick Jagger appeared as a greater threat to Western democracy than Karl Marx). Read now, the book seems slightly unhinged. Read then, it captured a hankering for philosophical certainty in an uncertain world, as well as pandering to the perennial democratic appetite to hear the worst of itself.

In the following year Bloom's thesis was overtaken by another academic blockbuster, Paul Kennedy's *The Rise and Fall of the Great Powers*, which told Americans that the good news was already over. Kennedy was an economic and military historian with no interest in Plato or Nietzsche, neither of whom feature anywhere in his book (Tocqueville is there, but only as the man who predicted that one day America's number one enemy would be Russia).[2] For Kennedy, the fact that the United States was a democracy was not the issue; the crucial fact was that it had acquired an empire and was therefore bound to suffer from the problem of imperial overstretch. Great powers decline because the economic and technological advantages that bring them to dominance cannot sustain the military commitments needed to keep them there. The United States was no different. Its days at the top were numbered. It would not be able to keep its rivals (the EU, the USSR, Japan, China) at bay for long. How long? Kennedy was unwilling to say, not least because he knew full well the Soviet empire was in even more trouble than the American one. Neither was finished quite yet. Despite its economic woes, Kennedy was adamant: "This does *not* mean the USSR is close to collapse."[3] He foresaw superpower rivalry lasting for perhaps another twenty years. But then all bets would be off.

Kennedy's book became one of the talking points in the 1988 US presidential election. George H. W. Bush found himself defending the ongoing promise of America's global reach against the gloomier take of his Democratic rival, Michael Dukakis. Gloom sells books, but optimism wins elections. By the time Bush had been in office for a year, Kennedy's argument already seemed hopelessly out of date. The Cold War was over, and with no plausible rivals in place, the United States and its political system looked to have the field to itself. But if 1989 seemed to show Kennedy was wrong, who had been proved right? The fact that the doomsayers had dominated the period leading up to the collapse of the Soviet empire meant the true prophets had to be found further back. Much further back. The people who were credited with having seen it coming were the old men who had been waging the lonely struggle for years. In 1989, the prophetic heroes of the revolution on the Western side were Kennan and Hayek.

Kennan was lauded during 1989 as the wisest of the wise, the man who had foreseen it all. In April he appeared before the Senate Foreign Affairs Committee to be told by each of his interlocutors that they were privileged to be in the same room with him. Kennan, a vain man who had felt undervalued for forty years, enjoyed the appreciation. Nonetheless, the only question to which he responded with any real intellectual satisfaction was one that asked him whether victory in the Cold War might be bad news for America. Didn't the country need a challenge to keep it honest? Yes, Kennan agreed, it did.

The truth is that Kennan was not made happy by the fulfillment of his prediction about the demise of Soviet power.

People who did not understand what they were doing were winning the war. They had not learned their lesson, and now he feared they never would. "I see nothing hopeful in any of it," he wrote during the summer, shortly after being awarded the presidential Medal of Freedom for his contribution to the struggle.[4] When the Berlin Wall came down in November, he did not change his mind. It was all happening too fast, too impulsively, without restraint. Caution should be the watchword in times of dramatic change. No one should get carried away. No one should believe they had been proved right.

Kennan was particularly eager that America's political leaders should not feel they had been proved right in the policy they had adopted during the Cold War. Worst of all were the Reaganites. Kennan had despaired of the presidency of Reagan, whom he considered a prejudiced fool. He persisted with this view despite the fact that during his second term Reagan attempted many of the things Kennan most wanted to see done, including a big reduction in nuclear arsenals. Reagan's problem was that any prudential actions went along with a tendency to see the world in Manichaean terms, all too typical of unthinking democratic opinion. He represented the worst of democracy for Kennan: an irresponsible crowd pleaser, he ended up doing the right things for the wrong reasons, which could be as dangerous as doing nothing at all. The events of 1989 did little to persuade Kennan that the world had been made safer: there were still far too many nuclear weapons floating about. But it had made the world stupider, by allowing a simplistic tale of democratic triumph to prosper. The unseemly rush toward German reunification exemplified this stupidity. Ken-

nan thought the haste to claim the spoils of victory was grotesque, and absurd.

In 1947 Kennan had argued that the Soviets were trapped
by their inability to admit their own failings, because they
were precommitted to a deterministic framework that
confirmed their own virtue. Now he feared the West was
trapped in the same way. His personal misfortune, in 1989,
was that no one wanted to hear this message from him. The
man being lauded was the Kennan of 1947, who in a brief
moment of optimism had laid out a far-sighted vision of
the future, not the Kennan who had spent the next forty
years trying to qualify what he had said. To his own mind,
the long, lonely struggle to get American democracy to face
up to its limitations went on. Kennan was eighty-five in
1989, in full possession of his faculties, which is what gives
his distress a poignant quality. He was being treated as an
old man who had once been ahead of his time. As a *New
York Times* commentator had written a few years earlier,
the world no longer turned to Kennan for concrete advice
but "for glimpses of an uncommon, even mystical prophetic
power."[5] He wasn't a prophet unappreciated in his own land;
he was being appreciated as a prophet, when he wished he
could be recognized as something else.

Hayek was ninety in 1989, and for him the distress was
more acute. He had disappeared from public view in 1985,
suffering from illness and depression. He lived to see the
Berlin Wall come down, and a statement was issued on his
behalf celebrating its demise. But he could take no public
pleasure in it. Two years later Hayek was also awarded the
presidential Medal of Freedom, but he was too ill to come
to Washington to receive the award. His son accepted it for

him. Austen Furse, director of policy planning at the White House, said at the ceremony: "More than almost anyone in the twentieth century, this guy was vindicated by the events in Eastern Europe."[6] By this point Hayek was barely aware of what was being said and done in his name.

Would he have approved? Hayek was celebrated in 1989 for having provided the intellectual framework that explained the triumph of the market over the planned economy. He would have had no problem with that: it was his defining creed. Nor would he have been displeased with the idea that he saw the end coming before others. In 1983 he was asked at a public gathering at the Hoover Institution to justify his optimism that communism was failing. He answered with a personal anecdote about an event he said "had given him more hope than anything else." A visiting Russian scientist had dined with him at his club in London. Hayek asked his guest what had most surprised him about the West. The scientist answered: "You still have so many Marxists. We haven't any!"[7]

What mattered for Hayek was the battle of ideas. It was clear to him the Russians had thrown in the towel. But just because one side realized they had got it wrong didn't mean the other side could claim they had it right. The West was winning in spite of its own ideas, not because of them. In Britain, Margaret Thatcher—who had once banged a table brandishing a copy of Hayek's *The Constitution of Liberty* and declared: "This, gentlemen, is what we believe!"—was in the ascendancy.[8] But even Thatcherism did not represent a sustainable path for democracy in Hayek's terms. It still depended too heavily on the whims of the majority, and their attachment to cheap money and social security.

Hayek's lifelong mission had been to get democracies to see that they needed to rein themselves in, to discipline themselves. Thatcher was a free market evangelist but she was not an apostle of democratic restraint. The end of the Cold War did not signal that Hayek's warnings about democratic extravagance were being heeded. It threatened instead to let democracies think they had got away with it.

In this, Hayek would be proved right, though not in the way he thought. The year 1989 certainly did not draw a line under democratic excess; it marked the start of a new age of it. Where Hayek was wrong, as he had always been wrong, was in assuming that democratic excess was invariably a stage on the road to serfdom. He never got beyond the idea that democracies crave the siren securities of socialism, and that only constitutional safeguards could protect them from their own weaknesses. Without those safeguards, democracies would pander to their electorates and destroy their market freedoms. By the 1980s Hayek was happy to admit his affinities with Schumpeter, a man he had once derided as a fatalist. Democracies that lurched from election to election, their politicians saying and doing whatever it took to get elected, were on the road to ruin. Since he saw no signs of Western democracies setting constitutional limits to their politicians' powers, Hayek saw no real prospect of salvation. "I don't think an effort toward reform will come in time," he said in one of his last interviews in 1983. "So I rather fear we shall have a return to some sort of dictatorial democracy. . . . And if the system is going to break down, it will be a very long period before real democracy can re-emerge."[9]

What Hayek had failed to notice was that the democracies were not simply pandering to their electorates. They were also distancing themselves from them. During the 1980s a story began to take shape about how Western democracy had recovered from the crisis of the 1970s: it had been achieved by politicians who recognized the limits to their own powers. They could not defeat inflation; the voters wouldn't let them take the painful steps required. So they had entrusted the task to independent central bankers who, armed with anti-inflationary targets but freed from electoral pressures, did the job for them. It didn't take long for this story, in the words of one critic, to be "polished until it acquired the quality of a moral tale."[10] Franchising out key decisions to nondemocratic bodies had saved democracy from itself. The story did not fit in every case. In Britain, for instance, the government retained the power to set interest rates throughout the 1980s; independence for the Bank of England did not arrive until 1997. But the story could be made to fit. In the British case, the defeat of inflation simply proved the special qualities, and iron resolve, of the Hayek-touting Margaret Thatcher.

The morality tale was cemented by the events of 1989. The planned economy had failed. The free market had triumphed. Democracy had won because it had recognized its own weaknesses and learned how to temper them. Hayek became the hero of this story: he had shown the path to victory. But Hayek is the wrong hero for this story. The democracies had not learned their lesson in the way he wanted, because they had not chosen this path for themselves. The defeat of inflation, like the defeat of communism, was the result of a series of ad hoc decisions. Democratic politicians acted in mild desperation and a spirit of improvisation, not out of accumulated experience and constitutional wisdom.

Success in this sort of haphazard venture threatened to breed its own sort of fatalism. This was not the fatalism that Hayek had feared all his life—the drift toward soft democratic tyranny. It was the other kind of democratic fatalism that Tocqueville had warned about, and that Hayek had consistently neglected: the fatalism that comes from successful experimentation. The end of the Cold War encouraged the Western democracies to mistake improvisation for permanence and contingent arrangements for a settled understanding of how to manage their affairs.

Kennan had wanted the Cold War to be won by democracies that showed the discipline needed for containment; Hayek wanted it to be won by democracies that put their majoritarian powers beyond use. Instead, it was won by democracies that did not know what they were up to. They were scared, they were distracted, and they were profligate. All they could do was hope for the best. They had turned a blind eye as their central bankers got a grip on inflation, but they still didn't want to balance their budgets. To take their minds off nuclear Armageddon, they watched television and went shopping. And that's how the Cold War was won: by people whose attention was elsewhere. In a notorious interview he gave in 1976, Kennan, who throughout his life was morbidly obsessed with the link between democracy and pornography, had declared: "As things are, I see very little merit in organizing ourselves to defend from the Russians the porno-shops in central Washington."[11] The porno shops were still going strong when the Russians gave up the fight (and a ready access to pornography was one of the market freedoms the West soon exported to the new democracies of the East). Kennan wanted democracy to have earned its victory. So did Hayek. Both men were at heart moralists and political puritans. It meant that unthinking democracy was bound to disappoint them at the moment of its success.

Western democracy had not reined itself in. It had not even franchised itself out. It had simply kept going. Its victory relied on its underlying adaptability, not its self-control. Democracy had failed to take charge of its destiny, but it had taken whatever history could throw at it and come through, in ways no rival system could match. It was still standing when everything else had fallen down. The person who found cosmic significance in this resilience was Fukuyama. The grand political battles were over. Only small differences remained.

Amid the heady excitements of 1989, Fukuyama insisted on taking the long view.[12] On that view, liberal democracy now had the field to itself; it had won by default. It was the only political idea that had a plausible future ahead of it. Everything else had run out of road. This did not mean the world had deliberately chosen democracy as its preferred option, and Fukuyama did not think there was much point in trying to prove that embracing democracy would make everyone better off (the evidence, particularly in relation to democracy and economic development, was mixed). Instead, it was enough that all the other grand ideas of history had lost their capacity to inspire. First fascism, then Marxism-Leninism, had failed to deliver on their promises. They could not survive that failure; without the promise of some better future they were simply monuments to cruelty and inefficiency. Liberal democracy did not have to deliver on its promises in order to come out on top. It simply had to retain its promise, as something that it still made sense to believe in.

The end of history represented a victory for democracy in the realm of ideas, far removed from what Fukuyama called "the trivial election year proposals of American politicians."[13] He dismissed all the fuss about Paul Kennedy's *The Rise and Fall of the Great Powers* as beside the point. Kennedy's reductive history had missed something essential: beliefs matter. The fate of American democracy would not be determined by its material circumstances. Democracy is only doomed if people come to believe it is doomed; otherwise, it can survive anything. Moreover, democratic societies are able to adapt their beliefs to suit their circumstances; if nothing else, they remain flexible. So the end of history was also the victory of a flexible idea. But it was no more than that. It was not the victory of an idea over which anyone could claim control. It couldn't be used to fix the future. It did not predetermine what would happen in crisis situations like those of 1989, and it could not be harnessed in the heat of the moment. Its advantages were only visible at a certain distance.

Fukuyama's argument was a grandiose one, starting with its bombastic title, but he was careful to litter it with caveats. He never said the end of history would be neat and tidy. But Fukuyama's critics, of whom there were many, did not notice the caveats. All they saw was the bombast. In the words of the Indian economist Jagdish Bhagwati, Fukuyama's article appeared "like a primeval scream of joy from a warrior with a foot astride his fallen prey."[14] This was a caricature, but the caricature stuck. As the events of 1989 conformed more closely to an end of history script, Fukuyama became the man who wrote it. When events diverged from that script, as they were bound to do, he became the man who had got it

wrong. Ralf Dahrendorf, who had scorned the idea that democracy had failed in 1974, was equally scornful of the idea
that it had triumphed in 1989. He mocked Fukuyama for his
pretensions and his insufferable arrogance. He regarded him
as a dangerous idiot. No "system," Dahrendorf said, ever triumphs, because the only thing that wins in the long run is
experimentation and flexibility.[15] Attempts to crown liberal
democracy the victor of history would condemn it to go the
way of communism: it would become rigid, inflexible and
ultimately brittle. It would crack open and the experiments
would have to start again.

Dahrendorf was being unfair. Fukuyama was defending
an idea, not a system. He understood the great merit of the
idea was its flexibility: its ability to adapt. Liberal democracy
was still going strong at the end of the twentieth century because it had been able to accommodate what had happened
during the century, even if it could not control it. Democracy had made room for history; no other system of government could do that.

Yet if Fukuyama was defending an accommodating idea,
not a fixed system, his argument had two flaws. First, it was
a mistake to talk about the end of history. Of course, it was
not a mistake for Fukuyama personally. The phrase, which
obliterated all the subtleties of his case, made him rich and
famous; for a while, he was the most famous intellectual in
the world. But the phrase did not fit with the idea that democracy had endured because it had been able to accommodate whatever history had thrown at it. If that were true,
then there was no reason to suppose the victory of democracy would shut history down. Democracy always leaves
open the space for competing views, unexpected reverses,

unanticipated rivals. It doesn't foreclose the future. That is how it survives the vagaries of history. And that is why it doesn't end them.

Second, Fukuyama did not say enough about what it might be like to live with the triumph of an accommodating idea, one that operates beneath the surface of events, always elusive, impossible to capture in the moment, accessible only in the long run, an idea over which no one has any immediate control. The picture Fukuyama draws to capture this state of affairs is a world of banality and boredom. "The end of history," he says, "will be a very sad time. . . . In the post-historical period there will be neither art nor philosophy, just the perpetual caretaking of the museum of human history."[16] The quintessential inhabitants of this world were the people of Western Europe, whose postwar existence Fukuyama saw as "post-historical" before its time. Europeans were already living in "flabby, prosperous, self-satisfied, inward-looking, weak-willed states whose grandest project was nothing more heroic than the creation of a Common Market."[17] Europe was a nice place to live in which there was nothing significant to do. That was the democratic future.

It is a familiar image of democratic fatalism: passive citizens, living unimaginative lives, contented to drift along with their comfortable fate. It echoes some of Tocqueville's anxieties about conformism in the age of democracy. But it is only one side of democratic fatalism. Fukuyama entirely misses the other side. People who live with an idea of politics that governs their fate but remains outside their power to control can also become impatient, reckless, and cavalier. Far from eschewing grand schemes, they may embrace them, confident that history is on their side. The only way Fukuyama could see for history to start up again was if people got tired of their material comforts and rediscovered a sense of intellectual adventure. This is far too narrow a view (it is far too intellectualist a view). It ignores the restless quality of all democratic societies, including the most comfortable ones. It ignores the frustration of living with a victorious idea whose advantages are seemingly tangible but always just out of reach. In democracies, people keep grabbing for those advantages, they keep making mistakes, and history moves on. Even in the comfortable, boring old states of Western Europe.

THE OUTLIERS

In Europe, it was clear who had won and who had lost by the end of 1989. The communist governments of Eastern Europe were the losers, as were their Soviet backers. Within the space of a few months these regimes fell apart in Poland, Hungary, East Germany, Bulgaria, Czechoslovakia and, finally, Romania. The winners were the people of Eastern Europe, who had got rid of their oppressors with minimal bloodshed, along with the democracies of the West, which had stayed the course long enough to see them do it.

However, this neat picture only holds for a certain time and place. The further you move out from 1989 the messier things look. People power quickly frayed in the new democracies of Eastern Europe; old communists returned in new guises, and won elections; democracy soon resumed its mixed and muddled ways. The picture also blurs the further you move away from Europe. This was as true during the dramas of 1989 as it was in their aftermath. The distinct pattern that had emerged in Europe by the end of the year did not fit with the wider world. Globally, it was much less obvious who were the real winners and losers from the demise of the Soviet empire.

"The Cold War is over and Japan won." This mock headline, which began its life as a joke, had turned into something like a truism by the close of the 1980s. Japan was the democracy that had most obviously grown in strength and stature during the ups and downs of the Cold War. It emerged from the struggle stable, secure, militarily unencumbered, and above all, very, very wealthy. At the end of 1989, when the Tokyo-based Nikkei stock index peaked at a level of nearly 39,000, it accounted for almost 40 percent of the total value of all global stock markets. Japanese multinational corporations were busy acquiring businesses and real estate across the globe, including in America, where they had even started to buy up Hollywood. Japanese tourists were an increasingly familiar sight in the West. In 1965, three hundred thousand Japanese holidaymakers took trips overseas. By 1989 that figure had reached ten million. Japanese consumer products, particularly at the cutting edge of the new technology, had invaded every marketplace. The 1980s, far from bogging Japan down in its own version of the 1970s, had seen the country forge ahead. The question was no longer whether Japanese democracy was going to catch up with the problems that had afflicted the rest of the world, it was whether the rest of the world was going to be able to catch up with Japan.

The 1980s saw a steady stream of books published in the West that predicted coming Japanese dominance, with titles ranging from *Japan as Number One: Lessons for America* (1980) to *Trading Places: How We Allowed Japan to Take the Lead* (1988). In *The Rise and Fall of the Great Powers*, Kennedy identified Japan as the rising power that was by far the most likely to win "the glittering prizes of the twenty-first century."[18] Not only, Kennedy said, did Japan hold the obvious advantages in both computer hardware and software (a common misapprehension at the predawn of the Internet), but also Japan's high national savings rate, along with America's growing burden of debt, would soon make Tokyo "the banker to the world." What Japan lacked was a military strategy commensurate with its growing economic power. The test of its ultimate destiny, Kennedy said, would be whether it acquired one.

In mid-1989 an article appeared in the *Atlantic Monthly* under the title "Containing Japan." Its author was James Fallows, a former speechwriter for President Carter. He argued that America needed a new strategy of its own to counter the growing Japanese threat. In many ways, this threat was the opposite of the Soviet one. Where that had been driven by ideology, the Japanese expansion was marked by a lack of ideological purpose, indeed the absence of any "principles" at all. Fallows stated that what made Japan so dangerous was its belief that it was merely acting pragmatically and taking advantage of business opportunities wherever it found them. Japan was behaving with the unconstrained ruthlessness of the "postideological" superpower.

As if on cue, some Japanese political and business leaders had started asking whether it was time for Japan to be more open about its growing strength. Shintaro Ishihara, a government minister, and Akio Morita, one of the founders of the Sony Corporation, published a widely noticed essay in the summer of 1989 called "The Japan That Can Say No." They argued that Japan had no need to assume a position of subservience to the United States, a tottering giant beset by problems of its own making. Japan's economic advantages meant it should no longer pretend to be without wider geopolitical ambitions. The moment had come for Japan to set its terms for participating in the new world order.

The rhetoric of US-Japanese rivalry became increasingly heated during 1989, just as US-Soviet rivalry was winding down. The United States and Japan had ostensibly been on the same side in the Cold War. They were both democracies. So why couldn't they both be winners? Part of the answer is that democracies need enemies, and they will fill that void whenever it appears: a democracy that wins an ideological struggle against its major rival creates a vacancy. Part of the answer was cultural (and indeed racial) antipathy, which the Cold War had suppressed but had not extinguished. Japanese "otherness" made its success threatening to the West, and Japanese "politeness" did nothing to allay those fears; it merely confirmed the impression that something inscrutable was taking place before the eyes of the world. Japan's global presence, Fallows suggested, had done nothing to puncture the inherent insularity of the Japanese character. The millions of Japanese who traveled overseas went about in "tightly organized and highly insulated groups," cut off from the benefits of outside influence.[19] They were everywhere but they were nowhere. At the same time, Fallows wanted to know, why weren't more of them traveling abroad? Ten million was still less that 10 percent of the total population, which compared unfavorably with other democracies, whose populations went overseas in far greater numbers (even 15 percent of the famously insular Americans were taking trips abroad by 1989). It sounded like the old Woody Allen joke. "The food is terrible here." "Yes, and such small portions."

There was another source of Western mistrust of Japan: the growing suspicion that Japan was not really a democracy. Although the country had seen frequent changes of personnel at the top, the same party (despite some alterations of name) had been in charge for almost the entire duration of Japan's postwar history. In forty years, the Liberals had never lost an election. If the test of a democracy is the peaceful hand-over of power when the voters decide it is time for a change, Japan had never passed that test. Instead, Japanese politics was cliquey, corporatist, and, to outside eyes, impenetrable. The key decisions were made by self-selecting elites, who could destabilize each other but appeared immune to democratic control. In the words of one commentator, Japanese politicians rose and fell "in the shifting sands of factional politics, not from any popular vote or mandate."[20] Prime ministers came and went, often brought down by scandal. But the same people remained in charge. Japan gave substance to the graffito complaint against democracy that had been popular during the 1970s: it doesn't matter who you vote for, the government always gets in.

The Japanese state had multiple, overlapping ties with big business, and the Japanese economy was closely regulated. Large players got government support and also government protection. This was what was coming to be known as "Asian capitalism." Not all the successful Asian capitalist states were democracies: South Korea was at this point only intermittently democratic; Singapore was a mild but unequivocal autocracy. In Japan the outward forms of democratic life—elections, the rule of law, a critical press—appeared to hide the true story. Democracy looked like a surface feature of Japanese life: formal, elaborate, and empty. Something more powerful and, from a Western perspective, more alien was going on underneath.

In the context of these sorts of suspicions, 1989 saw the publication of one truly prescient book that stood out against the prevailing mood. It was called *The Sun Also Sets*, written by a young British journalist (and future editor of the *Economist*) Bill Emmott. Japan was not so different from the West, Emmott contended. The Japanese were not hiding some secret formula for economic domination behind the formalities of democratic life. The impression that the country's elite lacked political vision was no smoke screen; it was the truth. They really didn't know what they were doing. Japan was surfing along a tide of prosperity with little idea of where it was heading. Its economic success, built on a remarkably high savings rate, was producing increasing amounts of speculation and recklessness; those savings had to find somewhere to go. The price of Japanese real estate, like the value of the stock market, was reaching unsustainable heights. At the same time, Japan's aging population was placing growing demands on the resources of the state. Japan needed to bolster domestic investment to provide for its future, but instead it was exporting capital: short-term opportunities trumped long-term needs. This was not evidence of a cunning master plan; it was evidence of the complete absence of one.

Emmott compared Japan's situation in the period from 1985 to 1989 with that of the United States in the period from 1925 to 1929, in the run-up to the Wall Street crash. Then, the Federal Reserve kept interest rates low in part to support the value of sterling; now, the Japanese central bank had been keeping interest rates low in part to support the value of the dollar. In both cases, the desire to prop up a convenient international economic order took priority over other concerns; in both cases, this preference for the devil you know was myopic. Such arrangements could not last forever, and when they broke down, it was best to be prepared. Japan was not prepared, any more than the United States had been. Emmott also compared Western fears about creeping Japanese domination in the 1980s to European (and particularly French) fears of creeping American domination in the 1960s. These fears had been overblown. First the Nixon shock, then the oil shock, dispelled them; it turned out the Americans were as vulnerable as everyone else. So too were the Japanese.

One of the ironies of the 1970s is that Japan had reacted to the shocks of that decade in the adaptable, self-sufficient way Nixon had hoped the Americans might. The end of Bretton Woods pushed Japan from being a low-tech, low-wage producer of mass consumer goods for the West (much like China today) to a high-tech, cutting-edge manufacturer of marquee products, from cars to computers. At the same time, the hike in oil prices prompted the oil-poor Japanese to explore alternative energy supplies and to commit to a program of nuclear-power stations. However, the success of these experiments had come at a cost. It produced a new inflexibility. Adaptable Japan, as it grew richer, had become cautious and set in its ways. The next shock might not turn out so well, because a country that was now prosperous and secure would be far more reluctant to admit the need to try something different.

Seen in this light, the steady state of Japanese politics was a handicap, not an advantage. "Japan is suffering from its political stability," Emmott wrote.[21] What the country needed was more of the regular upheavals of democratic life: the querulousness, the periodic revulsions against the status quo. Japan was a somewhat atypical democracy in its extreme attachment to deal making away from the prying gaze of the voters (though no democracy is immune to this). But Japan was also a typical democracy. It needed something to wake it up to its underlying strengths, yet the circumstances that might wake it up—a shock to the system—were also liable to expose its weaknesses. Emmott thought Japanese democracy was bound to face a crisis sooner rather than later. He did not think the crisis would destroy it; Japan had become too strong for that. But nor did he think the Japanese had any special qualities that would see them through. It would be touch and go for them, as it is for everyone.

Conventional wisdom said Japan would be the big winner from the end of the Cold War; conventional wisdom was wrong. Conventional wisdom also said the big loser would be India. The demise of the Soviet Union had finally exposed Indian ambitions to find a middle way between the rival systems of the two superpowers, drawing the advantages from each and dependent on neither. In international affairs the idea of nonalignment had long been on shaky ground, stretching back to the Sino-Indian war of 1962. Now, in economics, the Indian way had been undermined by the abject failure of the Soviet model, which robbed it of both financial support and intellectual inspiration. During the 1980s, India faithfully persisted with its five-year plans (the sixth began in 1980, the seventh in 1985), just as the rest of the world was coming to regard such planning as the ultimate symbol of Soviet-style sclerosis and inefficiency.

The Indian economy certainly did not look very dynamic in this period. Managed growth turned out to mean limited growth, averaging around 3.5 percent per annum from 1950 to 1980, increasing to around 5 percent per annum during the 1980s. This was far from a disaster; life expectancy in India rose dramatically over the same period (from thirty-three at independence to fifty-eight in 1989). But for a country with a rapidly expanding population and starting from a very low base (per capita income in 1950 was less than $500), it was a very modest performance. Some, derisively, termed it "the Hindu growth rate," implying that it had it roots in the fatalism of the East. This was glib. India was being left behind by other Asian economies, including not only Japan but also South Korea and Taiwan, which had been growing at twice that rate. Even communist China had grown faster than India.

South Korea had become a relatively rich country by the end of the 1980s. India was still very poor. South Korea also had its five-year plans. But the South Korean plans were not inspired by the Soviet Union. They were designed to promote rapid export growth and greater competitiveness, on the Japanese model. The Indian economy remained deeply uncompetitive by comparison. In trying to bridge the ideological divide of the Cold War, India had been dragged down by the losers.

In 1989 there was a widespread sense that India would have to change. But was it capable of change? The problem had nothing to do with Hindu fatalism. The problem was Indian democracy. It appeared stuck in a rut. This was nothing like the rut of Japanese democracy. India was caught in the trap of political populism. The state was paralyzed by its need to pander to the popular mood and to play off competing electoral factions. Although one party and indeed one family had governed India for most of its independent history—the prime minister in 1989 was Rajiv Gandhi, Indira's son and Nehru's grandson—the size and scale of Indian democracy had left it in the grip of multiple competing forces, from minor parties to local bosses to entrenched sectional interests. This had produced, in the title of one book published at this period, a "crisis of governability" for the Indian state.[22] It was unclear whether anyone was really in charge. In some respects, mid- to late twentieth-century Indian democracy resembled the early to mid-nineteenth-century American democracy that Tocqueville had encountered. All the action was happening at the surface, where there was wild exuberance, particularly around election time, and a fixation on short-term effects. But underneath, nothing much was moving. In Tocqueville's America political paralysis was at least able to coexist with economic dynamism. Indian democracy appeared to lack even that.

But Indian democracy did have one big success story to its name. By this time Amartya Sen's dictum that no famines happen in democracies had started to gain circulation. Sen's primary evidence was the contrasting experience of India and China since 1947. He had made the claim in an article in the *New York Review of Books* in 1982, where he also pointed out the deficiencies of India's performance over the same period, above all the failure to deal with rising inequality and widespread poverty.[23] Indians did not die in famines, but millions still died from malnutrition every year. Democracies like India's responded quickly to one-off threats of disaster, but too often they allowed the calamities of everyday life to pass under the radar. Was there any way to translate the responsiveness of a democratic state in worst-case scenarios into more routine benefits?

Sen contended there was. He sought to extend the negative advantages of famine avoidance into the positive gains of poverty reduction. If democracy empowered ordinary citizens to inform their rulers about impending disaster, increased empowerment should produce better information and greater responsiveness to a whole range of pressing needs. Basic democracy prevented famines; more democracy should prevent all sorts of other bad things from happening. This is the ongoing dream of democratic fulfillment: to harness the underlying benefits that only appear sporadically at times of crisis and turn them into solid, enduring gains. The problem, though, is that crisis politics does not map onto routine political decision making in a democracy. The threat of famine, once it becomes serious enough to demand attention, pushes other considerations to the margins: democratic politicians act when they have no choice. In everyday politics, other considerations will continue to jostle for attention, making coordinated action difficult. India's ability to avoid famines was consistent

with India's failure to make progress on other fronts; or-
dinarily, the wake-up calls get drowned out by the noise of
democracy in action.

That democratic India had been better than communist
China at preventing famine was pretty clear by 1989. There
was less agreement about how it had happened. Sen emphasized the importance of the free circulation of information, a crucial resource that autocracies lack. But potentially as important is the flexibility of democracies to take
help from wherever they can get it. Democratic leaders are
not proud when faced with calamity; they will compromise
their principles for practical help. Indian democracy, in an
emergency, sourced its grain, like its weapons, from across
the ideological divide, both inside and outside the country.
It was adaptable, which is something different from, and
something less than, being truly responsive. The optimal
way for India to get out of its rut was for it to become more
responsive to the needs of its citizens, as Sen wished. The
alternative was to let things carry on as they were, wait for
the next crisis to hit, and see what happened. That was less
inspiring. But it was more consistent with the way democracies tend to behave.

If Japan was perceived as the winner in 1989, and India as
the loser, the great unknown remained China. The Tiananmen Square student protests, which had been ruthlessly
brought to an end by armed force at the beginning of June,
could be interpreted to fit most narratives. The appetite for
democratic reform in China was evident. So too was the
capacity of the regime to suppress it. But which was stronger? Fukuyama was right about the tendency of excitable
commentators to overinterpret events. The *Economist*, in
an editorial pooh-poohing "The End of History" (which the

newspaper compared unfavorably to "1066 and All That"), contended that China proved Fukuyama wrong. The paper wrote: "Tiananmen Square showed that plenty of people in China still believe there is life in the old dog of communism yet."[24] This was an overstatement. All it showed was a frightened and brutal regime fighting for its life.

Yet if the massacre did not mark a resurgence of communism, neither did it signal the ultimate brittleness of the regime. Many were tempted to hope that it might. Hendrik Hertzberg, writing in the *New Republic*, argued that the violent repression of popular protests had exposed the ruling party's rhetoric of "the people's this and the people's that" as a lie. The people's army had been deployed to kill the people. "The words the party-state used to buttress its authority," Hertzberg wrote, "have become, thanks to its own actions, its mortal enemy. . . . That is why, even beyond the economic consequences of their brutality, China's shadowy rulers will ultimately proved to have destroyed themselves. Deng and company have committed the political equivalent of suicide."[25] As events subsequently unfolded in Eastern Europe, this became a common view. The Chinese leadership had merely put a temporary dam in the way of an unstoppable tide. Their turn to be swept away could not be long delayed.

What then was the model for China's future? Was it the Soviet Union, where freedom was on the march and the center could not hold? Was it Japan, where the outward appearance of democracy provided the cover for rapid economic expansion? Was it India, where democracy had bogged down the country in petty power struggles?

None of these models was right. China turned out to be China, and the rest of the world would have to watch and wait to discover what that meant.

THE AFTERMATH

The Japanese stock market hit its peak on December 29, 1989. Then the bubble burst. Within a year the Nikkei had halved in value. Japan's real estate bubble burst at the same time, leaving the country's banks sitting on mountains of bad debts. Such a sudden shake-up was unnerving, but few saw the need to panic. This was simply an inevitable correction at the end of a decade of unparalleled prosperity and a necessary stage on Japan's road to political and economic maturity. The American stock market had suffered an equally brutal reverse in 1987, when for a few days it fell further and faster even than it had in 1929, but unlike in 1929 it soon recovered. The panic turned out to be short-lived and the march of the insatiable consumer economy resumed. Japan was likely to prove equally resilient, aided by continuing American demand. The financier George Soros suspected that the Japanese authorities must have welcomed the crash, and might even had engineered it, as a short, sharp shock to aid in the rebalancing of the Japanese economy.[26]

It didn't turn out like that. 1990 was not a correction but the beginning of a slow, steady reversal of fortune. The bubble of Japan's coming domination of the twenty-first century had burst as well. The country was insufficiently adaptable to meet the challenge of changing course. The state propped up bad banks and networks of clients kept failing industries on life support. Timid Japanese consumers tightened their belts, and deflation took hold. The authorities responded calmly to each setback with measured, piecemeal attempts to spark the economy back into life. It was never quite enough. Japan remained a prosperous, comfortable place to live; life expectancy kept rising and unemployment was not allowed to get out of hand. Japanese voters even threw the Liberals out of office in 1993, only to see them return a year later. Things were never quite bad enough to spark a crisis of confidence in the system, and therefore never bad enough to force the politicians to attempt something dramatically different. Japan was stuck.

In India Rajiv Gandhi and the Congress Party were defeated in elections held at the end of 1989. This ushered in a new period of political instability, with four different prime ministers in two years, as coalitions fractured and rival factions jockeyed for position. Gandhi was assassinated while campaigning in the 1991 elections, which saw Congress returned to power. Meanwhile the Indian economy had reached a crisis point. By 1991 the country's budget and balance of payments deficits had reached alarming levels, and the government was running out of hard currency to repay its debts. A default threatened. The new prime minister, P. V. Narasimha Rao, and his finance minister, the academic economist Manmohan Singh, turned to the IMF for help.

Together they embarked on a series of economic reforms designed to make the Indian economy globally competitive. Subsidies, tariffs, and state-controlled monopolies were dismantled; a fixed exchange rate was abandoned; foreign investment was encouraged. The Indian public did not vote for these reforms; they merely watched them happen and acceded to the change, in that they did nothing to prevent it. The crisis, coming just after the election, gave the new government the scope it needed to act. The IMF provided the carrot and the stick. In 1991, without having planned it, and without having much control over the outcome, India's politicians decided to try something new. The crisis had produced a change of course. Indian democracy was embarked on a new path, even if the voters had been little more than bystanders as the change took place. The country was moving again.

The Chinese regime had not committed suicide in 1989. It had done what it thought necessary in order to survive. Autocrats cannot experiment with democracy in a crisis. The regime would almost certainly not have survived if the Tiananmen Square protests had been allowed to run their course. But autocrats can learn from each other's mistakes. In fact, autocracies may be better at this than democracies. Tocqueville had hoped that democracies might be able to draw educational benefit from each other's example, but this does not often happen. Democracies tend to do their own thing regardless. Autocracies, which are more adept at ruthless short-term decisions, can look and learn from the insufficient deployment of ruthlessness elsewhere. The Chinese communist party saw what was happening in the Soviet Union and Eastern Europe and chose not to go down that route. The door to greater democratic freedoms remained firmly shut. Instead, the door to greater market freedoms was flung wide open, while the party retained tight control of the decision-making process. The economic reforms that had begun under Deng Xiaoping in the 1980s were accelerated. Any popular appetite for political change was placated with rapid growth. This was not the promise of democracy being used as a cover for economic transformation. This was no democracy at all.

As Japan, India, and China all confounded the expectations for them that had been established in 1989, Germany cemented its place at the heart of the new world order by becoming a single state again. The country was reunified in 1990 as a constitutional democracy on the ordoliberal model: a powerful and politically independent central bank; devolved federal government; limits on political populism (including powerful barriers to entry for political extremists). This was, in many ways, the great democratic triumph of the late twentieth century. Germany, the country that had posed the biggest threat to the democratic peace of the world for much of that century, was now the shining beacon of democracy's ultimate durability. Many onlookers, watching from around Europe, could scarcely believe it. Adam Michnik, the Polish intellectual and political dissident, called it "a miracle."

Not everyone was satisfied. Plenty of German intellectuals believed it was all happening too fast and too unreflectively. The novelist Günter Grass argued for the two separate states to live on within one nation in order to allow the German people a meaningful choice between the free market and socialism.[27] What had once been a forced settlement could become an open experiment in ways of living. What could be more democratic than that? It was a pipe dream. Socialist East Germany was quickly folded into the capitalist West, a transaction paid for with Deutschmarks, which were exchanged for the now defunct East German currency at the remarkably generous rate of 1:1. As one commentator wrote: "Bonn Inc. has taken over bankrupt Prusso-Marx."[28]

East Germany's nascent democratic movements were also rapidly overtaken by the political imperatives of West German electoral politics. In 1989, democracy in East Germany had meant vast crowds on the street, impromptu political alliances with names like Democracy Awakening and

Democracy Now, mass protests, people power. By the time of the first unified German election of December 1990 little of this remained. The crowds had dispersed and the movements had fractured. Democracy meant slick advertising, stage-managed rallies, well-oiled party machines. Above all it meant money. East Germans were given the opportunity to vote for the DM and they took it.

Writing in the run-up to reunification, the towering German public intellectual Jürgen Habermas despaired of what he saw happening. He asked: "Will the DM now become the object of libido, emotionally re-valued so that a kind of economic nationalism will overwhelm republican consciousness?"[29] Habermas believed that a golden opportunity was being wasted to refound German democracy in a true republican spirit, based on a public embrace of democratic principles. He wanted a constitutional referendum to be held across the two Germanys to bind the inhabitants of the new state into their chosen destiny. An authentic democracy could not simply be allowed to stumble into the future, distracted by cheap promises and short-term gains. But that is what democracies do. Authenticity, like self-control, stays somewhere out of reach.

Disappointed by his homeland, Habermas turned his attention to the European Union as the political entity that offered the best prospect for a rebirth of the republican spirit. Here, in this new, experimental political space, the people of Europe might be given the chance to fashion something truly democratic. Again, Habermas was to be disappointed. Europe's politicians had more prosaic ambitions. The new Germany loomed as a threat. Her neighbors were determined not to repeat the mistakes of the past. A unified Germany had to be bound in to a wider European community that could constrain its ambitions and share its prosperity. France in particular made sure that enhanced European ties would be the price the Germans paid for becoming a single state again. The best way the French saw to retain control of their destiny was to annex it to Germany's.

The grand plan for the European project became the creation of a single currency for the member states of the European Union, which would replicate the strength of the DM but spread its benefits across the continent. Germany, having used its powerful currency to secure reunification, would now be required to give it up for the sake of the wider community to which the country belonged. It is easy to deride the idea of the Euro as a bureaucratic fantasy, foisted on the people of Europe by grandiose schemers lacking a popular mandate. But the people of Europe, for the most part, shared the dream. The Euro was a product of democratic wishfulness: a desire to have it both ways. It was born of recklessness and fear. The fear of German prosperity coincided with a dauntless desire to share in it. This was not a "posthistorical" piece of technical engineering. It was a rickety construction built on a faith that the tide of historical progress would keep it afloat. Europeans were doing more than simply curating the museum of political history, as Fukuyama had predicted. They were experimenting with an untested future.

In 1992 Fukuyama eventually published the book-length version of his 1989 article. He called it *The End of History and the Last Man*. It is a strange and unhappy book. When the original article first appeared in the *National Interest*, the magazine had commissioned a series of instant responses

from a range of thinkers, which it published alongside Fukuyama's piece. Fukuyama seems to have taken to heart the
one written by his former teacher, Allan Bloom. Bloom had
two complaints about the way Fukuyama presented his case.
First, Fukuyama had anchored his ideas to the thought of
the early nineteenth-century German idealist philosopher
Hegel ("It is doubtful whether he has even read Hegel,"
Dahrendorf noted dismissively). Bloom thought his ex-pupil
needed another German to complete his argument. The philosopher he wanted was Nietzsche, the true prophet of the
hollowness that lay at the heart of democratic life. Second,
Bloom suggested that Fukuyama had missed the likeliest
contemporary model for the "posthistorical" future. It was
not Western Europe that offered a glimpse of the emptiness
lying in wait at the end of history. It was Japan, the land of
tea ceremonies and technical proficiency. Japan was a prosperous, elegant, vapid society that exemplified the democratic spirit at the close of the twentieth century, the new
model of the good life where nothing meaningful ever happens. Its only rival was American consumerism, which was
equally empty but more restless. The contest of the future,
Bloom wrote, would be "the Americanization of Japan vs.
the Japanization of America. Nothing is at stake."[30]

Fukuyama followed Bloom to the letter. The End of History
repeats Bloom's line on Japan, almost word for word (both
men were echoing the arguments of the French philosopher
Alexandre Kojève, whose pupil Bloom had been). At the
same time, the book is awash with Nietzsche, from its sub-
title on ("the last man" was Nietzsche's term for the inhabitants of modern societies, lacking in all passion and vision:
comfortable, at peace, and spiritually dead). Fukuyama be-

moans the hollowness that looks set to accompany the end of history, and although he refuses to give in to nihilism, he sounds pretty gloomy about the cultural desert that lies before him. The German he unconsciously echoes is Thomas Mann, writing in 1918, when Mann too had been reading more Nietzsche than was good for him. At the moment of democracy's triumph, it is always tempting to give way to the mild satisfactions of intellectual despair.

The End of History is not all Nietzsche. The other thinker Fukuyama hitches to his argument is Tocqueville. However, he runs him together with Nietzsche: these are the men who foresaw that the triumph of democracy sounds a death knell for the creativity of the human spirit. Successful democracies get stuck in the rut of mediocrity. At his gloomier moments, Tocqueville believed this. But by turning Tocqueville into a forerunner of Nietzsche—just another aristocratic critic of democratic stupidity—Fukuyama makes a mistake. He jumbles up two fundamentally different views of democracy. Nietzsche thought democracy was a big lie, a blanket of empty ideas we use to console ourselves for our inadequacies. All it ever does is stifle. Tocqueville knew that with the mediocrity went exuberance and crazy ambition. Democracy has substance, but a substance no one can control. Nietzsche thought democracy was too good to be true. Tocqueville thought it was too true to be good. Nietzsche doesn't really explain what happened next. Tocqueville does.

CHAPTER 7

2008

Back to the Future

THE CRISIS

THE ECONOMIC CRISIS THAT BROKE WITH FULL FORCE following the collapse of Lehman Brothers in September 2008 threw up some memorable vignettes of political confusion and panic. President George Bush, faced with the disintegration of the entire banking system, announcing to a room of ashen-faced advisors: "This sucker could go down."[1] His secretary of the treasury, Hank Paulson, going down on one knee before Speaker of the House Nancy Pelosi to implore her not to scupper his desperately improvised rescue efforts ("Gee Hank," she responded, "I never knew you were a Catholic"). Republican presidential candidate John McCain suspending his campaign to come to Washington to help sort out the mess; arriving at a hastily arranged meeting with leaders from both main parties and simply sitting there in silence; the meeting breaking up in acrimony and disarray, with Democrats taunting McCain: "What's the plan? What's the plan?" There was no plan.[2]

The last few months of 2008 brought politicians, bankers, and business leaders face to face with the prospect of catastrophe. At times, they appeared to be fending it off day by day, even hour by hour. There were scenes at the epicenter of the crisis that came close to the exquisite terrors of late October 1962. As then, the threat of ultimate disaster, which had been bubbling up for some time, nonetheless seemed to come out of the blue. Almost everyone was taken by surprise by the scale of what they were facing. Dealing with the extraordinary danger fell on a small group of men (though, unlike in 1962, also a few women), meeting in cloistered (though no longer smoke-filled) rooms, holding the fate of the world in their hands.

Paulson, along with the chairman of the Federal Reserve, Ben Bernanke, and the head of the New York Federal Reserve, Timothy Geithner, wielded extraordinary power during the crisis and operated under intense, nerve-shredding pressure. A misstep threatened an escalation that might end in global calamity. There was even the looming possibility of mutually assured destruction, though this time America's partners in any dance of death were the Chinese not the Russians. By 2008 China's government had become by far the largest overseas holder of US treasuries and other government-backed securities. If the Chinese had decided to offload their dollar-denominated assets, whether in a panic or simply out of malice, the American government would have been powerless to contain the resulting havoc. The effects of the unraveling of the international economic order would have been devastating for the Chinese as well, which made any such threat appear senseless. But sense often seemed in short supply during the worst moments of crisis.

Yet what happened in September 2008 had nothing like the self-contained quality of the Cuban Missile Crisis. The world was not simply waiting on Washington to decide its fate. When Lehman Brothers collapsed governments everywhere made their own desperate efforts to deal with the chaos, as it spilled out and threatened them all with disaster. The ongoing crisis provided no single focus, no clear endpoint, no moment when it could be said that good sense had prevailed. The time was never quite right to exhale. Instead, the crisis dragged on, without either taking the global economy over the edge of the cliff or altogether pulling back from it. Part of the problem was that it was so hard to know where the brink of disaster lay.

The prospect of an international financial and economic collapse does not have the all-or-nothing quality of a nuclear war; it is less cataclysmic, but also more uncertain. It is difficult to picture the consequences because no one can be sure what they are. Mass unemployment, yes, along with widespread hardship. But shuttered banks? A return to barter? Civil breakdown? Armed gangs roaming the streets? The specter of another Great Depression was regularly conjured up in 2008. But in the fissile, complex, frighteningly interconnected world of the twenty-first century, even that could appear a quaint notion. The nameless terror was of something worse.

In this crisis no one could doubt that democracy was deeply implicated. Although many of the leading actors were unelected officials (Paulson, Bernanke, Geithner had no more of a popular mandate than their Chinese counterparts), they were heavily constrained by what public opinion would and would not stomach. No rescue was possible without the support of elected politicians, which was why Paulson had to bend the knee before Pelosi. The voters would have to be part of the solution. At the same time, it was clear that democracy was part of the problem. It was not simply that a fear of the wrath of the voters was making many elected politicians reluctant to adopt some of the drastic measures needed to stave off disaster. The crisis had its origins in the mistakes and misjudgments made by politicians and officials in the democratic West. This was a disaster the democracies had brought on themselves.

That is what made the crisis different. It was born out of the success of democracy, not out of some ongoing external threat to it. In the first decade of the twenty-first century democracy confronted no serious ideological rivals. Al-Qaeda was a threat but not a rival. China was a rival, but not an ideological threat. The idea that Chinese state capitalism offered a plausible alternative to Western democracy was a consequence of the 2008 crisis, not a presage to it. Some tried to blame China for the disaster, arguing that Chinese reliance on cheap exports had unbalanced the global economy and tempted Western consumers and governments to overleverage themselves in an effort to keep the fun going. But if this was temptation, very few tried to resist it. The democracies were entirely complicit in their own fate. A self-created crisis posed an obvious question: would the people who made the mess know how to fix it?

They had one resource they had not possessed in the past: the accumulated experience of previous crises. A reason to suppose this would not turn out to be a rerun of the 1930s was that the 1930s were there to serve as a warning. Ben Bernanke's academic specialty was the study of the Great Depression.[3] He famously announced in 2002 that there need never be another Depression because the Federal Reserve now knew how to avert one; they had learned their lesson. (The occasion was Milton Friedman's ninetieth birthday. "You're right, we did it," Bernanke told Friedman in a speech in his honor. "But thanks to you we won't do it again."[4]) Yet when the crisis hit, Bernanke's promise sounded like hubris. Knowledge of how to avoid past mistakes had not provided protection against disaster; it had produced complacency in the face of it. Knowing that we could get out of the mess had, if anything, encouraged us to get into it.

There was also the problem of knowing which past crisis was in fact the best model for the present one. In 2007, policy makers at the Federal Reserve, conscious of spiking oil prices, thought they might be reliving a version of the 1970s, when the gravest threat came from inflation. After the storm broke, Bernanke and his central banking colleagues did what they could to fend off a rerun of the 1930s. But so too had the Japanese authorities in the 1990s, with the unintended consequence of miring the Japanese economy in two decades of stagnation. Perhaps America was going to turn out to be Japan after all.

One way in which America was still America was in its faith in democratic renewal. Part of the reason the politics of the 2008 crisis were so fraught was that it coincided with a presidential election. This election raised memories of 1933, when a change in the White House had finally broken the logjam of the economic crisis. In 2008, unlike in 1933, the nature of the change was obvious to everyone. Roosevelt, to start with, was just another politician. Obama was always something more than that: the first African-American in the White House. No change could have been more visible or carried greater symbolic value. Yet in democracies, the changes one can see, the ones that are invested with the most hope, often turn out to be illusory. Democracies can renew themselves without really changing, just as they can sometimes change without anyone really noticing. Obama was not the agent of change in this crisis. In many ways, he came to embody the intractable nature of the crisis itself.

The aftereffects of the 2008 crisis are still being played out at the time of writing (early 2013). It was a moment of high drama, but also the beginning of an uncertain and open-ended period of transition. So much has changed since and yet so little has changed. To live through this time is to see how the two sides of democracy can interact: impatience and resignation. What we have not yet discovered is how to deal with the tension between them.

THE RECKONING

The period from 1989 to 2008 was marked by continuity and rupture. The continuity was in economic affairs. The rupture was in international affairs. Continuity is bad for democracies because it produces complacency and drift. Rupture is bad for democracies because it produces impulsiveness and aggression. The combination proved toxic.

This was the age of what came to be known as the Great Moderation, when the major economies (with the exception of Japan) enjoyed remarkably steady growth combined with low inflation and rising stock markets. Regular lurches from boom to bust appeared to be a thing of the past, at least in the West; the last significant recession before 2008 had been the one that brought Bill Clinton to the White House in 1992. Independent central bankers now had the tools to manage impending crises. Elected politicians understood the importance of letting them get on with it. Everything had been smoothed out, calmed down, regularized. The end of the Cold War appeared to have produced a magical elixir that finally stabilized mature capitalism. In 1999 the Euro was launched without mishap, and the continent continued to prosper. There were still violent upheavals around the edges of the new global prosperity, the most severe being the East Asian crisis of 1997. But the West rode out these disturbances relatively calmly. For those with money, the new financial order looked like a one-way bet.

Yet this was also the age of the Great Disruption: the attacks of September 11, 2001. The result was a sudden transformation in the climate of international politics. Almost overnight, a world that had appeared to be at peace found itself at war. The Western democracies, despite their growing economic security, suddenly felt vulnerable and exposed; they were being menaced by an enemy that might be everywhere or nowhere. They were also increasingly at loggerheads. American attitudes to the threat Al-Qaeda posed differed markedly from the popular mood across Western Europe, where there was almost no appetite for a military response. The disaster of 9/11 succeeded in frightening the leading democracies and in dividing them. In that respect, it had achieved some of the aims of its perpetrators.

The full-blown war on terror that began in 2001 with the American-led invasion of Afghanistan and continued with the invasion of Iraq in 2003 was a costly mistake. It was driven by fear, anger, and a desire for retribution. An enemy that was everywhere and nowhere had to be found a home so that there might be somewhere to attack, though in the case of Iraq it turned out that the enemy wasn't there (at least not until after the Americans moved in). The war provided an opportunity to showcase America's technological military might, though what it really demonstrated was that even the most sophisticated weaponry is still too blunt and indiscriminate to do its work without extensive collateral damage.

But the war was also driven by higher motives: a desire to spread the advantages of democracy to those parts of the world where it had not yet taken root. A number of the leading actors, including George Bush and British Prime Minister Tony Blair, believed that the defeat of the terrorist threat was inextricably bound up with the promotion of democracy. For Western democracy to feel safe it would have to spread its wings. "The best hope for peace in our world is the expansion of freedom in all the world," Bush said in his second inaugural address in 2004. "The concerted efforts of free nations to promote democracy is the prelude to our enemies' defeat."[5]

Bush's response to the threat to democracy after 9/11 had clear echoes of Wilson's response to the threat to democracy in 1917 (not least because in both cases it represented something of a volte-face: presidents who had wanted to keep their distance from the world's trouble spots turned into committed interventionists). Scholars argue about whether it makes sense to call Bush a Wilsonian, or even a neo-Wilsonian. The consensus is probably not: Wilson's vision of a secure democratic future was founded on the idea of collective international institutions bringing nations together; Bush disdained such organizations, including the United Nations.[6] Wilson wanted to make the world safe *for* democracy; Bush wanted to make the world safe *through* democracy, by expanding its reach. Central to Bush's vision was the idea that democracies promote peace through their own actions, not through some superimposed legal framework. And central to that view was the idea that no two democracies will ever go to war with each other (a.k.a. "democratic peace theory"). Hence, the more democracies, the fewer wars. By that reasoning, wars to spread democracy were an investment in future peace.

Democratic peace theory was not a new idea. The eighteenth-century German philosopher Immanuel Kant had laid down a version of it in his 1795 essay on "Perpetual Peace" (though Kant was careful to distinguish the irenic qualities of constitutional republics from the impulsive warmongering of some untamed democracies). Wilson himself had floated it in his speech announcing America's entry into the First World War, where he declared that if the states of Europe had been truly democratic the war would never have happened. But the idea gained a new lease on life in the 1980s when historically minded political scientists started to put it to the empirical test. The evidence of the twentieth century indicated that liberal democracies do not go to war with each other: it had never yet happened. This, like the idea that democracies do not suffer from famines, quickly became one of the great political scientific truisms of the age. Margaret Thatcher cited it ("Democracies don't go to war with one another," she said on a visit to Czechoslovakia in 1990). So did Bill Clinton ("Democracies don't attack each other," he said in his State of the Union Address in 1994). So did George Bush ("Democracies don't go to war with each other," he said in a press conference in 2004).

When Wilson had claimed that democracies do not fight each other he was not relying on the historical record; there were not enough democracies in existence back then to supply the evidence. His was a philosophical position based on a reasonable extrapolation from his own understanding of politics and international law (in that sense, he was following Kant). Bush, by contrast, did have the historical evidence. Where Wilson's belief in the peaceful propensity of democracies was essentially a declaration of faith, Bush's was an empirically based statement of fact. But that did not make Bush's position more considered or better grounded. Pushing the democratic peace through war required, if anything, an even greater a leap of faith. It assumed that the complexities of the present could be trumped by the sweeping lessons of the past. Democratic peace theory provided no evidence to support that assumption. Still, Bush believed he had the weight of history on his side and so could afford to take some risks.

Bush revealed himself to be an optimistic fatalist: the evidence he had been given of the advantages of democracy over other systems of government made him cavalier and reckless. This is what Mill had called "modified fatalism," which results from the knowledge we have that the world operates according to regular patterns of cause and effect. It was the fatalism that Tocqueville feared might result from democratic political science. Democratic peace theory turns out to be both true and dangerous. It is dangerous because it is true: it encourages crass and unreflective political action. History does not supply a magic recipe for engendering democratic peace. All it tells us is that it happens. It doesn't tell us what to do with that knowledge. Like Wilson, Bush wanted to harness the long-term, underlying strengths of democracy. Unlike Wilson, who knew some of the risks, Bush simply discounted the short-term perils of doing so.

Democracies may not fight each other but that doesn't mean they know how to promote peace. If anything, the attempt to apply democratic peace theory in practice runs afoul of familiar democratic weaknesses: impatience, jitteriness, inattention. This had been Lippmann's point back in 1947: democracy promotion around the world has deleterious effects on the democracy doing the promoting. Democratic politicians and their publics are bad judges of other countries' aptitude for democracy because they see the world through their own, limited experiences. They do not look and learn; they either look away or jump right in. Successful democracies are not curious; they are cloistered and myopic. The wars in Afghanistan and Iraq ran into trouble because of bad planning, insufficient local knowledge, and the political divisions they generated at home. This is what happens when democracies try to take advantage of their historical advantages. They mess up.

One person to recognize this was Fukuyama. In the late 1990s he had been a cheerleader for the Project for a New American Century, which was an aggressively upbeat take on the prospects for expanded American influence around the world (the project was, in some ways, an extravagant riposte to Paul Kennedy). By the time of the Iraq war, Fukuyama had reverted to his gloomier mindset of the early 1990s, though with a twist. American political life had not become placid and trivial, as he had feared. It had become reckless and hubristic, drawn to sweeping solutions and grandiose schemes. The success of democracy had generated a vision of its possibilities that was grossly simplistic and a hostage to fortune. State-building in a country like Iraq required a disaggregation of the complex array of competing factors on which success was likely to depend.[7] Bundling them all up in a general idea like "democracy promotion" was bound to be counterproductive at best, and potentially catastrophic. Fukuyama was now championing a fine-grained political science that prioritized contingency over destiny and detail over generality. But democratic public opinion doesn't really go in for fine-grained political science. That's for the political scientists. What the pundits noticed was that the man who had announced the end of history was now having doubts about what he had done.

Bush was reckless in another way. He believed America could afford the vast costs of the wars in Afghanistan and Iraq, which ended up exceeding those of the war in Vietnam. This belief was buoyed by a faith in the elixir of unstoppable economic growth that had been uncorked at the end of the Cold War. In *The Rise and Fall of the Great Powers* Paul Kennedy had pointed to annual US budget deficits of more than 5 percent of GDP during the mid-1980s as evidence that the country was on an unsustainable path. But then came victory in the Cold War, which made those concerns look like nitpicking. As Dick Cheney later remarked, "Reagan proved that deficits don't matter." During the 1990s the dividends of peace and prosperity meant that Bill Clinton, with some skillful political maneuvering, could balance the budget. In the following decade the Bush prescription of tax cuts plus costly wars tipped public expenditure back into the red. It was affordable so long as nothing else went wrong. And what else could go wrong?

What went wrong was a mixture of inadequate financial regulation, short-term political interference, and far too much wishful thinking. The Great Moderation turned out to be an extended boom and it led to an almighty bust. The boom was presided over by arrogant central bankers, meddlesome politicians, complacent economists, and greedy investors, none of whom wanted to call time on its benefits. The proximate causes of the crash of 2008 are still the subject of heated controversy; though there is little disagreement about the range of factors that contributed to the disaster there is no consensus about where the primary blame should lie. Is it with the investment banks that packaged and sold debt instruments they could neither control nor understand? Is it with the regulators, who let them do it? Is it with the politicians, who wanted to extend the advantages of home ownership to their poorer constituents, many of whom could not afford it? Is it with the central bankers, who failed to spot the warning signs of the impending crash? Or is it with the economists whose theories of efficient markets provided a justification for letting things take their course? Your answer will depend on your politics, and depending on your politics there is an answer to suit every taste.

In general terms, however, the crisis that unfolded in 2008 was a failure of democracy. That is, it was a failure by the leading democratic states to face up to what was wrong until it was too late. The excesses of the boom years manifested themselves differently in different places: in some, like the United States, Ireland, and Spain, the primary symptom was a real estate bubble; in Britain, it was a massively overleveraged banking sector; in others, like Italy and Greece, it was a bloated and inefficient public sector; in yet others, like Germany, it was an overreliance on the cheap export market the Euro created. But nowhere did the system correct itself in time; only when things had got out of hand was an attempt made to rectify the situation. By then, the damage was done.

This was a double failure. The democratic system that had emerged triumphant at the start of the twenty-first century was meant to have two safety valves. On the one hand, democratic public opinion was there to act as a corrective against the excesses of politicians and other public officials: when their rulers go too far, the voters can stop them. On the other hand, public officials, including independent central bankers, were there to guard against the excesses of the voters: when the public goes to far, the technocrats can stop them. It didn't work like that. What seems to have happened is that instead of guarding against each other, the two sides of democratic life—public opinion, expert opinion—cosseted each other. Each relied on the other to signal when things had got out of hand.

The morality tale that had emerged since the 1980s said that democracies would be stable if they franchised-out key decisions to unelected officials. These officials would then use their freedom from the day-to-day pressures of democratic political life to scrutinize and correct for the failings of democracy. But in fact, officials are just as likely to use their freedom from the day-to-day pressures of politics to indulge their own prejudices. The key official during the period of the long boom was Alan Greenspan, the chairman of the US Federal Reserve from 1987 to 2006. The formative experiences of Greenspan's tenure happened early on: first, the short-lived stock market crash of 1987, which came when he was six weeks into the job, and showed that even the biggest shocks could be overcome with a steady nerve and sound technical judgment; second, the fall of the Berlin Wall in 1989, which showed that free societies always triumph over planned economies in the long run.[8] The system had revealed itself as sound, so long as it had a man like Greenspan at the helm. This was a fatal conceit. Past successes blinded Greenspan to the possibility of failure.

Bernanke, his successor, was less convinced of his own rectitude but no less committed to the idea that technical adjustments could stave off a full-blown crisis. He too believed the system was sound and that the warning signs would be heard. He too was wrong. When the warnings came in 2007 he and his colleagues missed them, because technocrats delegated with the task of steering a steady course learn to discount prophecies of doom. In a democracy, there will always be some people predicting disaster. That is one of the democratic excesses that unelected officials are there to guard against. Democracies produce a surfeit of noise. But unelected officials, cut off from daily alarums of electoral politics, are not thereby sensitized to the sound of impending danger. They grow, if anything, increasingly deaf to it.

The relatively good times for Western democracy that lasted for nearly twenty years after the end of the Cold War seemed to indicate that a successful balance had been struck between the insistent demands of the public and the moderating influence of the experts. Each had learned to live with the other. The divisive effects of the war on terror came as a disruption rather than a derailment. But this was not a settled state of affairs. The balance had not been responsible for the good times. The good times had been responsible for the balance. When things unraveled in 2008, Western democracy reverted to type. A settled arrangement gave way to improvisation and experimentation. Mutual understanding morphed into mutual recrimination. It turned out that the age of prosperity was not what it seemed and that its benefits had been very unequally distributed. The losers far outnumbered the winners. People started looking for someone who could provide them with a fresh start.

THE REDEEMER

In a crisis, elections can be a godsend or a curse. They are a godsend if they provide a chance to ditch the people responsible for the mess. They are a curse if they make it impossible for anyone to take the tough decisions needed to get out of the mess for fear of being turfed out by the voters. The 2008 elections in the United States were both a godsend and a curse.

When the crisis erupted in September, George Bush had fewer than five months of his presidency still to run. He was by this point one of the most unpopular presidents in US history. His approval ratings the week before Lehman's went under were hovering just above 30 percent; two weeks later they were nearing 25 percent, a level only matched by just two other presidents in the age of modern polling, Truman in 1952 and Nixon in 1974. Bush's unpopularity meant he had no mandate for radical political action. But it also meant he had very little to lose. It is only in democracies that you get lame duck leaders, since autocrats must retain control until the moment they lose control. Yet lame duck presidents can sometimes display the attribute that autocrats possess: unaccountable executive power.

When the crisis hit, Bush betrayed many of his political principles, and infuriated many in his party, by endorsing the bailout of failed institutions, including Fannie Mae, Freddie Mac, and the giant insurance group AIG. As Paulson scrabbled to improvise solutions to problems that no one had anticipated even a few weeks earlier, Bush effectively gave him a blank political check to "do whatever it took." Paulson's main difficulties were with members of Congress who stuck to their ideological guns in the hope of currying favor with their electorates. His great fear was that one or other of the presidential candidates might be tempted do the same. In the seven weeks between the failure of Lehman's and voting day either presidential candidate could have pandered to the popular dislike of bailouts, making a politically treacherous rescue act a whole lot more dangerous. But McCain, who flirted with populist anger, never succumbed to it. And Obama didn't need to.

For Obama, the crisis was a blessing. It crystallized the failings of the Bush years in the public mind and cemented the idea that it was time for a change. Obama's message of hope and renewal suited a moment when the status quo had revealed itself to be unsustainable. What's more, Obama's candidacy was the literal embodiment of change: here was a man unlike any other to stand for the highest office. A black president had long seemed unthinkable in a democracy like the United States. Suddenly it became almost inevitable. A country that could make such a shift had reason to have faith in its powers of regeneration.

The timing of the 2008 election was just right for Obama. But that was what made it wrong. The symmetry was too neat. He could surf along with the appetite for something new without addressing the intractable difficulties any democracy has in making a fundamental change of course. He did not have to confront American democracy with the challenge of facing up to its self-created predicament, nor point the finger anywhere than at the discredited outgoing administration. He did not have to flesh out the rhetoric of hope with a concrete plan for effecting change. He symbolized change, which meant he did not need to specify it.

Democracies feed off hope. That is why they are poor judges of those peddling it. The people who look like they represent a fresh start, because they offer something obviously new, often turn out to mean more of the same. The two American presidents in the twentieth century who arrived in office with the best credentials to symbolize a fresh approach to politics were Herbert Hoover and Jimmy Carter, the western engineer and the southern farmer; both were, in their different ways, breakers of the mold. They were undone by bad luck, by inflated expectations, and by the very outsider qualities that had made them so attractive: they had an insufficient idea of how to change the system from the inside. The leaders who come to be known as the saviors of democracy rarely arrive in office marked out as something

new. Often they come with low expectations and a check-
ered past. To start with, Lincoln was just another political
lawyer. Reagan was just another political actor (the fact he
had also been a real actor didn't make him fresh; it made
him the embodiment of the superficiality of democratic politics). Roosevelt was just another political operator.

Obama went out of his way during his campaign to compare himself to Lincoln, Reagan, and Roosevelt. These were
false comparisons. He was equating the expectation of his
presidency with the reputation of theirs, when in fact their
ultimate reputations had confounded many early expectations. Lincoln didn't start out as Lincoln. So if Obama was
going to start out as Lincoln, then he was going to end up as
someone else.

The most enticing comparison was with Roosevelt, another president who inherited an economic crisis that had
exposed the incompetence and drift of the previous regime.
Like Roosevelt, Obama had an opportunity to experiment
with something new, in the knowledge that the public had
tired of the old. But there were big differences in the situations the two men found themselves in. Roosevelt inherited a crisis that had dragged on for four years and had seen
off a series of attempts to manage it. Obama was inheriting a crisis that had barely got going, yet that had already
prompted a series of rapid improvisations to guard against
economic collapse. In some ways, Obama was stymied by
the accumulated experience of past crises. The technocrats
had already used their knowledge of the mistakes that led
to the Great Depression to part-stabilize the situation by
the time Obama took office. Cheap money was being made
available; vulnerable institutions were being maintained on

life support. The worst-case scenarios had been fended off for now, which gave Obama less room for maneuver. He was not taking charge of a sinking ship, but of one that was just about being kept afloat.

The crisis of 2008 was bad enough to bring Obama to office but never so bad as to give him a free hand once he got there. The three months between the election and the inauguration did not have the same effect as the five desperate months between Roosevelt's election in 1932 and his inauguration in 1933. Then the dying days of the Hoover administration had provided Roosevelt with the perfect backdrop for a radical new beginning. Obama, by contrast, was tempted by continuity. In November 2008 he announced his intention to nominate Geithner as his secretary of the treasury to replace Paulson, the man with whom Geithner had been working hand in glove during the interregnum. The appeal of continuity is partly a matter of temperament and experience. Obama was an intellectual and an inexperienced politician. He wanted to avoid unnecessary risks. Roosevelt was not an intellectual. But he was an experienced politician who liked to take his chances.

Obama faced a similar difficulty when confronted with the legacy of the war on terror. He was inheriting an intractable mess but not an outright disaster. The conflict had confirmed a number of Tocqueville's edicts about democracies at war. Democracies often choose the wrong wars to fight; they misjudge the stakes and bungle their objectives. Yet when democracies find themselves bogged down in drawn-out struggles they don't know how to win, they have the advantages of their adaptability. They keep looking for something new, experimenting with different military leaders, different tactics, different objectives. They are flexible. In any drawn-out struggle, the two sides of democratic life will be in tension: on the one hand, a restless impatience with failure on the part of those doing the fighting; on the other, a growing disenchantment and detachment on the part of the wider public. Both were on display in the Iraq and Afghan wars. In Iraq, the Bush administration staved off collapse in 2007 with new military leadership, new tactics, and new resources ("the surge"). In Afghanistan, the NATO operation kept meeting reverses and kept trying to learn from them. Victory remained elusive but defeat was being deferred. Meanwhile, public commitment to both wars continued to wane.

The war on terror was a mistake, but it was not a straightforward mistake. In 2008 Obama campaigned on a promise to end the conflict in Iraq ("the bad war") and to concentrate resources on the conflict in Afghanistan ("the good war"). Nonetheless, in both cases, he faced the temptations of continuity. Experimentation and adaptation had taken root, which made it hard to draw a clean line under what had gone before. Outright disasters produce new beginnings. Successful firefighting tempts you to keep putting out fires.

Obama faced another difficulty that made his predicament different from Roosevelt's. Obama had portrayed himself during his campaign as a postpartisan politician who offered the chance of a new era of civility and cooperation in American politics. Yet he faced a Republican opposition that was deeply partisan, resistant to compromise, and firmly opposed to his agenda. Roosevelt was in many ways a more overtly partisan politician, yet plenty of the radical measures he undertook in office were able to capture cross-party support. The crisis of 1933 helped to muffle some of the partisanship of American politics. The crisis of 2008 helped to entrench it. Why?

Part of the answer is the different nature of the crises. The situation in 1933 had become more desperate than in 2008, the international tensions were far more acute, and the fate of democracy more precarious. Part of the answer is changes in the conduct and technology of politics. Twenty-first-century legislators are exposed to ever blunter and more strident expressions of public opinion, fashioned by the new information technology and fueled by speed of the news cycle; it can be hard to find the room for compromise when the noise is so unrelenting. But part of the answer is the cumulative experience of the intervening seventy-five years. American democracy had survived its near-death experience in 1933. It had survived everything that had been thrown at it since. It had proved its adaptability and its resilience. There is less incentive for politicians to compromise if they believe the system can withstand most forms of confrontation. Just as knowing how to avoid a Depression helped bring the country to the brink of one, so knowing the system was resilient encouraged intransigence in its politicians.

The irony is that this intransigence manifested itself as a claim that the system could not survive what Obama was proposing. Republican opposition to the Obama program coalesced around the question of debt. The country was said to be on an unsustainable path, having already racked up too many future obligations to be able to afford large outlays of public money to stimulate the economy. Republicans accused Obama of short-term pandering in the place of long-term prudence—the classic democratic vice. Yet the politicians who made this argument were guilty of most of the democratic vices themselves: grandstanding, brinkmanship, disinformation, and chicanery. It is easy to deride politicians who claim they are thinking of the long-term future of their country while presenting their case in a way that indicates they are thinking of their own short-term electoral prospects.

You can put this mismatch down to hypocrisy, mendacity, or stupidity. You can bemoan it is as a betrayal of democracy. Yet it is in fact a quintessential feature of democracy. Everyone does it. Democrats do it too. They take the long view and tailor it to suit their short-term objectives. They do it because they know they can get away with it.

This is the confidence trap. Democracies are adaptable. Because they are adaptable, they build up long-term problems, comforted by the knowledge that they will adapt to meet them. Debt accumulates; retrenchment is deferred. Democracies are also competitive, which means that politicians will blame each other for their failure to tackle the long-term problems. However, they do it in a way that gives the lie to the urgency, because if it were truly urgent, then they would compromise to fix it. Instead they squabble. They are comforted as they squabble by their knowledge that the system is resilient.

So democracy becomes a game of chicken. When things get really bad, we will adapt. Until they get really bad, we need not adapt, because democracies are ultimately adaptable. Both sides play this game. Games of chicken are harmless, until they go wrong, at which point they become lethal.

The Aftermath

President Obama took the oath of office on January 20, 2009. The new president's inaugural address was eloquent, civil, and unmemorable. He began by praising his predecessor and thanking him for his help during the transition (Roosevelt had nothing to say in his inaugural about his predecessor, whom he seemed to regard as the embodiment of fear itself). Obama's first day in office was in keeping with what was to follow. His administration, guided by many of the officials who had presided over the Great Moderation and its unraveling, proceeded to steer a steady course through the ongoing crisis, eschewing radical measures, relying on the tried and tested where possible, and trying to retain a sense of balance. Wall Street was helped through its troubles and so too was the auto industry. Homeowners were given some relief with their mortgages, but only in small doses. A stimulus package of $800 billion was passed. This was a compromise figure that was too high for conservatives and too low for liberals, which left Obama hoping he had got it about right. The budget deficit remained large but never got out of hand. Unemployment kept going up, then it flatlined, then it began a very slow decline. The overall federal debt continued to rise. It was a mixed bag. Nothing too good, nothing too bad, nothing broken beyond repair, nothing fixed beyond some future reckoning.

The piecemeal nature of the response, hemmed in by electoral considerations, limited by short-term time horizons, guided by a pragmatic urge to grasp fleeting opportunities, was in keeping with the fidgety, humdrum quality of modern democracy. But democracies do not like to see themselves reflected in that mirror; they want something more. As Obama tried to manage the crisis he appeared to be simply surfing along with it. The call went out, as it so often does at times of crisis, for "real" democracy, something that might signal a genuine rebirth. Movements sprung up in America, on the right and on the left, that sought the authentic version that had been buried beneath the unsatisfactory outer shell of democratic life. For the Tea Party, authenticity lay with the origins of American democracy at its founding, and in the promise of popular independence from remote central government. For "Occupy Wall Street," authenticity lay in reassertion of popular control over the institutions of wealth and power that had made American society increasingly unequal over the previous generation. The slogan of Occupy Wall Street—"We are the 99%"—implied that American democracy had become a kind of confidence trick, through which the few had enriched themselves at the expense of the many by means of underhanded practices. After all, if the 99 percent had been aware of what was happening, they could hardly have allowed it. In democracies, 1 percent of the population cannot get their way unless everyone else is being duped. Now, with the crisis, was a chance for the truth to out.

For all their differences, these populist movements had one thing in common: they needed the crisis to get a lot worse for their message to stick. Yet if the crisis got a lot worse, more democratic improvisation would be required, trumping the claims of "real" democracy. The populists were caught in a bind. The idea of the "99%" was both a brilliant slogan and a vapid concept; in democracies, there are never coalitions of the 99 percent; majorities fracture long before they reach such a figure. The 99 percent have far too little in common, except in moments of extremis, at which point emergency action takes over from the long-delayed promise of popular politics.[9] For the Tea Party, Obama's health care legislation, which was passed in highly acrimonious circumstances in 2010, offered the possibility of another focal point for public mistrust of central government. But the inadvertent qualities of democratic politics prevailed: the US Supreme Court eventually endorsed the legislation, with its conservative chief justice crossing partisan lines to rule in its favor. Chief Justice Roberts's motives remain obscure; he may have wanted to provide himself with cover for even more partisan judgments on even more contentious issues he planned to deliver down the line.[10] But the fact remains that in the complex moral and political economy of a long-standing democracy, the search for an authentic popular politics is always liable to run up against the capacity of the system to accommodate piecemeal change.

While the Obama administration was feeling its way, the crisis continued to evolve and spread around the world. Its impact was neither consistent nor uniform: some democracies fared much better than others. In previous global economic crises elected governments everywhere found it very hard to hold on to office. In both the early 1930s and the mid-1970s almost none managed it. This crisis was different. The countries that were shielded from the worst effects of the global recession did not turn on their governments.

By 2012, four years after the crisis broke, many elected leaders who had been in office from the beginning were still around: Manmohan Singh in India, Angela Merkel in

Germany, Fredrik Reinfeldt in Sweden, Stephen Harper in Canada, and Recep Erdoğan in Turkey had all retained power for the duration, in contrast to the four years following the Wall Street Crash of 1929, when every democratic state in the world changed its government at least once, and many gave up on democracy altogether. Of the members of the G20, ten still had the same governments at the end of 2012 that they had at the start of 2008, and of these only two were straightforwardly undemocratic (China and Saudi Arabia). In this crisis, democracy did not necessarily represent instability and autocracy continuity. By 2012 China's political leadership, rocked for the first time by a major scandal involving a party chief, his wife, his police chief, and a murdered British businessman (the "Bo Xilai affair"), and facing the possibility of a delayed economic downturn, looked less stable than some of its democratic counterparts.

The exception to this picture of relative stability was in Europe, outside of Germany and Scandinavia. Once the crisis had spread to infect the Eurozone in 2010, governments across the continent were exposed to the wrath of the voters. Incumbents were defeated in Britain, France, Portugal, Spain, Ireland, Italy, Greece, the Netherlands, Denmark, Belgium, Hungary, and Slovakia. In two of these countries, Italy and Greece, democracy was briefly suspended for a form of technocratic executive rule: appointed experts were given temporary powers to stabilize the economy and pass budget reforms. These experiments with autocracy did not signal the abandonment of democracy; instead, they signaled the propensity of established democracies to try anything in a crisis. The problem, though, was that the respective fates of

Italy and Greece were by this point no longer in the hands of their own governments. The Euro had bound them in to an arrangement that left them waiting to be rescued by the country it had been designed to protect them from: Germany. And German democracy, still relatively prosperous, still relatively secure, was in no mood to experiment with radical solutions. German democracy remained set in its ways, which meant European democracy was at its mercy.

The Euro had been intended to provide a framework of financial stability for the continent as a whole, marking a definitive break with Europe's long history of conflict and misadventure. However, the promise of stability produced inattention and complacency. Countries that had been used to hard choices took advantage of the new arrangements to take the easy option. Some borrowed, some spent, some consumed, some saved, but each followed the path of least resistance within the contours of the new system. This was not a morality tale. Europe's southern democracies did not indulge in greed or sloth at the expense of the Germans any more than the Germans indulged in greed or duplicity at the expense of their southern neighbors. It was simply a tale of drift. The Euro, designed to prevent wild fluctuations of fortune, created the conditions in which difficult questions could be shirked. If democracies can shirk difficult questions, they will. But eventually they have to be faced.

The crisis exposed the unresolved tension at the heart of the Euro, between the collective fate of a union of democracies and their continuing ability to determine their own fate. Usually, this is expressed as the tension between monetary union and fiscal disunion; countries that shared a common currency nonetheless retained the freedom to decide for themselves how much they could tax and spend (rules intended to set some constraints to that freedom—in the form of budget deficit limits—having been routinely ignored). The result was a set of imbalances. Germany saves and exports; southern Europe spends and imports; France stands somewhere in between. There is now no avoiding some very hard choices: either European states like Greece and Spain, which can no longer export their way out of recession because of the currency they share with the Germans, face the prospect of years of grinding austerity; the alternative, which is for Germany to allow the collectivization of European debt, means large transfers of resources from north to south. The Euro, which was meant to cement European solidarity, has instead exposed its limits.

But there is another tension at work between different ideas of the urgency of the crisis itself. Does it require an all-or-nothing solution or a wait-and-see approach? Before one of the interminable series of make-or-break summits that have marked the Euro crisis since 2010—this one in Brussels in December 2011—the two leading political actors in the drama expressed opposed views on this question. Nicolas Sarkozy, then president of France, announced "that Europe has never been in so much danger." Action had to be taken now; get it wrong and "there will be no second chance." Angela Merkel wanted people to know that it was important not to be rushed. "The European crisis will not be solved in one fell swoop," she declared. "It is a process and this process will take years."[11]

Here are the two sides of the democratic mindset: it is too soon to act and it is never too soon to act. This is another version of the confidence trap. The knowledge that democracies can adapt encourages delay; delay encourages drift; fear of drift encourages precipitate action; precipitate action encourages mistakes; mistakes encourage caution. So it goes on. There is always reason to try the piecemeal approach and there is always reason to reject it. We muddle on because we know that muddling on has been sufficient in the past; we also know that muddling on increases the risk that we will lose control of events.

This predicament remains unresolved. And so, for now, does the Euro crisis.

EPILOGUE

The Confidence Trap

THE LONG AND THE SHORT

THE HISTORY OF DEMOCRACY AND CRISIS OVER THE last hundred years shows repeated patterns of behavior: misapprehension, confusion, brinkmanship, experimentation, recovery. Democracies are not good at spotting crises before they occur. They ignore the warning signs of impending trouble. At the same time, they overreact to the routine hiccups of political life, which adds to the air of distraction. Scandals grip democracies while systemic failings get overlooked. Democracies lack a sense of perspective. This produces repeated crises as mistakes mount up. But it also enables democracies to escape from crises, because no single mistake is ever conclusive. Democracies continue to adjust, adapt, and find a way through. This process is not pretty, and it creates a pervasive feeling of disappointment. In crises there is always the hope that something more fundamental will be revealed. The search goes out for real democracy, the true story concealed behind the mess of democratic life. This quest is invariably fruitless. The confusion that produces the crisis is the same confusion that dissolves it over time. Alongside the disappointment and frustration comes a lingering complacency. Democracies survive their mistakes. So the mistakes keep coming.

The current crisis fits this pattern. It was not anticipated. It was caused by a mixture of complacency and skittishness. It has generated a series of improvised solutions that have prevented the worst from happening. At the same time, frustration with all this improvisation has continued to mount. We want something more: a resolution that is in keeping with the scale of the problem and with the scale of the greed and ineptitude that brought it about. The hope persists that we might achieve a fundamental rescue of democracy, one that finally breaks the cycle of crisis and recovery. But that hope has to compete with a corresponding fear that piecemeal solutions are merely papering over the cracks. At some point the repeated failings of democracy will catch up with it. As we muddle our way through this crisis, from summit to summit and election to election, it is tempting to think the real story about democracy is being concealed. The reckoning is still to come.

If the pattern repeats itself, these hopes and fears will remain unrealized. Muddling through is the true story; the reckoning never arrives. When they have no choice, democracies adapt, often reluctantly and almost always inadvertently. In the adjustment there are winners and losers, though these rarely correspond with the heroes and villains of the drama. It is one of the unavoidable frustrations of modern democracy that we don't get to dole out punishment commensurate with the scale of the crisis. Defeated dictators can be torn apart by the mob; defeated democratic politicians retire in comfort to compose their self-justifying memoirs. Elections reinforce the inconclusive quality of democratic life; they bring change, but they do not bring closure. Because we prevent our leaders from doing their worst, we never get to decide which ones deserve the ultimate sanction. Max Weber remarked in 1919 that his idea of democracy was a system in which elected leaders are given absolute powers, on the understanding that if they fail the people can send them to the gallows. That is not how modern democracy works. In democracies, there is no final settling of accounts. There is just an endless putting off of the evil day.

But how can we be sure the pattern will keep repeating itself? We can't. We should not assume that democracies will always be able improvise a solution to whatever challenges they face. There is nothing about democracy that guarantees this will happen; it is simply more likely to happen under democracy than any other system of government. The assumption that it is bound to happen increases the likelihood it will stop happening. It breeds the sort of complacency that allows dangerous crises to build up, invites decisive action to be deferred, and encourages brinkmanship. This is tempting fate. Crises do not come in neat packages waiting for democracies to work out how to solve them. Their dimensions vary, their causes vary, and their consequences vary. Some are more dangerous than others. The crises I have described in this book all contained moments of real peril, even if the perils were ultimately overcome. The next crisis might take a form that makes it much harder to overcome. And if we do overcome the next crisis, there is always the one after that. Because on this pattern there is no final crisis, it is hard to see how the sequence can continue indefinitely. No end to crisis means a never-ending risk of encountering the crisis that is too great to solve.

As well as being cyclical, the history of democracy and crisis in the modern age is cumulative. The experience of crisis builds up over time: no crisis is quite like the one before, because the one before is always there to serve as a warning and a temptation. The repeated sequence of democratic crises over the past hundred years also describes a single, overarching narrative. It is, as I said in the preface to this book, an obvious success story. The democracies of the West emerged from the twentieth century as the richest and most powerful states the world has ever seen, having overcome the many challenges they encountered on the way. They defeated their enemies and enabled their citizens to prosper. But success on that scale comes at a price. It has helped blind the democracies to the enduring threats they face. On this version of events, the iterated pattern of democratic crisis—the endless quickstep from failure to success, from success to failure—is a distraction from the underlying story. The cumulative success of democracy has created the conditions for systemic failure. The time may be past for muddling through. Democracies must either confront their endemic indebtedness, their growing inequality, and their environmental irresponsibility, or they will find themselves beyond rescue.

Here are two ways of thinking about the current state of democracy: On one view the present crisis is not so different from previous crises, which means we will eventually stumble across a solution. The alternative view is that the present crisis is the cumulative result of previous crises, in which case we will need to make a more fundamental adjustment. Which is right? Is this crisis a temporary glitch or a permanent watershed? One reason to think it might be a watershed is that it signals the unraveling of an extended political/economic experiment. In this book I have concentrated on relatively short cycles of crisis and its aftermath: one every ten to fifteen years, or half a generation (which was Kennan's original estimate for the likely span of the Cold War). But there are also transgenerational shifts. The forty-plus years of the Cold War was one. Another is the near-forty-year arc from the birth of the post–Bretton Woods order in the 1970s to its apparent demise in the current crisis.

This was the age of "neoliberalism": open markets, deregulation of finance, rapid currency flows, regressive taxation.[1] Many people have come to see it as a prolonged conspiracy against democracy: unfettered global capitalism enriched the few at the expense of the many. Now we have a once-in-a-generation opportunity to rebuild democracy from the ground up, to make it more equal, more livable, more stable. However, neoliberalism still has its champions, who draw a very different moral from its failure. The real story of the last forty years has been the inability of advanced democratic societies to tackle their propensity to overspend. The damage of the previous forty years of Keynesianism has never been undone. The current crisis is a crisis of democratic indebtedness, not of oligarchic greed. It provides a once-in-a-lifetime opportunity to retrench.

This argument has been played out in many different forms: it's Nancy Pelosi vs. Paul Ryan, Paul Krugman vs. Niall Ferguson, Ed Balls vs. George Osborne, François Hollande vs. Angela Merkel.[2] It is a version of the argument that has always accompanied democracy. The doubters think democracy is in danger of becoming a confidence trick. Its champions think it has been the victim of a confidence trick. Both are looking to the crisis as a moment of truth. But one big difference between the twenty-first-century version of this argument and earlier incarnations is that where both sides would once have hesitated to call themselves democrats (for most of the nineteenth century even the supporters of democracy were careful to distance themselves from the classical form of politics known as "democracy"), now both sides call themselves democrats, even the doubters. Notwithstanding the current crisis, few people in the West are giving up on democracy just yet. The ideological alternatives remain deeply unappealing. There is a pervasive fear that China is gaining the upper hand. Countless books forecast coming Chinese dominance. But the fellow travelers of Chinese state capitalism in the West are very thin on the ground. We worry about the Chinese threat; we don't want to emulate it. When western states experiment with technocracy, it is in the cause of preserving their democracies, not abandoning them. For most of us, democracy is still the only game in town.

This is the other overarching story of the last hundred years: our growing knowledge of the lasting appeal of democracy. At the start of the twentieth century democracy was a largely untried and untested form of politics. It aroused wild hopes and equally wild fears. No one really knew what it might bring. Each crisis was expected to be the last. But over time and through a succession of crises, democracy has spread, strengthened, and endured. Now, in many parts of the world, it looks entrenched. During that time, and particularly during the past few decades, we have learned a lot about how this process works. There does appear to be a confidence threshold for any successful democracy. Once the threshold is passed, it becomes very unlikely that the move to democracy will be reversed.

This threshold is confirmed by the empirical data. No democracy has reverted to autocratic government once per capita GDP has risen above $7,000.[3] When it reaches a certain level of prosperity, democracy reinforces itself; with the arrival of material comforts the high risk, high stakes game of authoritarian politics loses its appeal.[4] There also seems to be a demographic threshold for stable democracy. Countries where the median age is in the twenties or below are much less likely to wait out a democratic crisis than countries where it is in the thirties or above.[5] Young people, especially young men, are impatient and reckless: they want immediate results. Older people are more willing to give things time; they learn to live with the tentative, experimental quality of democratic politics.

There are still many parts of the world that fall well below both these thresholds, including in Africa and much of the Middle East. (For comparison, per capita GDP [PPP] in Egypt is currently around $6,500, and the median age is twenty-five; the figures for Iraq are $4,000 and twenty-one; for the Democratic Republic of the Congo, one of the least stable states in the world, they are $400 and eighteen.) In many of these places democracy looks fragile, and in some it looks practically impossible. But where it is established, it looks secure.

The existence of these thresholds is hard to square with the apparent uncertainty generated by repeated democratic crises in the West. Where is the risk for democracy if it is so secure? One way to keep the doubts about democracy alive is to raise the threshold for what counts as proof of durability. In 1951 the economist Kenneth Arrow argued that democratic decision making would have to be heavily constrained if it was not to be entirely arbitrary; on his account there could be no such thing as a stable democracy. This work earned him a Nobel Prize. In 2008 the octogenarian Arrow was asked in an interview how he reconciled his views about the "impossibility" of democracy with its enduring strength over the course of his professional lifetime. Didn't the success of democracy show he had been wrong? No, Arrow replied. It simply showed that it was too soon to pass final judgment. The instability was just getting going.[6]

It is always possible to adjust the time frame to suit the argument you want to make about democracy. Any lasting success can be made to seem temporary by expanding your time horizons (look at the ancients!), just as any fleeting failure can be made to look definitive by fixating on the present (look at us!). Nothing gets resolved this way. The real story of democracy is that the long view and the short view must coexist. One never trumps the other. The ongoing success of democracy creates the conditions for repeated failures, just as repeated failures are a precondition for its ongoing success. It is a permanent relationship. It is also an unstable one. The instability is where the real risks lie.

This claim is consistent with what we know about democracy, and with what we still don't know. It fits with our growing knowledge of the existence of a confidence threshold. The academic focus has been on the threshold itself, that magical line that divides stable from unstable societies, the rich from the poor, the secure from the insecure. Given the vast differentials that continue to exist between parts of the developed and the developing world—the world's richest and poorest countries are as far apart as they have ever been—it is understandable that social scientists should want to pin down what makes the difference.[7] But as we discover more about the line that separates out successful states from the failures—and the role that democracy can play in crossing it—we still know next to nothing about what it means for successful democracies to fail. We remain ignorant of the risks that come with living on the other side of the confidence threshold.

In this book I have looked at the crises that afflict democratic societies that have crossed the threshold. There, as Tocqueville saw, it is impossible to find the line that separates success from failure. They go hand in hand. Lots of little failures combine to produce lasting success. What we don't know is whether the little failures might yet combine to produce lasting failure. There may be a point past which the repeated distractions of democratic life turn into a cumulative disaster. We can't be sure. It has never yet happened that a prosperous, stable democracy—one with plenty of wealthy, long-lived citizens—has ceased to be a democracy. But it would be absurd to think it could never happen.

Present-day Greece is well above the relevant thresholds for democratic stability. Its per capita GDP, though falling fast, is still over $25,000. The median age of its population is forty-three, one of the highest figures in the world. It seems highly unlikely that if the present crisis worsens, and Greek GDP continues to fall, Greek democracy would remain secure all the way down to the threshold of $7,000. It is just as hard to see how Greek democracy can remain secure if the median age continues to rise; societies with an imbalance of pensioners to wage earners will always have great difficulty paying their way. Is there a median age threshold above which democracy becomes unsustainable? For now, we have no idea.

Political scientists answer the big questions for which they have the historical evidence, questions about the move from disorder to order, from war to peace, from the democracies that fail to the democracies that succeed. They want to know, as Fukuyama put it in a recent book, "how to get to Denmark," perhaps the most livable society on earth, a prosperous, stable, experimental, law-abiding, well-governed state.[8] Is it worth asking what happens when Denmark ceases to be Denmark? Perhaps not; we have so little to go on. But that doesn't mean we should discount the possibility.

Stable democratic societies focus on the details of their politics and how to improve them. There is room to improve any democracy, even Denmark. Small problems can be addressed with patience and perseverance; we can recalibrate voting systems, try to render welfare more efficient, find new ways to promote social cohesion. The evidence political science supplies can help in making these improvements. But political science cannot help us discover when choosing to concentrate on little improvements is evidence, not of progress, but of fatal complacency.

Secure democracies are not all alike. Denmark is very different from the United States; both are very different from Japan. The spread of democracy over the past hundred years has greatly increased the variety of democratic experiences. The single, overarching narrative of the success of democracy has multiple different strands. There is more experimentation going on than ever. Many democracies are now in the position that Tocqueville thought was a unique privilege of the Americans, with the ability to make reparable mistakes.

The evidence of those different experiments is growing all the time, offering more examples of what is possible. Want an education system that works? Try Finland. A banking system that works? Try Canada. Environmental safeguards? Try Australia. Each of these experiments is subject to its own forms of democratic skittishness (many Finns think their education system in is crisis; many Canadians think their economy is underperforming; many Australians think their environmental safeguards are oppressive). Democracies remain bad at learning from each other's example; they still tend to privilege their own experiences. But for the democracies that want to learn, there are plenty of examples to choose from.

At the same time, the world's democracies are more interconnected than ever before. They are bound together by complex financial instruments, shared institutional arrangements, and global technological networks. Failure in one place can have wholly unexpected repercussions somewhere else. A bad bank in one country can infect confidence in the entire system. So there is always a danger that the proliferation of experimentation will create unsustainable collective risks. A world in which everyone feels they have the ability to make reparable mistakes may be one in which no one is safe.

The spread and growth of democracy has generated the possibility of collective failure. Yet the spread and growth of democracy remains our best bet against the possibility of collective failure, because democracies are always trying something new. The advantages of democracy are inseparable from the risks. There is no way to access the former without incurring the latter. The long-term strength of democracy comes from its short-term restlessness; it is also at risk of being undermined by its short-term restlessness. The short-term restlessness is at risk of being undermined by the knowledge of its long-term strength. Democracies succeed because they fail and they fail because they succeed. There is no way around this.

The future for democracy remains open. There are grounds for hope and there are grounds for fear. Often these are the same grounds; a single event can be the source of both optimism and pessimism. That is true of the present crisis. It does not fit into one or the other of the stories I outlined earlier. It fits into both. It is part of a repeated pattern of crisis and recovery. It is consistent with an overarching narrative of cumulative success and eventual failure. I do not know what will happen. No one does (and anyone who says they know what the future holds for democracy is either deluded or lying). But it is possible to say where the challenges lie.

FOUR CHALLENGES

In the preface I identified four areas where the established democracies have performed poorly over the past decade: they have fought unsuccessful wars, mismanaged their finances, failed to take meaningful action on climate change, and seemed frozen in the face of China's growing power. The present crisis has highlighted these failures. Yet the present crisis is not the end of the story. These are the four fundamental challenges that any political system has to face: war, finance, environmental threat, and the existence of a plausible rival. Whatever the result of the present crisis, the challenges are not going away. I will briefly consider each in turn.

War

There is solid evidence from the past century for two general conclusions about democracy and war. First, democracies do not go to war with each other. Second, in the wars they do fight, democracies win far more often than they lose (most estimates put the success rate at above 75 percent).[9] The recent struggles of the Western democracies to prosecute wars in Iraq and Afghanistan illustrate some of the limitations of these maxims, but they do not refute them. Democratic peace theory helped to promote a reckless optimism about fighting wars for peace. These wars did not end in victory and they have not resulted in peace. Nonetheless, they have not been outright defeats. The democracies have fallen out among themselves, but they have not started fighting each other. The wars of the past decade have been relative failures, not absolute ones.

The reason that democracies do not fight each other is connected to the reason that democracies do not often lose the wars they fight. The structure of democratic politics (regular elections, a free press, civilian control of the military) makes democratic politicians wary of needless conflicts. They are regularly reminded of the costs and risks. When they do find themselves at war, they are less likely than autocrats to fall prey to wishful thinking and double down on their mistakes. They will adapt rather than lose.

But it does not follow that democracies have learned how to avoid unwinnable wars. The evidence of recent years is sufficient to disprove that idea. The successes of democracy in war and peace have more to do with what Tocqueville called the "untimeliness" of democratic life than with any superior grasp of what is at stake. Democracies find it harder than autocracies to commit to war; there are too many competing interests that have to be aligned first. When those interests are eventually aligned, democracies have a range of resources to draw on that makes them formidable adversaries. This provides double insulation against war between democracies. It is very difficult for any two democracies to get their act together to fight each other at the same time, and if they did, both sides would be given pause by the thought of what they were up against.

Democratic untimeliness is not simply a delaying device. It also means that mistakes will keep happening. The fractured and inattentive quality of democratic life provides opportunities for reckless behavior as well as caution. Political systems that make it difficult to gather the resources needed for war make it tempting to fight wars on the sly. Democracies increasingly find themselves engaged in military conflicts being conducted away from the public glare, fought by proxies, special forces, unmanned drones. The institutional barriers in the way of garnering public support for war can result in bypassing the public instead of bypassing the war.

Equally, the difficulty of holding together public support means that long wars are dangerous for democracies. Attention starts to drift, distractions get in the way, indifference mounts. The same qualities that make democracies reluctant to fight can get them stuck fighting wars they lack the ability to end.

The spread of democracy has lessened the likelihood of war in many parts of the world. But this is not a story about growing wisdom or self-control on the part of the democracies. It is an inadvertent achievement, which makes it an endlessly frustrating one. Why can't we access the peaceful benefits of democracy more directly? It is always tempting to try. But forcing the advantages of democracy tends to undermine them. It does not work to accelerate the progress of democracy in the hope of accelerating the progress of peace. The democracies that do the accelerating squander the benefits of caution. Yet simply waiting for the peace to unfold at its own pace encourages passivity and fatalism. It makes it more likely that needless wars will slip between the gaps of democratic attention spans.

The current crisis in Europe has led to some dire warnings of a return to the wars and violence that scarred the continent for most of its history. This is scaremongering. Europe's democracies will not be going to war with each other any time soon. It is almost impossible to imagine the circumstances in which their interests could be so fundamentally misaligned as to allow their people to think it was worth it. Or rather, it is impossible to imagine those circumstances without also envisaging that democracy had ceased to function. Some future economic or environmental catastrophe could push Europe back to a state of internecine war. But the catastrophe would have to be on a sufficient scale that Europe's democratic institutions had been destroyed first.

Peace between democracies is not an illusion; it is real and it is robust. The clock is not going to turn back to the start of the twentieth century. But the relationship between democracy and war will continue to be unstable. There are two reasons for this. First, as democracies distance themselves from war—as their people become less tolerant of it and less used to it—they create the space for more, not fewer, military misadventures. Small-scale wars, proxy wars, clandestine wars, wars that go by another name ("peace operations"), are all likely to continue to proliferate in an age of public disengagement from military conflict. Second, where a preference for peace is entrenched, only major shocks will be capable of generating the popular support required for outright war (the sort of war in which democracies can make the most of their advantages of adaptability and resourcefulness). A future war between the European Union and some external foe is possible to imagine (it is certainly easier to imagine than any renewal of hostilities between Germany and France). But given the inherent difficulties of aligning the people of Europe for war, it would take a very significant disruption to bring it about. Disruptions on that scale have unpredictable consequences. The deeper the peace that precedes them, the more unpredictable the consequences will be.

The democratic peace is self-reinforcing but it is not self-fulfilling. As peace becomes the default option for democracies, war does not disappear. Instead it becomes harder to control. Democratic stability always creates the conditions for complacency and recklessness. War and peace are no exceptions.

Finance

The pattern of behavior I have identified for democracies has clear parallels with the way financial markets behave. The benefit of having free markets goes along with repeated short-term failures. This produces growth in the long run punctuated by regular crises and other mishaps. Market participants are not good at spotting which are the real crises and which are the mishaps. There is a tendency to talk up the imminent prospect of collapse; at the same time, there is a tendency to discount it, because so much of it turns out to be talk.

As the old joke says, economists have predicted six of the last three recessions (just as political commentators have predicted at least six of the last three crises of democracy). Over time, this breeds complacency. Like democracies, markets go through endless minor dislocations that often serve to conceal their underlying problems. Well-functioning markets can be broadly efficient. But knowing about the efficiency of markets causes participants to behave in ways that undermine it. Confidence in the market turns to overconfidence; overconfidence leads to a crash; the crash provokes a crisis of confidence; the crisis of confidence requires adaptation; adaptation sooner or later leads to recovery; recovery creates new forms of moral hazard.

At moments of financial crisis it is tempting to think the market has been exposed a confidence trick. Its critics, from Marx on, have always hoped that each crisis will prove to be the moment of truth. But it is more accurate to say markets get caught in a trap. They fall victim to their own successes: feedback loops inflate the value of good news to the point where bad news gets drowned out.[10] As the economists George Akerlof and Robert Schiller point out in their book *Animal Spirits*, market failures do not prove that market behavior is irrational. Markets run on confidence, and there are often good grounds for that confidence. But even when we have good grounds for confidence in something, we can quickly become overconfident, because confidence is a form of trust, "and the very meaning of trust is that we go beyond the rational."[11] The better markets work, the more trust people have in them; the more trust people have in them, the more likely they are to go wrong.

The investor George Soros has coined the term "reflexivity" to describe the inbuilt tendency of financial markets to distort the information they supply. Writing in 1994, he saw an obvious political parallel. Market failures were analogous to the systemic failure of the Soviet Union, which had been unable to escape its own informational biases, to the point where the information it was supplying had become entirely detached from reality.[12] Soros argued that the answer to reflexivity was more democracy, which would ensure that closed feedback loops are opened up to competing sources of information. However, democracies are also subject to reflexivity. They too place excessive faith in the evidence they have of their own reliability. Because that faith is better grounded than the faith people place in autocratic systems of government—and because democracies are better at recovering from crises than autocracies—it is harder to correct for. Soros was wrong; markets do not fail like autocracies fail. The Soviet Union was a confidence trick and it eventually fell apart like a house of cards. Markets fail like democracies fail.

To say that democracies are analogous to markets is not to say that democracies *are* markets: markets for influence, markets for votes. Politics cannot be reduced to economics in this way. Democracies do things that markets can't. Democracies fight wars. Markets don't. What's more, democracies are able to correct for market failures; the long history of the adaptability of democratic politicians at times of economic crisis is evidence of that. Democracies operate to their own cycles of confidence, overconfidence, and failure. These can work against market cycles. But not always.

In the aftermath of democracy's triumph in the Cold War, and the victory of the free market over the planned economy, economists came to believe in democracy at the same time that politicians came to believe in markets. As a result, no one wanted to say that things were getting out of hand: the bankers did not want to call out the politicians; the politicians did not want to call out the bankers. This is a particularly dangerous form of reflexivity. It is unlikely to happen again for a while, but when it does the consequences could be devastating.

Democracies do not only go wrong when they come to place excessive faith in markets. The successful regulation of markets is also subject to the inherent tendency of democracies to be spoiled by success. Lessons learned always create the room for more mistakes. The system of international financial regulation that emerged after the Great Depression and the Second World War eventually fell apart in the 1970s. The discipline of Bretton Woods gave the democracies room to follow the path of least resistance. When the United States pulled the plug on Bretton Woods, Western democracy did not fall apart. It groped its way toward a new system and adapted to make it work; then the democracies pushed that system to its limits and beyond. Now we are groping for something else. On these forty-year cycles, the next global financial crisis will come at the midpoint of the century. But only if nothing else goes seriously wrong first.

There are bigger cycles than the forty years' ones. Democracies have very long-term advantages when it comes to finance.[13] Over their modern history, established democracies have gained credibility for the repayment of debts, which means they are able to borrow more cheaply. The institutional constraints that operate on democratic leaders make it hard for them to behave with sustained fiscal irresponsibility. Democracies do still sometimes default, but much less often than autocratic regimes. At the same time, the short-term pressures that operate on democratic leaders make it hard for them to impose fiscal discipline. The voters don't like it. So they will take advantage of the long-term credibility of democracies to follow the path of least resistance and push the system to its limits.

The most apocalyptic warnings coming out of the present crisis argue that this tendency to push their luck will lead the democracies to ruin in the end. Eventually, not just fringe players like Greece but also major democracies like the United States will have to default, because their debt burden will become unsustainable. This too is scaremongering. American democracy is not going to indulge itself to the point where a full-scale default becomes the only option. The institutional constraints on sustained fiscal irresponsibility would kick in before then. The real problem is not that the United States will knowingly walk off a cliff. It is that no one knows where the edge of the cliff is, or which of the intermediate ridges along the way—the lesser "fiscal cliffs"—pose real danger.

Democracies do not morph into giant Ponzi schemes like the Soviet Union. The idea, sometimes floated, that American social security has become such a scheme is absurd. But democracies do find it hard to distinguish false alarms from real ones. The danger is that US democracy will get itself into more trouble than it realizes because it will be unable to tell apart the point when deferring retrenchment keeps its options open from the point when deferring retrenchment closes them down. Credible systems, like credible banks, can find they lose credibility quickly and unexpectedly. At that point, the democratic ability to adapt is likely to run up against the lack of available options. No functioning democracy will choose to prop up its unaffordable social security system beyond the point that it can make the payments on its debt. But a democracy may find that it props up its social security system beyond the point where it gets to make that choice for itself. We simply don't know how robust democracy will prove under those circumstances.

As I say, the next financial crisis is due in about forty years. But only if nothing else goes wrong first.

Environment

Why have the democracies done so little to tackle climate change? There have been frequent summits, endless warnings from experts, and numerous pledges from politicians. But decisive action has been almost entirely absent. One explanation is that the science of climate change is too complicated for democratic publics to understand. Faced with complexity most people retreat into what they think they can understand for themselves. The full effects of climate change will not be experienced for a long time; for now, there is no clear pattern of disruption. Meanwhile, the short-term costs of taking action can be immediately felt, in the form of taxes on energy consumption and a drag on growth. Given a choice between a vague threat of future disaster and a clear threat to present prosperity, democracies will always plump to avoid the latter.

This is the traditional complaint against democracy: people don't know what's good for them. Democracies prioritize immediate over future experiences, simplicity over complexity, gut instinct over science. The openness of democratic societies doesn't simply encourage the free exchange of ideas; it also allows room for antiscientific prejudices to flourish. The Victorian lawyer and historian Henry Maine, in one of most widely read nineteenth-century laments against the coming age of democracy, made this point. In the contest between science and democracy, science is always the loser. He wrote:

> The gradual establishment of the masses in power is the blackest omen for all legislation founded on scientific opinion, which requires tension of mind to understand it and self-denial to submit to it.[14]

However, this is hard to square with the evidence of the twentieth century. Western democracies promoted scientific achievement and technological advance; their publics more or less happily submitted to the advantages these brought. It was autocracies that ended up stifling science, because they couldn't adapt to accommodate its benefits. Autocratic regimes are the worst polluters and the greatest squanderers of natural resources. Over time democracies make far better use of their resources because they are far more resourceful.

So there is an alternative explanation. The democracies have failed to act not because they are stupid, but because they know they are not stupid and will take the necessary action when it is required. In his 2007 film *An Inconvenient Truth*, Al Gore rejects the idea that climate change is simply too difficult for democracies to know how to address. Democracies have overcome all of the most serious challenges they faced in the past, as Gore reminds his American audience at the end of the film.

Are we as Americans capable of doing great things even though they are difficult? Are we capable of rising above ourselves and above history? Well, the record indicates that we do have that capacity. We formed a nation. We fought a revolution and brought something new to this Earth, a free nation guaranteeing individual liberty. America made a moral decision that slavery was wrong and that we could not be half free and half slave. We, as Americans, decided that of course women should have the right vote. We defeated totalitarianism and won a war in the Pacific and the Atlantic simultaneously. We desegregated our schools and cured some diseases like polio. We landed on the moon, the very best example of what's possible when we are at our best.[15]

Gore intends this stirring peroration as a call to arms: we did all that, so surely we can do this. But it can be read the other way. The fact that we did all that could make us think that we'll get around to dealing with this when we need to, confident that we have always got our act together in the past. And that could be a recipe for disaster if climate change (unlike the various challenges Gore listed) requires preemptive action.

One of the dangers of overconfidence is an assumption that any difficulty you face is simply a replication of some difficulty you have overcome in the past. Gore is not the only one to fall into this trap. Climate change is routinely characterized as a "moon-shot" challenge, or as a "greatest generation" challenge, or as a technology/innovation challenge like the eradication of a disease. The hope is that this familiar frame of reference will give us the impetus to act. The risk comes if climate change doesn't fall into any of these categories. Drawing encouragement from the historical record makes it hard to know whether this time is different. If it is different, we may not find out until it's too late.

Another risk is that bundling together the accomplishments of democracies in meeting past challenges ignores how different those challenges were. Tackling climate change may require a combination of forms of democratic adaptability that don't sit easily together. Established democracies have two basic strengths in the face of existential threats. The first is their ability to pull together when the threat becomes too big to ignore, for instance when they find themselves under direct attack. The second is their ability to keep experimenting and adapting to the challenges they encounter, so that no danger becomes overwhelming.

In the first case, democracies face up to the threat, but only when it gets really serious. In the second, they sidestep it.

In the case of climate change, these two possibilities may work against each other. Optimists insist that technological innovation will solve the problem.[16] They point to repeated warnings in the past about imminent environmental catastrophe that have turned out to be hot air. Open societies trade on prophecies of doom. In the 1860s Britain was warned that it was ruined because it was running out of coal (John Stuart Mill was one of the doom-mongers). Yet in the 1860s coal production had barely got going. In the 1890s New Yorkers were told they faced being buried under a tide of horse manure. Then someone invented the motorcar. In the 1960s the world faced disaster from "global cooling." In the 1970s it was the collapse of the food supply in the face of a population explosion. In the 1980s it was the hole in the ozone layer. These problems were solved by adaptation and innovation rather than by extreme measures and political coercion. Politicians can encourage innovation. But they can also stifle it by overreacting to perceived threats. When environmental disaster looms, your best bet is to keep your options open.[17]

Optimism, however, can also be a form of fatalism. Just because democracies have been guilty of crying wolf in the past doesn't mean there is no wolf out there. Keeping your options open also means closing them down in one crucial respect, because it rules out decisive political action. Or rather, it rules it out until the wolf is so close no one could doubt its existence. In the case of climate change, that would be waiting too long. If at some point we need to draw on the collective resilience of democratic societies to combat climate change—their ability to adapt to straitened circumstances when they have to—then an overreliance on their experimental qualities will be a barrier to action. If one keeps sidestepping a challenge, it becomes hard to know when it is time to face up to it.

Gore was right that democracies have the capacity to deal with climate change. They have the experimental adaptability, and they have the collective resilience under duress. The problem is that they don't know which one they need first. The knowledge that democracies have of their long-term strengths does not tell them how to access those strengths at the right moment. If anything it makes it harder. That is why climate change is so dangerous for democracies. It represents the potentially fatal version of the confidence trap.

Rivals

China is sometimes said to have an advantage over the West when it comes to tackling the challenges I have been discussing: war, finance, climate change. The Chinese authorities are not hamstrung by the need for public consultation. They can take decisive action without fear of the electoral consequences, allowing them to impose short-term costs for the sake of long-term benefits. This is the advantage of autocratic systems that Tocqueville identified: they are better at thinking about the long term in the short term. But it is only a limited benefit because they get stuck with the choices they make. Autocratic regimes are far less likely to own up to their mistakes and change course when required. They are more likely to change course on a whim. Nor is it true that autocratic regimes can simply ride roughshod over public opinion. Unelected leaders are often more nervous of public opinion than elected ones, because they have even less of an idea of what the public is thinking.

We are caught between a sense of our relative weakness compared to China and our relative strength. The Chinese have a range of short-term advantages. Unlike past communist regimes, they are not constrained by ideology. Unlike democracies, they are not constrained by constitutional checks and balances. They can enforce technocratic solutions to economic problems more easily than we can. For now, the Chinese authorities have been relatively successful in managing the effects of the crash of 2008 (certainly they have been more successful than the Europeans). In this they are greatly helped by the limits they have imposed on the investment opportunities available to ordinary Chinese citizens— central policy is more effective when the escape routes are closed off. China does not feel tempted to fight wars for the sake of justice and morality, as some Western democracies have been doing over the past decade. The Chinese can be as pragmatic (that is, unprincipled) as they like in seeking to expand their global influence. Yet we also know that in the long run autocratic regimes struggle to match the rising expectation of their populations and to meet their growing demand for a greater say in their government. China is still a relatively poor country in terms of per capita GDP, and it has a vast population. It is hard to see how the present regime can keep a lid on its discontents as it continues to grow.

China stands in relation to the West in the twenty-first century as Tocqueville thought European monarchy stood in relation to American democracy in the nineteenth. Democracy had the long-term advantages, but in the interim it risked being outmaneuvered by less consultative and more decisive autocratic regimes. This creates a dangerous world in which both sides are liable to miscalculate: democracies might shirk an immediate challenge in the hope that their long-term strengths would tell eventually; autocracies might try to preempt their disadvantages by seeking a confrontation in the short term. The relationship between democracy and autocracy is always unpredictable and unstable.

Nonetheless, Tocqueville saw some benefits from the mismatch. Democracies needed plausible rivals in order to puncture their complacency. In the nineteenth century America's role was to show Europe that democracy was possible; Europe's role was to show America that it was not inevitable. Tocqueville hoped each side might learn something from the other. But a kind of paradox was at work here: democracies needed autocracies to keep them honest and stop them drifting along with their fate, but the existence of autocracies was dangerous for democracies because it drew them into volatile relationships. Anything that can puncture the complacency of democracies threatens them with challenges they may not know how to deal with. The rise of China places the West in a similar position today.

Of course, there are big differences between then and now. One is the spread of democracy beyond Europe and the United States to many other parts of the world. It may be that democratic India's rivalry with China will turn out to be the central political contest of the twenty-first century. But Indian democracy is hardly immune from the promise and temptations of democracy that Tocqueville identified. In some ways India is the contemporary state that most closely fits the nineteenth-century American version Tocqueville encountered: formally egalitarian but deeply hierarchical; a relatively weak center; chaotic but robust. India has been growing almost as fast as China over the past two decades, but it has not caught up with China on many quality-of-life measures: life expectancy in India is around ten years lower (64.4 to 73.5) and the country lags behind on various standards of health and education.[18] India is running into difficulties as its current economic model strains to accommodate the multiple demands of its democratic politics. But that politics remains more adaptable than its Chinese counterpart. The hope is that India will outperform China in the long run. The fear is that the short run will get in the way first.

Since Tocqueville wrote, there has been a multiplication of different models of autocratic government, especially in the period since the end of the Cold War. The contest is no longer with monarchy, nor simply with dictatorship. Autocrats have learned to cherry pick some of the tools of democracy to blur the edges between the two systems. These hybrid regimes have acquired various different names: "competitive authoritarianism," "exclusionary democracy," "semiauthoritarianism," "defective democracy," or simply "mixed regimes." Vladimir Putin's Russia exemplifies one version: repression is combined with liberalization, and elections coexist with entrenched power elites. Predictions that Russia would be swept along by the democratic tide following the collapse of the Soviet Union have turned out to be mistaken. Russia has not turned into a democracy. It has turned into a pseudo-democratic kleptocracy, in which people use money to get power and power to get money.

Autocrats have turned out to be better at picking up tips from their democratic rivals than the other way round. Putin has learned to mimic some of the flexibility of democratic leaders in order to maintain his hold on power. His regime has an air of permanence born of its brutal adaptability. The Chinese authorities have learned from the West (many of the present generation of leaders studied in the West), and also from their own mistakes in the past: a calamity like the famine of 1958–62 is highly unlikely to be repeated.[19] During the Arab spring, some autocratic regimes have proved more adept than others in discovering how to cling on: intransigence does not pay; flexibility does, particularly when it contains its own forms of ruthlessness.

Nonetheless, this is flexibility within limits. Autocracy remains a one-way bet, even when it is combined with elements of democracy. Autocrats can experiment with democracy but they can never let democracy experiment on them. Hybrid regimes face the basic problem that comes with trying to utilize the strengths of democracy in dangerous situations. It can't be done without losing control. That is why, in a crisis, semiauthoritarian regimes will revert to authoritarianism, while democratic regimes can try something new.

Democracy's current rivals are less encumbered by ideology than would have been the case during the twentieth century and better able to draw on technical expertise. But they still lack adaptability. As information technology spreads and adapts at breakneck speed, this is a major weakness. The Chinese regime can devote vast resources to regulating the Internet and to monitoring the threat it poses. It can use the Internet as a tool of power. What it can't do is modify its own power to make the best use of the Internet. It remains vulnerable to any technology that is more adaptable than it is.

This does not mean that Internet is bound to democratize China. The regime retains the capacity to take ruthless short-term decisions. States can do things that information networks can't. States fight wars. Google doesn't, and not just by choice. A regime that cannot find ways to accommodate the forces of change can try to channel them to particular ends. The question of how the Chinese regime decides to face up to its weaknesses is unresolved. Chinese state capitalism is unlikely to collapse like a house of cards: it is not just a confidence trick. It would be a mistake to assume that the demise of the Soviet Union is a reliable guide.

Democracy still has the advantages. But it is no better than its rivals at accessing its advantages when it needs them. As the world speeds up, it remains an untimely form of government. The Chinese state has discovered how to take advantage of the Internet but doesn't know how to accommodate it. Democracies can accommodate the Internet but they haven't discovered how to take advantage of it. Predictions that the new information technology would work to democracy's benefit have proved premature. The advanced democracies have access to multiple new sources of information. They just don't know what to do with it all.

The triumph of democracy in the twentieth century was inadvertent and incomplete. It may well become more complete during the twenty-first century. But it will not be any more advertent, which means that history goes on.

The Confidence Trap

Politics is sometimes described as a tragic mode of life. We face irresolvable dilemmas and the long term certainty of failure; there are no happy endings. This is too bleak. Democracy is not a tragedy; it is too inadvertently comical for that. It is a trap. We are not doomed. We are boxed in.

People have to believe in democracy for it to work. The better it works, the more they believe in it. But the more they believe in it, the less likely they are to know when something is wrong. Democracy lives in the moment and displays its strengths over time. This mismatch produces confusion and uncertainty. We can't wait out the confusion and uncertainty because waiting them out gives them the room to grow. We have to live with them, from crisis to crisis, and from recovery to recovery. It is always possible that we will encounter the crisis that overwhelms us. But it does not make sense to assume this is bound to happen. If we assume it we more or less guarantee it, because we will have become fatalistic. It is better not to assume it. That too is a form of fatalism, but it is at least fatalism of the adaptable kind.

The history of writing about politics is full of images of escape from our bounded horizons. On the final page of *The End of History and the Last Man*, Fukuyama describes history as a long wagon train, progressing over the hills and deserts, making its way into town. Some wagons will get there and some won't; a few will break down or get attacked by Indians. But the majority will make it in the end. The day will come when enough wagons have pulled into town, "such that any reasonable person would be forced to agree that there had only ever been one town and one destination." We are not there yet, Fukuyama insists. Nor can we know, once the wagons do arrive, "whether their occupants, having looked around at their new surroundings, will not find them inadequate and set their eyes on a new and more distant journey."[20]

It is a nice image, but it is not a convincing one. It imagines a moment when the democracies finally recognize where they are and where they have come from—the moment of truth. That moment will never arrive. The long view and the short view do not come together like that. There is no ultimate moment of recognition. Democracies are always prone to mistake their surroundings and stumble on.

Nietzsche has an even more compelling image of emancipation. In *The Gay Science*, he writes of the moment when we recognize that the dead past is behind us and the future is ours to make for ourselves.

At long last the horizon appears free to us again, even if it should not be bright; at long last our ships may venture out again, venture out to face any danger; all the daring of the lover of knowledge is permitted again; the sea, our sea, lies open again; perhaps there has never yet been such an "open sea."[21]

Nietzsche was talking to philosophers—the "daring lovers of knowledge." He certainly did not think a democratic society could ever take to the open seas. It would be held back by its timidity and lack of endeavor. Democratic societies are much more daring than Nietzsche imagined. But he was right that they do not see the free horizon, even dimly. They

set sail without much idea of what is out there. They don't
see that far ahead.

Tocqueville, at a time of personal gloom following the political disasters of 1848, conjured up a very different image
of what it meant to be at sea politically. As he wrote in a letter to a friend, he felt as though he were crouched in the bottom of a boat, without a rudder, without a compass, without
oars, no longer even clear where the shore lay. All he could
do was huddle up and await the future. He was powerless in
the face of fate.

But Tocqueville was not always so gloomy. A better image
comes from the best book ever written about democracy.
In *Democracy in America*, Tocqueville invokes the idea of democracy as a river flowing through history.[22] We are afloat
on a rickety craft (perhaps one of the American steamboats
that Tocqueville so hated). The river is wide and fast moving
but it is also hemmed in by the banks on either side. It is
heading out to sea, but the sea is a long way off and no one
is thinking about that. The waters are choppy and there are
hazards ahead. How do you steer? If you fix on a point on
the shore you risk losing sight of what is in front of you. If
you fix on the eddies and currents in front of your craft, you
risk losing sight of where you are heading. There is no easy
way to do it, just a constant back and forth. Without the
back and forth the ship will eventually go down.

This is the democratic predicament. Knowing the difficulties doesn't tell us how to steer. But it is better to know.

AFTERWORD TO THE PAPERBACK EDITION

IN THIS BOOK I TRY TO DESCRIBE THE INTERPLAY OF three patterns of change at work in modern democracies: the relentless, surface noise of political argument and adjustment (who's in, who's out, who's up, who's down); the underlying and much more infrequent shifts in the deep-rooted structures of power and economic organization (who really gets to call the shots); and the sudden pressure of unexpected events- -or, as we have come to call them, crises.[1] What's been striking since I finished writing it in early 2013 is just how persistent the press of events has become. In the past year the ongoing catastrophe in Syria has morphed into the horror of the Islamic State in Iraq and Syria (ISIS); there have been further crises in Crimea and what remains of Ukraine, with the potential to spill over into other parts of the former Soviet Union; in Libya, the state has collapsed; and in Gaza, a costly and deeply contentious Israeli invasion has been concluded, for now at least. The explosion of instability and violence in all these trouble spots has led some commentators to compare the summer of 2014 to the summer of 1914. Is the world stumbling on the brink of disaster again? These are not all democratic crises—no one, for instance, would describe Libya in its present state as a functioning democracy—but they all represent crises for Western democracy, which has had to decide what to do about them (especially in those places where it feels some responsibility for having brought them about). As of yet, the answer has been very inconclusive. No one knows what to do about them, though the noise of political infighting about who might be responsible is as relentless as ever.

Western leaders are stuck in the familiar bind of trying to find an appropriate scale of response for an unfolding and uncertain threat. But what is appropriate? British Prime Minister David Cameron spent the summer of 2014 interrupting his regular holidays to convene crisis meetings in Downing Street. He takes the holidays to show that the civilized routines of democratic life remain unaffected; he interrupts them to show that they are nonetheless not to be taken for granted. One minute he is sober and serious in a dark suit; the next he is photographed on a surfboard. For President Obama the pattern has been the same, though in his case it has been back and forth from the golf course. Democratic politicians can hardly be blamed for thinking they can't win. In a crisis, the space between over-reacting and under-reacting remains narrow and hard to find.

However, the real question is how these crises interact with the other patterns of democratic change: surface adjustments and structural shifts. In this book, I describe a wide variety of different ways in which events, noise, and structure can interact in a democracy. Some are benign and lead to progress. Others are malign and open the door to stagnation and ultimate decay. The good version happens when crisis triggers the kind of surface adjustments that make structural change possible without threatening systemic collapse. Something like this took place in the 1930s and again in the 1970s: the experimental, impatient side of democratic life enabled change while guarding against a total collapse of confidence. This kind of shift is rarely apparent as it is unfolding. Democratic impatience often looks like the harbinger of democratic failure, whereas in fact it is a sign that no failure will last for long enough to do terminal damage. The noise of democratic life can provide the necessary smokescreen for adjusting to a new reality. But sometimes it is simply a smokescreen for doing nothing. The malign forms of change occur when surface happenings are mistaken for deeper shifts: elections get treated as turning points; making-do gets substituted for mending; anger gets confused with decisive action. This is the fundamental problem of democratic life: a system that is making the necessary adjustments looks remarkably similar to one that is failing to make those adjustments, because in both cases all that you can hear is the noise and all you can see is the muddle of democracy in action.

In this book, most (though by no means all) of the changes I describe are of the good kind. Over the last hundred years, established democracies have eventually adjusted to the challenges they faced, however ugly the process appeared as it was unfolding in real time. But this is only visible in retrospect. What, then, of the present spate of crises? There are two possibilities here. It may be that what looks like muddle and confusion will in due course reveal itself to have been clearing the ground for real change. Or it may be that what looks like real change will turn out to have been nothing more than muddle and confusion. Muddling through is the best and the worst of democracy, which is why it is so hard to know where the present crisis will lead.

The space for secure democracy in Europe has started to shrink. Europe is not about to fall back into a continental civil war: warnings that we are facing a return to the 1930s remain as luridly unconvincing as they were at the height of the Eurozone crisis. Nor is 2014 anything like 1914: the main European players are far too stable and prosperous to stumble down that route. But civil war is raging round the edges of this comfortable world. The crisis in Ukraine is a reminder, among other things, of just how stark the dividing line is between democracies that have crossed the confidence threshold and those that have not. In countries such as Ukraine, where democratic division fuels conflict rather than substituting for it, almost nothing can be taken for granted, including the survival of democracy itself. The hybrid authoritarian alternative offered by Putin's Russia is gaining ground, in some places by force of arms, in others simply by sowing the seeds of political uncertainty. As far as Western Europe is concerned, Putin's example is not something that anyone wants to emulate: there may be intermittent envy of his dictatorial decisiveness, but almost no one is pushing for Western governments to adopt his political practices.[2] The evidence of the last century suggests that democratic adaptability works best when the alternatives present a realistic challenge to the status quo. That is not true in the West at present. The instability lapping at the borders of European democracy represents a threat, but it does not offer a coherent vision of an alternative future.

The gulf in political understanding between the two sides of the confidence threshold is nowhere more apparent than in another of the world's primary sites of political instability. Israel and Gaza exist side-by-side in a condition of unbreakable interdependence but they remain worlds apart. The political experiences of their inhabitants are too remote from each other to provide the impetus for any of the benign forms of change. Israel, once the model of democratic adaptability, is increasingly trapped by short-sightedness. The noise of its democratic politics—party infighting, electoral imperatives, coalition building and dismantling—stifles the opportunities for a shift of priorities. So too does the quiet comfort of a democratic existence. During the Gaza invasion of the summer of 2014 the Israeli public was simultaneously gripped by the conflict and by the drama of its favorite reality TV show, *Big Brother*, whose contestants were isolated in a house with no knowledge of the violence taking place outside. A society that can watch *Big Brother* during a time of war is blessed and cursed: blessed to have a secure means of escape, cursed to have it as well.

That is the presiding impression of the recent round of crises pressing in on Western democracy. They impinge and they disturb; but they don't connect with our own sense of what is politically possible. There is a gulf between what threatens us and what we experience, a gulf that grows through these crises rather than diminishes. Western politicians routinely describe the violence unleashed by ISIS as the worst thing imaginable; yet in fact, for many democratic citizens, it is beyond imagining and in that respect beyond comprehension. The worst of our own politics—its pettiness, its hypocrisy, its dithering—though trivial by comparison, seems far more real.

The crises swirling round the edges of Western democracy do not seem likely to trigger significant change for the better. They are consistent with drift and low-level adaptation that patches up what can be patched up but doesn't address what can't. We are not on the cusp of World War III. Rather, as the historian Margaret Macmillan puts it, we are entering the era of "low grade, very nasty wars that will go on and on without clear outcomes, doing dreadful things to any civilians in their paths." This is not a scenario that plays to the strengths of democracy. Muddling through major crises that threaten democracy itself is a major achievement. Muddling through a series of lesser crises that spell catastrophe for their victims but leave the secure parts of the world relatively untouched is not: it is a form of failure.

However, external pressures to Western democracy are not all that is driving change at present. There is also growing impetus from internal discontent. This mounting pressure has been noticeable even in the brief period since I finished this book. Public frustration with the structural failings of democratic politics—the seemingly inexorable grip of oligarchic elites, technocratic solutions, and plutocratic outcomes—is widespread. It is manifested not only in the traction achieved by parties that burnish their anti-Establishment credentials outside the political mainstream, on the left and on the right,[3] but also in the appetite for books and ideas that promise the possibility of doing things radically differently. The ecstatic reception many reviewers and readers gave to Thomas Piketty's *Capital in the Twenty-First Century* is the most striking example of this: a critique of the inherent trend towards inequality in capitalist societies, it challenged democracy to find new ways of reversing it.

There is an unquestioned appetite for this kind of talk. Yet nothing in Piketty's book gets around the fundamental difficulty of meeting the challenge he sets: the need for a crisis severe enough to trigger the requisite impetus for change. The crisis of 2008 wasn't bad enough: it created the space for a book like Piketty's to be a runaway success but not the conditions to act on what it recommends. That would probably take something bigger and even more dangerous. Declining inequality during the middle part of the twentieth century coincided with the massive destruction of human lives and property: WWII was what made the social democratic restraint of *"les trentes glorieuses"* (the golden age of welfarism from 1945–75) possible. In the absence of WWIII, it is hard to see how to repeat this feat. In that sense, Piketty's proposed solutions—including a global wealth tax—look out of kilter with the size of the task, as seen from both ends of the scale: it represents too big an adjustment for stable democracies to adopt any time soon, yet too small a measure to tame the self-destructive instincts of global capitalism on the march.

The same problem holds for those solutions to our democratic discontents that look to embrace the emancipatory potential of new technology. Again, there is a rising appetite for this kind of talk on both sides of the political divide: left and right see in the explosion of new ways to communicate the possibility of new forms of democratic empowerment, particularly at the local level.[4] In more extreme libertarian circles, especially in Silicon Valley, the chatter is about using technology to circumvent tired old democratic politics altogether. (The sea-steading movement, whose Floating City Project seeks to give tech pioneers the opportunity to experiment with new forms of governance without the inconvenience of conventional elections or political parties, is emblematic of this.) The vision here is of change on the model of the innovative disruption that propels the tech industry itself. But politics doesn't work like that. Its disruptions are experienced as crises. The consequences of a genuine crisis of the new technology—systemic failure with runaway effects—is not something anyone contemplates with equanimity. We don't know what would happen to our politics under conditions of technological breakdown. What we have had so far are tech scandals rather than crises—like the Edward Snowden scandal, which revealed the extent of surveillance being undertaken by the NSA and other Western government agencies. As with all democratic scandals, these tend to get described as crises in the heat of the moment (as the Snowden revelations were), but scandals don't generate the same pressures for change. They are an outlet for voicing discontent rather than a means of channeling it (as has been true of the Snowden affair so far). A technological crisis sufficiently serious to trigger the benign forms of democratic adaptability is hard to envisage: something bad enough to do that would likely be bad enough to do something worse than that. If our technology breaks down, our politics might break down with it.

Yet without something to trigger the risk of systemic collapse, it is hard to see what will shake democratic politics out of its current rut. Europe is trapped, unable to move forward or back because the risks of decisive action—for instance, dismantling the Euro—are too great. Without running greater risks nothing much will change. In the United States, partisanship cripples the prospects for reform, even though the need for some reform is apparent to almost everyone. American politics is trapped in a space where anger and complacency feed off each other. This was most apparent during the government shut-down late of 2013, an event that rested on the twin assumptions that American democracy is broken and at the same time sufficiently secure that nothing can break it. Faced with the current stalemate, American politics is already engaged in the game of waiting for whoever comes after Obama. That is very unlikely to be the fork in the road. The "crisis of the election" is almost always an illusion.

As well as being the centenary of the outbreak of the First World War, the summer of 2014 was also the twenty-fifth anniversary of the publication of Fukuyama's "End of History." This provoked a round of commentary pointing out the ways that Fukuyama turned out to be wrong: history has rarely looked more alive than it did during 2014. Nonetheless, I still think he was broadly right: that is, broadly right to be gloomy about the consequences of democracy's triumph. The success of democracy during the twentieth century was both unarguable and the source of its current travails. Democracy is stuck with the knowledge of its accomplishments, which has left it slower to adapt to the need for change. Now Fukuyama has a new book out: the second volume of his account of origins of political order and decay.[5] It is also gloomy, and it also seems right. He is pessimistic about the capacity of American democracy to reform itself without the imperative of war to give it the necessary impetus. American politics is trapped in a pattern of partisan and

legalistic disputation that shackles the capacity of the executive to take decisive action when it is needed. Fukuyama
does not think this negates his claim that liberal democracy
is the best idea out there. But even the best ideas get stuck.

I originally wrote this book because I felt torn between
the good news and the bad news about democracy and
wanted to understand how they might be related: democratic short-termism and complacency seemed finely balanced
against democratic adaptability and experimentalism. I
feel less torn now. The bad news outweighs the good. The
appetite for change is unquestionably there. But so are the
barriers to acting on it. In this book I tried to resist psycho-
analytic analogies. But the line that therapists sometimes
use about what's holding their patients back—"they want to
change but not if it means changing"—applies to contemporary Western democracy. Crisis is what breaks through
those barriers. It will take a bigger crisis than anything we
have seen in recent years to get democracy out of its rut.
But, in this age of crisis, no one can wish for worse than
what we have had and remain sanguine about what might
follow.

ACKNOWLEDGMENTS

THIS BOOK WAS RESEARCHED AND WRITTEN WHILE I held a Leverhulme Major Research Fellowship from 2009 to 2012. I am deeply grateful to the Leverhulme Trust for its support, which enabled me to undertake and complete this project. I am also very grateful to my colleagues in Cambridge who covered my undergraduate teaching during this period, particularly Chris Brooke in POLIS and Alastair Fraser in Trinity Hall.

During the initial part of the project I had research assistance from Caroline Ashcroft, Katrina Forrester, and Jamie Martin. At the end I had assistance from Freddy Foks. Katrina Forrester also commented on a draft on the manuscript. The book has benefited a great deal from their help.

An early stage of the research was undertaken at the Australian National University in Canberra in 2010, where I was able to try out some of these arguments. Bob Goodin was a generous host and I am very grateful for his help then and since. I have also given versions of the argument in this book at seminars and lectures in Cambridge, Oxford, London, Jyvaskyla, and Uppsala. I would like to thank everyone who commented on those occasions.

I have published a number of essays based on some of the themes in the book: In *Political Quarterly*, "Can Democracy Cope?" (2011), which derives from the Princeton in Europe lecture I gave in the same year. In the *London Review of Books*, "Will We Be Alright in the End? Europe's Crisis," "Confusion Is Power: Our Very Own Oligarchs," and "Stiffed: Occupy" (all 2012). I am very grateful to Mary-Kay Wilmers and the staff of the *LRB* for their continued encouragement and support. Many thanks, also, to my agent, Peter Straus.

At Princeton, Al Bertrand has been a patient and encouraging editor throughout. The book has benefited enormously from his careful attention. Ian Shapiro provided very helpful comments on a draft of the manuscript and has been supportive in many ways. I am also grateful for the comments of an anonymous Princeton reviewer. Dawn Hall supplied expert copyediting of the manuscript. The mistakes that remain are of course my own.

Finally, as always, I would like to thank my children, Tom, Natasha, and Leo, and my wife, Bee, for their help and support, Bee above all. The book is dedicated to her.

NOTES

NOTE ON SOURCES

In the endnotes I list the references for particular passages and themes as they appear in the main text. In addition I want to flag up some of the books that were most useful to me overall. This is intended as a very brief guide to some further reading.

The main influence on this book, which developed about half-way through the period I was researching it, came from Tocqueville. This meant *Democracy in America* (Tocqueville 2000) became the key source, but the other book that was very important to the development of my argument was Tocqueville's *Recollections* (Tocqueville 1948), his troubled memoir of his experiences in 1848. Most influential of all was Stephen Holmes's essay on Tocqueville's recollections of 1848, titled "Saved by Danger / Destroyed by Success" (Holmes 2009). This brilliant essay gave me the confidence to develop the themes of this book.

There is a lot of good writing on Tocqueville in English, and he continues to be the subject of heated debate. Along with Holmes, the readings I found most helpful were from Jon Elster, in his recent book on Tocqueville as a social scientist (Elster 2009) and in his earlier writings on the problems of constraint and license in democratic politics (Elster 1979, 1983, 1993, 2000). Elster has many interesting things to say about some of the ideas I only touch on in this book, including the problem of leaving the future open in politics. An excellent recent guide in English to Tocqueville's own intellectual formation is in the translation of Lucien Jaume's book about him (Jaume 2013).

On the general history of the twentieth century, I was strongly drawn, for reasons of style and content, to the work of Tony Judt. His *Postwar* (Judt 2005) remains a model of how to write about politics in a way that does justice to the people and to the ideas. On the current predicament of democracy, two books that influenced my thinking were Jacob Hacker and Paul Pierson's account of the way inequality developed in the United States over the past forty years (Hacker and Pierson 2010) and Alasdair Roberts's account of the turn to technocracy over the same period (Roberts 2010).

For the individual crisis years I discuss, some books were disproportionately useful. One was the *Cambridge History of the Cold War* (Leffler and Westad 2010). Another was the collection of essays about the 1970s called *The Crisis of the Global* (Ferguson et al. 2010). On the current financial crisis, there are many interesting books. Two I found particularly useful for the themes of this book were Akerlof and Schiller 2009 and Posner 2010.

A central theme of the book is the role of fatalism in political life. I discuss this idea through the thought of Tocqueville, but it is a theme addressed by many other writers who approach it somewhat differently. Three important books on this subject that I do not discuss here are Herbert Croly's *The Promise of American Life* (Croly [1909] 1965), Judith Shklar's *After Utopia* (Shklar 1957), and Arthur Schlesinger's *The Cycles of American History* (Schlesinger 1986). The problem of fatalism is also an important strand in the work of Reinhold Niebuhr and Raymond Aron, and of Albert Hirschman, from whom I draw one of my two epigraphs. In the book I deal with these authors only in passing, if at all. They are all worth reading.

Preface

1. For some commentators these setbacks are sufficient to constitute a counternarrative of democratic decline to set against the "end of history" story. See, for example, Kurlantzick 2013.

INTRODUCTION: TOCQUEVILLE: DEMOCRACY AND CRISIS

1. Tocqueville 1985, 56.

2. Tocqueville 2000, 221.

3. It is true that many other French observers in the 1830s were interested in American democracy and in what it said about the prospects for democracy in Europe. In that sense, Tocqueville was taking part in a widespread debate. Some French commentators believed that American democracy had been maligned, and that it had virtues from which France could learn. Others believed that its apparent strengths were being undermined by its deep-seated failings, above all the continuation of slavery. In these debates, as in similar debates in Britain, people tended to take sides: American democracy was either a good thing or a bad thing. What was unique about Tocqueville was his ability to see both sides; he provided fresh insights into the ways that the good and bad of American democracy went together. On rival French views of America around the time Tocqueville wrote *Democracy in America*, see Craiutu and Jennings 2004. On the intellectual background to Tocqueville's own thought, see Jaume 2013. On competing British attitudes to the United States in the period leading up to the civil war, an excellent recent account is Foreman 2010.

4. Quoted in Jardin 1989, 118.

5. Tocqueville 2000, 234.

6. Paine 2000, 181–82.

7. Paine was writing from his home in London in the late winter of 1791/92. "It is now toward the middle of February. Were I to take a turn into the country, the trees would present a leafless, wintry appearance. As people are apt to pluck twigs as they go along, I perhaps might do the same, and by chance might observe that a *single bud* on that twig has begun to swell. I should reason very unnaturally, or rather not reason at all, to suppose that this was the *only bud* in England which had this appearance. Instead of deciding thus, I should instantly conclude that the same appearance was beginning, or about to begin, everywhere; and though the vegetable sleep will continue longer on some trees and plants than on others, and though some of them may not *blossom* for two or three years, all will be in leaf in the

summer, except those that are *rotten*. What pace the political summer may keep with the natural, no human foresight can determine. It is, however, not difficult to perceive that spring is begun" (Paine 2000, 262–63).

8. Tocqueville 2000, 617.

9. Ibid., 6–7.

10. Ibid.

11. Quoted in Jardin 1989, 165.

12. Quoted in Pierson 1996, 645.

13. Mill's fullest discussion of the varieties of fatalism is in *A System of Logic* (1843), in the chapter titled "Of Liberty and Necessity" (Mill 1963–91, vol. 7).

14. Mill 1963, 433.

15. Tocqueville 2000, 662.

16. Ibid., 472.

17. Ibid., 216.

18. Ibid., 265.

19. Ibid., 629.

20. Ibid., 621.

21. The United States had fought a number of lesser wars since then, including another war with Britain, the conflict of 1812. Tocqueville follows subsequent historical convention in downgrading the significance of this war. However, for a contrary view, which argues that the 1812 conflict was a significant event in the histories of both combatant nations, see Bickham 2012.

22. Ibid., 213.

23. Ibid., 127–28.

24. Ibid., 177–78.

25. There were other grounds of disagreement between them. Mill, like many readers of *Democracy in America* since, thought that Tocqueville had not properly defined what he meant by democracy, and he suspected that Tocqueville was blaming democracy for ills that really belong to the principle of equality (mediocrity, conformism). However, Tocqueville's most distinctive views do concern democracy (loosely defined), not equality: it was America's democratic spirit that produced its distinctive mix of surface activity and underlying drift. Mill and Tocqueville agreed about this.

26. Mill 1963, 460.

27. Tocqueville 1985, 151.

28. Quoted in Hadari 1989, 147–48.

29. He was more concerned about the possibility of conflict between blacks and whites in the South than he was about the prospect of armed conflict between the South and the North. Tocqueville's mordant views regarding race relations in America are laid out in the concluding section of volume one of *Democracy in America* ("Some Considerations on the Present State and the Probable Future of the Three Races That Inhabit the Territory of the United States"). His views on the improbability of a full-blown civil war taking place in a democracy are contained in volume two. This is one of the few topics about which the second volume seems less gloomy than the first.

30. Craiutu and Jennings 2009, 183. Tocqueville uses the Latin phrase *puer robustus*, meaning the child inside the man.

31. Bryce 1888, 2:235–36.

32. Ibid., 432.

CHAPTER 1: 1918: FALSE DAWN

1. Estaunié's views are discussed in Englund 2011, 464–65.

2. Quoted in Holroyd 1988–92, 1:613.

3. Wilson 1966–94, 41:524.

4. Lippmann 1917, 3.

5. Quoted in Figes 1996, 414.

6. H. L. Mencken, "Ludendorff," *Atlantic Monthly* 116, no. 6 (1917): 828.

7. Ibid., 832.

8. In late 1915, the London *Times* had published a series of letters comparing the advantages of autocratic regimes like Germany in wartime to the disadvantages of democracy in similar circumstances. One letter writer drew the comparison in these terms: "A monarchy or bureaucracy knows its men and their achievements and can make judicious selection if it pleases. A democracy has no such knowledge: it chooses its leaders because they are well-born, because they are skilful speakers, because they are good fellows" (Bampfylde Fuller, "Letters," *Times*, November 10, 1915). The context for this discussion was the recent failure of the Allied campaign in the Dardanelles, which

was being blamed on political incompetence. Its architect, Winston Churchill, resigned from the British Cabinet the following week, his political career apparently in ruins. At the same time, Ludendorff was first making a name for himself with a series of military victories in the East. These were the men the letter writer had in mind. The trouble with democracy in war as it appeared at the end of 1915 was that it promoted leaders like Churchill. The German system's great merit was that it promoted leaders like Ludendorff.

9. Leon Trotsky, "On the Publication of the Secret Treaties," November 22, 1917, "Soviet Documents on Foreign Policy," www .marxists.org.

10. Quoted in Kennan 1956, 263.

11. Lloyd George 1936, 5:2522.

12. See Schulzke 2005 for a full discussion of Wilson's attitude to crisis politics.

13. The idea of an association or "league" of nations to guarantee future peace had been floated before America's entry into the war, and it had supporters on the right as well as the left of American politics (though they tended to have very different ideas of what it might entail). Knock 1992 remains the best account of the complex political origins of the League of Nations idea in Wilson's thinking. The idea also had some unintended overlap with schemes being devised in Westminster that envisaged the British Empire as a model of future international security (one of the most influential of these schemes came from the South African Jan Smuts). On this side of the story, see Mazower 2009.

14. As it turned out the Germans never felt sufficiently confident about the situation in Russia to leave it to its own devices; significant numbers of German troops remained to "police" the peace, which continued to be violent and volatile. In this respect, the war continued on two fronts, despite the crushing terms of Brest-Litovsk: troops that might have made the difference in the West were stuck in the East for the duration of 1918.

15. Webb 1952, 115–16.

16. Ibid., 26.

17. Quoted in Macdonald 2003, 404.

18. Bourne 1992, 364.

19. Mann 1985, 180.

20. Ibid., 271.

21. Ibid., 223.

22. *New Republic*, April 27, 1918.

23. See Barry 2004, 207–9.

24. This was particularly true of the British army. See Sheffield 2002 and Hart 2010. The best recent account of the learning experience of 1918 is Stevenson 2011.

25. A version of this argument is given in Winter and Robert 1997.

26. All three men who ended up leading the Allies to victory had earlier established reputations as critics of militarism and imperialism at the turn of the century: Wilson as a critic of American policy after the Spanish-American war, Lloyd George as a critic of the Boer war, and Clemenceau as a critic of the French military during the Dreyfus affair. The reluctant warrior-politicians turned out to be the most adept warrior-politicians.

27. Wilson 1966–94, 51:318.

28. Ibid., 344.

29. Ibid., 339.

30. Knock 1992, 207–8.

31. Wilson 1966–94, 51:630.

32. Perhaps the most distinctive feature of the election was the number of servicemen standing as candidates; on some estimates nearly a quarter of all the candidates were in uniform. This is almost certainly the highest figure for any election in British history. The only occupation that was more widely represented in parliament after the 1918 election than army officers was lawyers (see Strachan 1997).

33. Masterman 1939, 307.

34. "Paying the Bill," *Economist*, December 14, 1918, 798.

35. Ibid.

36. Lippmann 1919, ix–x.

37. Shaw 1919, 94.

38. The Fiume episode is recounted in MacMillan 2001, 302–12.

39. Lippmann 1919, 56.

40. Wilson 1966–92, 62:390.

CHAPTER 2: 1933: FEAR ITSELF

1. Quoted in Clavin 1991.

2. Jan Smuts, "Address at Chatham House Dinner," *International Affairs*, July 11, 1933.

3. "Supply," HC Deb, April 14, 1932, vol. 264, cc. 1030–128, hansard.millbanksystems.com/commons/1932/apr/14/supply-1.

4. See Ortega y Gassett 1985.

5. Shaw, radio broadcast, December 10, 1931, http://walterschafer.com/atimesofshaw/articles/1931.html.

6. Harold Goad, "The Corporate State," *International Affairs* 12 (November 1933): 780.

7. George Bernard Shaw, "The Politics of Un-Political Animals," Fabian Society, October 12, 1933, http://walterschafer.com/atimesofshaw/articles/1933.html.

8. Keynes 2012, 21:86.

9. The line originally comes from *A Tract on Monetary Reform* that Keynes published in 1923 (see Keynes 2012, 4:65).

10. Keynes 2012, 21:86.

11. Ibid., 9.

12. The governor of the bank, Montagu Norman, put the failure to restore the gold standard once the war was over down to a combination of democratic ill discipline and wishful thinking. He wrote to his American counterpart, Benjamin Strong, in 1922: "Only lately have the countries of the world started to clear up after the war, two years having been wasted in building castles in the air and pulling them down again. Such is the way of democracies it seems, though a 'few aristocrats' in all countries realised from the start what must be the result of such hastily conceived remedies for such serious ills" (quoted in Ahamed 2009, 149.) By "aristocrats," Norman meant central bankers like himself.

13. A widely cited anecdote. See, for example, Cairncross and Eichengreen 2003, 5.

14. Nicolson 1933, 94.

15. Quoted in Steel 1980, 291–92.

16. Campaign address in Salt Lake City, September 17, 1932 (Roosevelt 1938–50, 1:713).

17. Roosevelt 1938–50, 2:35.

18. Roosevelt, "First Inaugural Address," http://www.bartleby.com/124/pres49.html.

19. Quoted in Brands 2011, 56.

20. During the 1920s Lippmann had established a reputation as a critic of democracy, specifically of democratic public opinion as the vehicle for progressive reform. In two books, *Public Opinion* (1922) and *The Phantom Public* (1927), he had made the case for experts to de-

cide on behalf of the untutored, indifferent, or plain ignorant voting public. Lippmann remained broadly on the left of American politics in this period. But he was increasingly skeptical about the educative power of democracy to effect change. Eventually this extended to having doubts about the ability of experts to moderate their own opinions: he worried that no one in a democracy was much good at learning from experience, including the decision makers. By the late 1930s he had started to become skeptical of some aspects of government itself, as they related to the control of the economy. This move is discussed in more detail in chapter 3, which looks at the links between Lippmann, Keynes, and Hayek.

21. Keynes 2012, 21:251–52.
22. Ibid., 253.
23. Roosevelt 1938–50, 2:264–65.
24. Keynes 2012, 21:271.
25. Ibid., 277.
26. Quoted in Dallek 1995, 57.
27. Keynes 2012, 21:281.
28. Ibid., 295.
29. Quoted in Skidelsky 1983–2000, 2:xx.
30. Wells 1933, 133.
31. Ibid., 128–38, 171.
32. "The Revolving Storm," *Economist*, March 11, 1933, 507.
33. "If Economists Were Kings," *Economist*, May 6, 1933, 955.
34. See Badger 2009.
35. "A World Adrift," *Economist*, June 4, 1932, 1223.

CHAPTER 3: 1947: TRYING AGAIN

1. "Parliament Bill," HC Deb, November 11, 1947, vol. 444, cc. 203–321, hansard.millbanksystems.com/commons/1947/No/11/parliament -bill.
2. Ibid.
3. Truman, "Address before Joint Session of Congress," March 12, 1947, http://avalon.law.yale.edu/20th_century/trudoc.asp.
4. Quoted in McCullough 1992, 653.
5. "Russia's Strength," *Economist*, May 17, 1947, 745.

6. Anon. [Kennan], "Sources of Soviet Conduct," *Foreign Affairs*, July 25, 1947, 571.

7. Ibid., 575.

8. Ibid., 582.

9. Lippmann 1972, 13.

10. Ibid., 39–40.

11. Some of it was personal. *Foreign Affairs* was edited by the man who had previously been married to Lippmann's wife (as often happens, Lippmann could never forgive the person he had cuckolded). Some of it was an accident of temperament. Neither Kennan nor Lippmann was cheerful by nature; pessimism came easily to them both. But as Kennan's biographer points out, Lippmann had caught Kennan at one of the few moments in his life when he was actually feeling quite hopeful about the future. In the summer of 1947 he took a trip to Europe and discovered that things were not as bad as they had been painted, if you were willing to take the long view. On the flight back he wrote a poem that ended: "Content / Be he whose peace of mind from this may stem / That he, as Fortune's mild and patient claimant / Has heard the rustling of the Time-God's raiment / And has contrived to touch the gleaming hem" (quoted in Gaddis 2011, 282). This sunny mood didn't last. Once he was back in America Kennan soon found plenty of things to be depressed about, including his newfound fame.

12. The title was inspired by this passage: "Among our contemporaries I see two contrary but equally fatal ideas. Some perceive in equality only the anarchic tendencies to which it gives birth. They dread their free will; they are afraid of themselves. Others, fewer in number, but more enlightened, have another view. Next to the route that, departing from equality, leads to anarchy, they have finally discovered the path that seems to lead men inevitably to servitude; and despairing of remaining free, at the bottom of their hearts they already adore the master who is to come" (Tocqueville 2000, 672.) For the details of Lippmann's influence on *The Road to Serfdom*, see Jackson 2012.

13. For an account of some of the political implications of "self-binding," see Elster 1979 and Elster 2000.

14. See Acton 1904.

15. On the early links between Hayek and German "ordoliberalism," see Friedrich 1955.

16. Aron 1990, 184.

17. Aron 2002, 159.

18. This is a theme of Milward 1987.

19. "Constituent Assembly Debates," 4:734, parliamentofindia.nic .in/ls/debates/debates.htm.

CHAPTER 4: 1962: ON THE BRINK

1. "Euroracle 1970," *Economist*, December 29, 1962, 1254.

2. Morgenthau 1960, 264.

3. Kennan 1958, 471–72.

4. Louis Halle, "Muddles That Might Lead to War," *New Republic*, January 22, 1962, 14.

5. Ibid.

6. The more extreme accusation, put forward subsequently by some Republicans, was that Kennedy contrived the timing of the crisis to suit his electoral purposes. This accusation is dealt with and rebutted in Paterson and Brophy 1986.

7. May and Zelikov 2002, 219.

8. Quoted in Beschloss 1991, 110.

9. See Gaddis 2011.

10. Quoted in Gopal 1975–84, 3:182.

11. Ibid.

12. Tocqueville 1948, 15.

13. Quoted in Gopal 1975–84, 3:223.

14. Quoted in Bark and Gress 1989, 508.

15. Ibid., 505.

16. On the distinctive democratic character of political scandals, see Thompson 2000.

17. Selig S. Harrison, "The Passing of the Nehru Era," *New Republic*, December 8, 1962, 16.

18. Morgenthau 1970, 345.

19. See, for example, Burns 1963.

20. Caro 2012, 222.

21. Quoted in ibid., 402.

CHAPTER 5: CRISIS OF CONFIDENCE

1. "And All That," *Economist*, December 28, 1974, 12.

2. Lippmann 1972, vii.

3. Quoted in Kissinger 1994, 665–66.

4. Aron 1974, 156.

5. Louis Halle, "Does War Have a Future?" *Foreign Affairs* 52 (October 1973).

6. Ibid.

7. Ibid.

8. Ronald Steel, "Interview with Walter Lippmann," *New Republic*, April 14, 1973, 16.

9. Morgenthau, "Nixon and the World," *New Republic*, January 13, 1973, 17.

10. Quoted in Ferguson et al. 2010, 173.

11. Kissinger 1994, 701.

12. Quoted in Mueller 1999, 214.

13. See Daggett 2010.

14. Nixon 1971–78, 3:264.

15. Oriana Fallaci, "Interview with the Shah of Iran," *New Republic*, December 1, 1973.

16. Nixon 1971–78, 5:976.

17. "The Great Priority," *Times*, June 22, 1974, 9.

18. "Gas Geben Wäre Tragisch," *Die Zeit*, October 4, 1974.

19. Friedman 1974, 32.

20. Buchanan 1975, 162.

21. "The Presidency Myth," *New Republic*, May 19, 1973.

22. Nicholas Harman, "Italy Goes Bust," *New Statesman*, July 12, 1974.

23. "The Plot Sickens," *New Republic*, May 18, 1974.

24. In his memoirs published twenty years later, Brandt complained that he had been bounced into the wrong decision by disloyal colleagues (see Brandt 1994).

25. This story is told in Shaxson 2011.

26. Stephen Kotkin, "The Kiss of Debt," in Ferguson et al. 2010, 89.

27. Crozier, Huntington, and Watanuki 1975, 8–9.

28. Ibid., 53–54.

29. Ibid., 188.

30. Ibid., 193–94.

31. Ford 1975, 27.

32. See Huntington 1991.

33. This story is told in Hacker and Pierson 2011.

34. The term *malaise* during this period came to be associated with the notorious televised address given by Jimmy Carter on July 15, 1979, commonly known as "the malaise speech." Carter was addressing the crisis of confidence that he saw afflicting American democracy. In fact, Carter did not himself use the word "malaise" (just as James Callahan never uttered the words fatefully attributed to him in the same year: "Crisis? What crisis?"). Carter's primary theme was the same as Nixon's had been in his televised addresses earlier in the decade: the need for energy conservation and independence.

CHAPTER 6: 1989: THE END OF HISTORY

1. Revel 1984, 3.

2. The reference is to the celebrated concluding passage of the first volume of *Democracy in America*: "There are two great peoples on the earth today who, starting from different points, seem to advance towards the same goal: these are the Russians and the Americans. . . . Their point of departure is different, their ways are diverse; nonetheless, each of them seems called by a secret design of Providence to hold the destinies of half the world in their hands" (Tocqueville 2000, 396).

3. Kennedy 1987, 513.

4. Quoted in Gaddis 2011.

5. Quoted in ibid.

6. Quoted in Sylvia Nassar, "Neglected Economist Honored by President," *New York Times*, November 19, 1991.

7. Quoted in Ebenstein 2003, 234.

8. For Hayek's influence on Thatcher, see Ranelagh 1991.

9. "Nobel Prize Winning Economist Oral History Transcript," http://www.archive.org/stream/nobelprizewinninoohaye/nobelprizewinninoohaye_djvu.txt.

10. Roberts 2010, 28.

11. Urban 1976, 36.

12. Fukuyama never claimed to be a prophet. He happily confessed that when he was working as a relatively lowly researcher in the US State Department in the mid-1980s he remained as convinced as anyone else that the Cold War order was entrenched. Nor did Fukuyama claim to be able to explain what was happening in 1989 as the drama unfolded. He was adamant that his argument did not operate at the level of surface events. Too many other commentators were getting overexcited about the here and now, which meant they were liable to overinterpret the twists and turns of political contingency. They would soon change tack if, say, "Mr. Gorbachev was ousted from the Kremlin or a new Ayatollah proclaimed the millennium from a desolate Middle Eastern capital" (Fukuyama 1989, 3). Fukuyama wouldn't.

13. Ibid., 5.

14. Bhagwati 2005, 13.

15. Dahrendorf 1990, 37–40.

16. Fukuyama 1989, 18.

17. Ibid., 5.

18. Kennedy 1987, 459.

19. James Fallows, "Containing Japan," *Atlantic Monthly*, May 1989, 54.

20. Emmott 1989, 204.

21. Ibid.

22. Kohli 1990.

23. Amartya Sen, "How Is India Doing?" *New York Review of Books*, December 16, 1982.

24. "Time to Call History a Day?" *Economist*, September 16, 1989, 98.

25. Hendrik Hertzberg, *Atlantic Monthly*, June 26, 1989, 4.

26. He also thought it might be welcomed as a toughening-up exercise: "I suspect that at least a fraction of the Japanese power elite would be quite pleased to see investors lose some money; it would prevent the Japanese from going soft before Japan has become great" (Soros 1994, 357).

27. See Grass 1990.

28. Joseph Joffe, "Reunification II: This Time No Hobnail Boots," in James and Stone 1992, 105.

29. Habermas 1991, 84.

30. Bloom, "Responses to Fukuyama," *National Interest* (Summer 1989): 21.

CHAPTER 7: 2008: BACK TO THE FUTURE

1. Sheryl Gay Stolberg, "Talks Implode during a Day of Chaos," *New York Times*, September 25, 2008.

2. Versions of both these stories are given in Paulson 2010.

3. See Bernanke 2000.

4. "Remarks by Governor Ben S. Bernanke at the Conference to Honor Milton Friedman, University of Chicago, Chicago, Illinois, November 8, 2002," http://www.federalreserve.gov/boarddocs/speeches/2002/20021108/default.htm.

5. Bush, "Second Inaugural Address," http://www.bartleby .com/124/pres67.html.

6. See Ikenberry et al. 2009. Smith provides the dissenting view.

7. See Fukuyama 2004 and 2006.

8. See Greenspan 2008.

9. For a fuller version of this argument, see David Runciman, "Stiffed: Occupy," *London Review of Books*, October 25, 2012.

10. For a version of this argument, see Ronald Dworkin, "A Bigger Victory Than We Knew," *New York Review of Books*, July 13, 2012.

11. For a more detailed account, see David Runciman, "Will We Be Alright in the End? Europe's Crisis," *London Review of Books*, January 5, 2012.

EPILOGUE: THE CONFIDENCE TRAP

1. The intellectual history of this movement in Britain and the United States is told in an evenhanded way in Stedman Jones 2012. For the paranoid version, see Klein 2007.

2. For an early version of the argument between Krugman and Ferguson (which has since become considerably more acrimonious), see "The Crisis and How to Deal with It," *New York Review of Books*, June 11, 2009.

3. See Przeworski et al. 2000.

4. There is some recent evidence that this relationship may no longer securely hold in those parts of the world—for example, Venezuela and Thailand—where democracy has been losing its appeal for

the struggling middle classes who had previously supported it. The story of this backlash is told in Kurlantzick 2013.

5. See Cincotta 2009.

6. Arrow, "Questions about a Paradox," in Weingast and Wittman 2008.

7. Of the very many recent books dealing with this question, see in particular Clark 2008; North Wallis, and Weingast 2009; Acemoglu and Robinson 2012.

8. Fukuyama 2011, 431–34.

9. See Reiter and Stam 2002.

10. On what happens when the bad news finally gets heard, and how its effects are magnified, see Geanakoplos 2010.

11. Akerlof and Schiller 2009, 5–6.

12. See Soros 1994, 5–6.

13. See Schultz and Weingast 2003.

14. Maine 1886, 98.

15. Gore, "An Inconvenient Truth," online transcript, http://www.veryabc.cn/movie/uploads/script/AnInconvenientTruth.txt.

16. See, for example, Ridley 2010.

17. A version of these arguments is currently being played out over fracking (the hydraulic fracturing of shale gas and "tight" oil), which has taken off in the United States. For its cheerleaders fracking represents the solution to inflated fears about "peak oil"— another example of the way technological innovation comes to rescue open societies at the point rescue is needed. For a skeptical view of this claim, see David Runciman, "The Crisis of American Democracy," *London Review of Books*, March 21, 2013. See also Janeway 2012.

18. See Amartya Sen, "Quality of Life: India vs. China," *New York Review of Books*, May 12, 2011.

19. The learning experience for the current generation of China's leaders is described in Pankaj Mishra, "The Hungry Years," *New Yorker*, December 10, 2012.

20. Fukuyama 1992, 340.

21. Nietzsche 2001, §343.

22. Tocqueville 2000, 7.

AFTERWORD TO THE PAPERBACK EDITION

1. "Events" used to offer an alternative to the vocabulary of "crisis"—it was, for instance, still "les événements" that gripped Paris during the crisis year of 1968—but no longer. I have not seen what's been unfolding in Ukraine described anywhere as the Ukrainian events; this is the Ukraine crisis. We now live in an unambiguous age of crisis.

2. That is less true further East, where Putinism has growing cachet in mainstream political circles; and you do not have to move far to the East to find it. In Hungary, for instance, Prime Minister Viktor Orban made clear during the summer of 2014 that he saw Putin's Russia (along with Erdogan's Turkey) as a model to be emulated in preference to the "liberal democracy" of Western Europe, which he claimed had been seen to fail.

3. In Britain, the beneficiaries of the anti-Establishment wave include both UKIP and the SNP, who between them represent opposite poles on a conventional ideological spectrum of liberal democratic politics. What they have in common is their desire to dismantle what are perceived to be the most unresponsive elements of the existing structures of power. This indicates that the conventional ideological spectrum no longer maps neatly onto contemporary democratic politics.

4. Roberto Unger, a post-Marxist social theorist, believes that information technology holds the key to democratic revival; so does Douglas Carswell, a libertarian Tory MP who defected to the anti-immigration party UKIP. They have almost nothing in common bar this.

5. Francis Fukuyama, *Political Order and Political Decay: From the Industrial Revolution to the Globalization of Democracy* (London: Profile Books 2014).

BIBLIOGRAPHY

Note: In this bibliography I do not list individual articles from the newspapers and journals that I have consulted most often. Where I cite particular articles in the main text these are listed in the notes. The following are the main publications I have used that cover a range of the different crisis years I study in this book.

NEWSPAPERS AND JOURNALS

American Journal of Political Science
American Political Science Review
Atlantic Monthly
Economist
Foreign Affairs
Foreign Relations
International Affairs
International Security
Journal of Democracy
London Review of Books
National Interest
New Republic
New Statesman
New York Review of Books

New York Times
New Yorker
Newsweek
The Guardian (*The Manchester Guardian*)
The Times of India
Der Spiegel
Time
Times (of London)
Die Zeit

BOOKS AND ARTICLES

Acemoglu, Daron, and James A. Robinson. 2006. *Economic Origins of Dictatorship and Democracy*. Cambridge: Cambridge University Press.

———. 2012. *Why Nations Fail: The Origins of Power, Prosperity and Poverty*. London: Profile Books.

Acton, J.E.E.D., Baron. 1904. *Letters of Lord Acton to Mary Gladstone*. London: Macmillan.

Ahamed, Liaquat. 2009. *The Lords of Finance: 1929, the Great Depression and the Bankers Who Broke the World*. London: William Heinemann.

Akerlof, George A., and Robert J. Schiller. 2009. *Animal Spirits: How Human Psychology Drives the Economy and Why It Matters for Global Capitalism*. Princeton, NJ: Princeton University Press.

Angell, Norman. 1910. *The Great Illusion: A Study of the Relation of Military Power in Nations to Their Economic and Social Advantage*. New York: Putnam.

———. 1933. *The Great Illusion, 1933*. New York: Putnam.

Aron, Raymond. 1947. *Le grand schisme*. Paris: Gallimard.

———. [1938] 1948. *Introduction to the Philosophy of History: An Essay on the Limits of Historical Objectivity*. London: Weidenfeld and Nicolson.

———. 1957. *The Opium of the Intellectuals*. London: Secker and Warburg.

———. 1966. *Peace and War*. London: Weidenfeld and Nicolson.

———. 1974. *The Imperial Republic: The United States and the World, 1945–1973*. New York: Little, Brown.

———. 1977. *In Defense of Decadent Europe*. South Bend, IN: Regnery.

———. 1990. *Memoirs: Fifty Years of Political Reflection*. New York: Holmes and Meier.

———. 2002. *The Dawn of Universal History: Selected Essays from a Witness of the Twentieth Century*. New York: Basic Books.

Arrow, Kenneth. 1951. *Social Choice and Individual Values*. New York: Wiley.

Babbitt, Irving. 1924. *Democracy and Leadership*. Boston: Houghton Mifflin.

Badger, Anthony J. 2009. *FDR: The First Hundred Days*. New York: Farrar, Straus, Giroux.

Bark, Dennis L., and David R. Gress. 1989. *From Shadow to Substance: A History of West Germany, 1945–1963*. Oxford: Wiley-Blackwell.

Barry, John M. 2004. *The Great Influenza: The Epic Story of the Deadliest Plague in History*. New York: Viking.

Bartels, Larry M. 2010. *Unequal Democracy: The Political Economy of the New Gilded Age*. Princeton, NJ: Princeton University Press.

Becker, Carl. 1941. *Modern Democracy*. New Haven, CT: Yale University Press.

Beinart, Peter. 2010. *The Icarus Syndrome: A History of American Hubris*. New York: Harper.

Bell, Daniel. 1962. *The End of Ideology: On the Exhaustion of Political Ideas in the Fifties*. Cambridge, MA: Harvard University Press.

Bernanke, Ben. 2000. *Essays on the Great Depression*. Princeton, NJ: Princeton University Press.

Beschloss, Michael R. 1991. *The Crisis Years: Kennedy and Khrushchev, 1960–1963*. New York: Harper Collins.

Bhagwati, Jagdish. 2005. *In Defense of Globalization*. Oxford: Oxford University Press.

Bickham, Troy. 2012. *The Weight of Vengeance: The United States, the British Empire, and the War of 1812*. New York: Oxford University Press.

Bloom, Allan. 1987. *The Closing of the American Mind*. New York: Simon and Schuster.

Bourne, Randolph. 1992. *The Radical Will: Selected Writings, 1911–1918*. Edited by Olaf Hansen. Preface by Christopher Lasch. Berkeley: University of California Press.

Brands, H. W. 2011. *Greenback Planet: How the Dollar Conquered the World and Threatened Civilization as We Know It*. Austin: University of Texas Press.

Brandt, Loren, and Thomas G. Rawski, eds. 2008. *China's Economic Transformation*. Cambridge: Cambridge University Press.

Brandt, Willy. 1994. *My Life in Politics*. New York: Random House.

Brendon, Piers. 2001. *The Dark Valley: A Panorama of the 1930s*. London: Bloomsbury.

Brown, Judith M. 1994. *Modern India: The Origins of an Asian Democracy*. 2nd ed. Oxford: Oxford University Press.

———. 2003. *Nehru: A Political Life*. New Haven, CT: Yale University Press.

Brown, Michael E., Sean M. Lynn-Jones, and Steven E. Miller, eds. 1996. *Debating the Democratic Peace*. Cambridge, MA: MIT Press.

Bryce, James. 1888. *The American Commonwealth*. 2 vols. London: Macmillan.

———. 1917. *The War of Democracy: The Allies' Statement; Chapters on the Fundamental Significance of the Struggle for a New Europe*. London: Doubleday.

———. 1921. *Modern Democracies*. 2 vols. London: Macmillan.

Buchanan, James M. 1975. *The Limits of Liberty: Between Anarchy and Leviathan*. Chicago: University of Chicago Press.

———. 1989. *Reaganomics and After*. London: Institute of Economic Affairs.

———. 1992. *Better Than Plowing, and Other Personal Essays*. Chicago: University of Chicago Press.

———. 1997. *Post-Socialist Political Economy*. Cheltenham: Edward Elgar.

Buchanan, James M., and Gordon Tullock. 1962. *The Calculus of Consent: The Logical Foundations of Constitutional Democracy*. Ann Arbor: University of Michigan Press.

Burke, Edmund. 1993. *Pre-Revolutionary Writings*. Edited by Ian Harris. Cambridge: Cambridge University Press.

———. [1790] 2009. *Reflections on the Revolution in France*. Edited by L. G. Mitchell. Oxford: Oxford University Press.

Burleigh, Michael. 2006. *Sacred Causes: Religion and Politics from the European Dictators to Al Qaeda*. London: HarperPress.

Burns, James M. 1963. *The Deadlock of Democracy: Four-Party Politics in America*. Englewood Cliffs, NJ: Prentice-Hall.

Byrne, Janet, ed. 2012. *The Occupy Handbook*. New York: Back Bay Books.

Cairncross, Alec, and Barry Eichengreen. 2003. *Sterling in Decline: The Devaluations of 1931, 1949, and 1967*. London: Palgrave Macmillan.

Caldwell, Bruce. 2005. *Hayek's Challenge: An Intellectual Biography of F. A. Hayek*. Chicago: University of Chicago Press.

Carey, John. 1992. *The Intellectuals and the Masses: Pride and Prejudice among the Literary Intelligentsia, 1880–1939*. London: Faber and Faber.

Caro, Robert. 2012. *The Years of Lyndon Johnson*. Vol. 4, *The Passage of Power*. London: The Bodley Head.

Churchill, Winston S. 1923–31. *The World Crisis*. 6 vols. London: Thornton Butterworth.

Cincotta, R. P. 2009. "Half a Chance: Youth Bulges and Transitions to Liberal Democracy." *Environmental Change and Security Report* (13): 10–18.

Clark, Gregory. 2008. *A Farewell to Alms: A Brief Economic History of the World*. Princeton, NJ: Princeton University Press.

Clarke, Peter. 2010. *Keynes: The Twentieth Century's Most Influential Economist*. London: Bloomsbury.

Clavin, Patricia. 1991. "The World Economic Conference 1933: The Failure of British Internationalism." *Journal of European Economic History* (20): 489–527.

Cockett, Richard. 1994. *Thinking the Unthinkable: Think-Tanks and the Economic Counter-Revolution, 1931–1983*. London: HarperCollins.

Coyle, Diane. 2011. *The Economics of Enough: How to Run the Economy as If the Future Really Matters*. Princeton, NJ: Princeton University Press.

Coyle, Diane, ed. 2012. *What's the Use of Economics? Teaching the Dismal Science after the Crisis*. London: London Publishing Partnership.

Craiutu, Aurelian, and Jeremy Jennings. 2004. "The Third Democracy: Tocqueville's Views of America after 1840." *American Political Science Review* (98): 391–404.

———. 2009. *Tocqueville on America after 1840: Letters and Other Writings*. Cambridge: Cambridge University Press.

Croly, Herbert. [1909] 1965. *The Promise of American Life*. Edited by Arthur Schlesinger Jr. Cambridge, MA: Belknap Press of Harvard University Press.

Crozier, Michael, Samuel Huntington, and Joji Watanuki. 1975. *The Crisis of Democracy: Report on the Governability of Democracies to the Trilateral Commission*. New York: New York University Press.

Curtis, Gerald L. 1988. *The Japanese Way of Politics*. New York: Columbia University Press.

Daggett, Stephen. 2010. "Costs of Major U.S. Wars." *Congressional Research Service* (RS22926).

Dahl, Robert A. 1963. *A Preface to Democratic Theory*. Chicago: University of Chicago Press.

———. 1989. *Democracy and Its Critics*. New Haven, CT: Yale University Press.

Dahrendorf, Ralf. 1990. *Reflections on the Revolution in Europe*. New York: Times Books.

Dallek, Robert. 1995. *Franklin D. Roosevelt and American Foreign Policy, 1932–1945*. New York: Oxford University Press.

———. 2003. *An Unfinished Life: John F. Kennedy, 1917–1963*. Boston: Little, Brown.

Dewey, John. 1927. *The Public and Its Problems*. Chicago: Swallow Press.

Diamond, Larry. 2008. *The Spirit of Democracy: The Struggle to Build Free Societies around the World*. New York: Henry Holt.

Dienstag, Joshua Foa. 2006. *Pessimism: Philosophy, Ethic, Spirit*. Princeton, NJ: Princeton University Press.

Dikötter, Frank. 2010. *Mao's Great Famine: The History of China's Most Devastating Catastrophe, 1958–62*. London: Bloomsbury.

Dowding, Keith, Jim Hughes, and Helen Margetts. 2001. *Challenges to Democracy: Ideas, Involvement, and Institutions*. Basingstoke: Palgrave Macmillan.

Doyle, Michael. 1983. "Kant, Liberal Legacies, and Foreign Affairs." *Philosophy and Public Affairs* (12): 205–35, 323–53.

Dunn, John. 1979. *Western Political Theory in the Face of the Future*. Cambridge: Cambridge University Press.

———. 2005. *Setting the People Free: The Story of Democracy*. London: Grove Atlantic.

Dunning, Thad. 2008. *Crude Democracy: Natural Resource Wealth and Political Regimes*. Cambridge: Cambridge University Press.

Dutton, David, ed. 2001. *Paris 1918: The War Diary of the British Ambassador, the 17th Earl of Derby*. Liverpool: Liverpool University Press.

Easton, David, John G. Gunnell, and Michael Stein, eds. 1985. *Regime and Discipline: Democracy and the Development of Political Science*. Ann Arbor: University of Michigan Press.

Ebenstein, Alan O. 2003. *Hayek's Journey: The Mind of Friedrich Hayek*. Basingstoke: Palgrave Macmillan.

Eichengreen, Barry. 1995. *Golden Fetters: The Gold Standard and the Great Depression*. Oxford: Oxford University Press.

Elster, Jon. 1979. *Ulysses and the Sirens*. Cambridge: Cambridge University Press.

———. 1983. *Sour Grapes: Studies in the Subversion of Rationality*. Cambridge: Cambridge University Press.

———. 1993. *Political Psychology*. Cambridge: Cambridge University Press.

———. 2000. *Ulysses Unbound: Studies in Rationality, Precommitment, and Constraints*. Cambridge: Cambridge University Press.

———. 2009. *Alexis de Tocqueville: The First Social Scientist*. Cambridge: Cambridge University Press.

Emmott, Bill. 1989. *The Sun Also Sets: Limits to Japan's Economic Power*. London: Simon and Schuster.

Encarnation, Dennis J. 1989. *Dislodging Multinationals: India's Strategy in Comparative Perspective*. Ithaca, NY: Cornell University Press.

Englund, Peter. 2011. *The Beauty and the Sorrow: An Intimate History of the First World War*. London: Profile.

Fenby, Jonathan. 2010. *The General: Charles de Gaulle and the France He Saved*. London: Simon and Schuster.

Ferguson, Niall. 2001. *The Cash Nexus: Money and Power in the Modern World*. London: Allen Lane.

———. 2008. *The Ascent of Money: A Financial History of the World*. London: Allen Lane.

———. 2011. *Civilization: The West and the Rest*. London: Allen Lane.

Ferguson, Niall, Charles S. Maier, Erez Manela, and Daniel J. Sargent, eds. 2010. *The Shock of the Global: The 1970s in Perspective*. Cambridge, MA: Belknap Press of Harvard University Press.

Fewsmith, Joseph. 2008. *China since Tiananmen: From Deng Xiaoping to Hu Jintao*. Cambridge: Cambridge University Press.

Figes, Orlando. 1996. *A People's Tragedy: The Russian Revolution, 1891–1924*. London: Jonathan Cape.

Fink, Carole, and Bernd Schaefer. 2008. *Ostpolitik, 1969–1974: European and Global Responses*. Cambridge: Cambridge University Press.

Finley, Moses I. 1985. *Democracy Ancient and Modern*. Rev. ed. New Brunswick, NJ: Rutgers University Press.

Ford, Gerald. 1975. *The Public Papers of the President*. Washington, DC: US Printing Office.

Foreman, Amanda. 2010. *A World on Fire: An Epic History of Two Nations Divided*. London: Allen Lane.

Friedman, Benjamin. 2005. *The Moral Consequences of Economic Growth*. New York: Knopf.

Friedman, Milton. 1962. *Capitalism and Freedom*. Chicago: University of Chicago Press.

———. 1963. *Inflation: Causes and Consequences*. Bombay: Council for Economic Education.

———. 1974. *Monetary Correction*. London: Institute for Economic Affairs.

Friedman, Milton, and Anna Jacobson Schwartz. 1971. *A Monetary History of the United States, 1867–1960*. Princeton, NJ: Princeton University Press.

Friedrich, Carl J. 1948. *Inevitable Peace*. Cambridge, MA: Harvard University Press.

———. 1955. "The Political Thought of Neo-Liberalism." *American Political Science Review* (49): 509–25.

Fukuyama, Francis. 1989. "The End of History." *National Interest* (16): 3–18.

———. 1992. *The End of History and the Last Man*. New York: Free Press.

———. 2004. *State-Building: Governance and World Order in the 21st Century*. Ithaca, NY: Cornell University Press.

———. 2006. *America at the Crossroads: Democracy, Power, and the Neoconservative Legacy*. New Haven, CT: Yale University Press.

———. 2011. *The Origins of Political Order: From Prehuman Times to the French Revolution*. London: Profile.

Fukuyama, Francis, ed. 2007. *Blindside: How to Anticipate Forcing Events and Wild Cards in Global Politics*. Washington, DC: Brookings Institution Press.

Gaddis, John Lewis. 2005. *The Cold War*. London: Allen Lane.

———. 2011. *George F. Kennan: An American Life*. New York: Penguin Press.

Galbraith, John Kenneth. 1969. *Ambassador's Journal: A Personal Account of the Kennedy Years*. Boston: Houghton Mifflin.

Gamble, Andrew. 1996. *Hayek: The Iron Cage of Liberty*. Cambridge: Polity Press.

———. 2000. *Politics and Fate*. Cambridge: Polity Press.

Ganguly, Sumit, and Rahul Mukherji. 2011. *India since 1980*. Cambridge: Cambridge University Press.

Gannett, Robert T. 2003. *Tocqueville Unveiled: The Historian and His Sources*. Chicago: University of Chicago Press.

Gat, Azar. 2009. *Victorious and Vulnerable: Why Democracy Won in the Twentieth Century and Why It Is Still Imperiled*. Lanham, MD: Rowman and Littlefield.

Gaubatz, Kurt Taylor. 1999. *Elections and War: The Electoral Incentive in the Democratic Politics of War and Peace*. Stanford, CA: Stanford University Press.

Geanakoplos, John. 2010. "The Leverage Cycle." Cowles Foundation Discussion Papers No. 1715.

Gelfland, Lawrence. 1963. *The Inquiry: American Preparations for Peace, 1917–1919*. New Haven, CT: Yale University Press.

Geuss, Raymond. 2001. *History and Illusion in Politics*. Cambridge: Cambridge University Press.

———. 2008. *Philosophy and Real Politics*. Princeton, NJ: Princeton University Press.

Ginsborg, Paul. 2001. *Italy and Its Discontents: Family, Civil Society, State, 1980–2001*. London: Allen Lane.

———. 2003. *A History of Contemporary Italy: Society and Politics, 1943–1988*. Basingstoke: Palgrave Macmillan.

Godkin, Edwin L. 1898. *Unforeseen Tendencies of Democracy*. Boston: Houghton, Mifflin.

Gopal, Sarvepalli. 1975–84. *Jawaharlal Nehru: A Biography*. 3 vols. Delhi: Oxford University Press.

Gowa, Joanne. 2000. *Ballots and Bullets: The Elusive Democratic Peace*. Princeton, NJ: Princeton University Press.

Grass, Günter, 1990. *Two States—One Nation?* New York: Secker and Warburg.

Gray, John. 1984. *Hayek on Liberty*. London: Blackwell.

———. 2009. *Gray's Anatomy: Selected Writings*. London: Allen Lane.

Greenspan, Alan. 2008. *The Age of Turbulence*. New ed. London: Penguin Books.

Grigg, John. 1985. *Lloyd George: From Peace to War, 1912–1916*. London: Methuen.

Grünbacher, Armin. 2010. *The Making of German Democracy: West Germany during the Adenauer Era, 1945–63*. Manchester: Manchester University Press.

Guha, Ramachandra. 2007. *India after Gandhi: The History of the World's Largest Democracy*. London: Macmillan.

Habermas, Jürgen. 1991. "Yet Again: German Identity—A Unified Nation of Angry DM-Burghers?" *New German Critique* (52): 84–101.

———. 2000. *The Postnational Constellation*. Cambridge: Polity Press.

Hacker, Jacob S., and Paul Pierson. 2010. *Winner-Take-All Politics: How Washington Made the Rich Richer and Turned Its Back on the Middle Class*. New York: Simon and Schuster.

Hadari, Saguiv A. 1989. "Unintended Consequences of Periods of Transition: Tocqueville's 'Recollections' Reconsidered." *American Journal of Political Science* (33): 136–49.

Hadenius, Axel, ed. 1997. *Democracy's Victory and Crisis*. Cambridge: Cambridge University Press.

Haidt, Jonathan. 2012. *The Righteous Mind: Why Good People Are Divided by Politics and Religion*. London: Allen Lane.

Hamby, Alonzo. 2003. *For the Survival of Democracy: Franklin Roosevelt and the World Crisis of the 1930s*. New York: Simon and Schuster.

Hanson, Russell L. 1989. "Democracy." In *Political Innovation and Conceptual Change*, edited by Terrance Ball, James Farr, and Russell L. Hanson, 68–89. Cambridge: Cambridge University Press.

Hart, Peter. 2010. *1918: A Very British Victory*. London: Hachette.

Hartwell, R. M. 1995. *History of the Mont Pelerin Society*. Indianapolis: Liberty Fund.

Hartz, Louis. 1955. *The Liberal Tradition in America*. New York: Harcourt, Brace.

Hayek, F. A. 1944. *The Road to Serfdom*. London: Routledge and Sons.

———. 1949. *Individualism and Economic Order*. London: Routledge and Kegan Paul.

———. 1960. *The Constitution of Liberty*. London: Routledge and Kegan Paul.

———. 1973–79. *Law, Legislation, and Liberty: A New Statement of the Liberal Principles of Justice and Political Economy*. London: Routledge and Kegan Paul.

———. 1978. *New Studies in Philosophy, Politics, Economics, and the History of Ideas*. London: Routledge and Kegan Paul.

————. 1990. *The Fatal Conceit: The Errors of Socialism*. Edited by W. W. Bartley. London: Routledge.

Hennessey, Peter. 2000. *The Prime Minister: The Office and Its Holders*. London: Allen Lane.

Herzog, Don. 1998. *Poisoning the Mind of the Lower Orders*. Princeton, NJ: Princeton University Press.

Hibbing, John R., and Elizabeth Theiss-Morse. 2002. *Stealth Democracy: Americans' Beliefs about How Government Should Work*. Cambridge: Cambridge University Press.

Hinshaw, Randall Weston, ed. 1972. *Inflation as a Global Problem*. Baltimore: Johns Hopkins University Press.

Hirschman, Albert O. 1982. *Shifting Involvements: Private Interests and Public Action*. Princeton, NJ: Princeton University Press.

Hobson, J. A. 1918. *Democracy after the War*. London: Unwin.

Hoffmann, Steven A. 1990. *India and the China Crisis*. Berkeley: University of California Press.

Hofstadter, Richard. 2008. *The Paranoid Style in American Politics*. New York: Vintage Books.

Holmes, Stephen. 2007. *The Matador's Cape: America's Reckless Response to Terror*. Cambridge: Cambridge University Press.

————. 2009. "Saved by Danger / Destroyed by Success: The Argument of Tocqueville's *Souvenirs*." *Archives Européennes de Sociologie* (50): 171–99.

Holroyd, Michael. 1988–92. *Bernard Shaw*. 4 vols. London: Chatto and Windus.

Horne, John, ed. 1997. *State, Society, and Mobilization in Europe during the First World War*. Cambridge: Cambridge University Press.

Huntington, Samuel P. 1968. *Political Order in Changing Societies*. New Haven, CT: Yale University Press.

————. 1991. *The Third Wave: Democratization in the Late Twentieth Century*. Norman: University of Oklahoma Press.

Ikenberry, G. John, Thomas J. Knock, Anne-Marie Slaughter, and Tony Smith. 2009. *The Crisis of American Foreign Policy: Wilsonianism in the Twenty-First Century*. Princeton, NJ: Princeton University Press.

Inkeles, Alex, ed. 1991. *On Measuring Democracy: Its Consequences and Concomitants*. New Brunswick, NJ: Transaction Publishers.

Isaac, Joel, and Duncan Bell, eds. 2012. *Uncertain Empire: American History and the Idea of the Cold War*. Oxford: Oxford University Press.

Ishida, Takeshi, and Ellis S. Kraus, eds. 1989. *Democracy in Japan*. Pittsburgh: University of Pittsburgh Press.

Jackson, Ben. 2012. "Freedom, the Common Good and the Rule of Law: Lippmann and Hayek on Economic Planning." *Journal of the History of Ideas* (73): 47–68.

Jackson, Julian. 2003. *The Politics of Depression in France, 1932–1936*. Cambridge: Cambridge University Press.

Jacobs, Alan M. 2011. *Governing for the Long Term*. Cambridge: Cambridge University Press.

James, Harold, and Marla Stone, eds. 1992. *When the Wall Came Down: Reactions to German Unification*. New York: Routledge.

Janeway, William H. 2012. *Doing Capitalism in the Innovation Economy*. Cambridge: Cambridge University Press.

Jardin, André. 1989. *Tocqueville: A Biography*. New York: Farrar, Straus, Giroux.

Jaume, Lucien. 2013. *Tocqueville: The Aristocratic Sources of Liberty*. Princeton, NJ: Princeton University Press.

Jervis, Robert. 1976. *Perception and Misperception in International Politics*. Princeton, NJ: Princeton University Press.

Johnson, Dominic D. P. 2004. *Overconfidence and War: The Havoc and Glory of Positive Illusions*. Cambridge, MA: Harvard University Press.

Judt, Tony. 2005. *Postwar: A History of Europe since 1945*. London: Heinemann.

———. 2008. *Reappraisals: Reflections on the Forgotten Twentieth Century*. London: Vintage.

Judt, Tony, and Timothy Snyder. 2012. *Thinking the Twentieth Century*. London: Heinemann.

Kalyvas, Stathis N., Ian Shapiro, and Tarek Masoud, eds. 2008. *Order, Conflict, and Violence*. Cambridge: Cambridge University Press.

Keane, John. 2009. *The Life and Death of Democracy*. London: Simon and Schuster.

Kellner, Peter. 2009. *Democracy: 1,000 Years in Pursuit of British Liberty*. Edinburgh: Mainstream.

Kennan, George F. 1956. *Russia Leaves the War*. Princeton, NJ: Princeton University Press.

———. 1958. *The Decision to Intervene*. Princeton, NJ: Princeton University Press.

———. 1983. *Memoirs 1950–1963*. New York: Pantheon Books.

Kennedy, Paul. 1987. *The Rise and Fall of the Great Powers: Economic Change and Military Conflict from 1500 to 2000*. New York: Vintage.
———. 1993. *Preparing for the Twenty-First Century*. New York: Vintage.
Keynes, John Maynard. 2012. *The Collected Writings of John Maynard Keynes*. Edited by Douglas Moggridge and Austin Robinson. 30 vols. Cambridge: Cambridge University Press.
Khilnani, Sunil. 1997. *The Idea of India*. London: Hamish Hamilton.
Kindleberger, Charles, and Robert Z. Aliber. 2005. *Manias, Panics, and Crashes: A History of Financial Crises*. Basingstoke: Palgrave Macmillan.
Kissinger, Henry. 1994. *Diplomacy*. New York: Simon and Schuster.
Kitchen, Martin. 1976. *The Silent Dictatorship: The Politics of the German High Command under Hindenburg and Ludendorff, 1916–1918*. London: Croom Helm.
Klein, Naomi. 2007. *The Shock Doctrine: The Rise of Disaster Capitalism*. London: Allen Lane.
Kloppenberg, James T. 1998. *The Virtues of Liberalism*. Oxford: Oxford University Press.
———. 2011. *Reading Obama: Dreams, Hope, and the American Political Tradition*. Princeton, NJ: Princeton University Press.
Knock, Thomas J. 1992. *To End All Wars: Woodrow Wilson and the Quest for a New World Order*. Princeton, NJ: Princeton University Press.
Koch, H. W. 1984. *A Constitutional History of Germany in the Nineteenth and Twentieth Centuries*. London: Longman.
Kohli, Atul. 1990. *Democracy and Discontent: India's Growing Crisis of Governability*. Cambridge: Cambridge University Press.
Kurlantzick, Joshua. 2013. *Democracy in Retreat: The Revolt of the Middle Class and the Worldwide Decline of Representative Government*. New Haven, CT: Yale University Press.
Kynaston, David. 2007. *Austerity Britain, 1945–51*. London: Bloomsbury.
Lanchester, John. 2010. *Whoops! Why Everyone Owes Everyone and No One Can Pay*. London: Penguin.
Lasch, Christopher. 1972. *The American Liberals and the Russian Revolution*. New York: McGraw-Hill.
Le Bon, Gustave. 1896. *The Crowd: A Study of the Popular Mind*. London: T. F. Unwin.

Le Bon, Gustave. 1916. *The Psychology of the Great War*. London: T. F. Unwin.

Lebow, Richard Ned. 2003. *The Tragic Vision of Politics: Ethics, Interests, and Orders*. Cambridge: Cambridge University Press.

Lebow, Richard Ned, and Janice Gross Stein. 1995. *We All Lost the Cold War*. Princeton, NJ: Princeton University Press.

Lecky, W.E.H. 1896. *Democracy and Liberty*. London: Longmans.

Leffler, Melvyn P., and Odd Arne Westad. 2010. *The Cambridge History of the Cold War*. 3 vols. Cambridge: Cambridge University Press.

Lewis, Michael, ed. 2008. *Panic: The Story of Modern Financial Insanity*. London: Penguin Books.

Lippincott, Benjamin E. 1938. *Victorian Critics of Democracy*. Minneapolis: University of Minnesota Press.

Lippmann, Walter. 1913. *A Preface to Politics*. New York: M. Kennerley.

———. 1914. *Drift and Mastery: An Attempt to Diagnose the Current Unrest*. New York: Henry Holt.

———. 1915. *The Stakes of Diplomacy*. New York: Henry Holt.

———. 1917. "The World Conflict in Its Relation to American Democracy." *Annals of the American Academy of Social and Political Science* (72): 1–10.

———. 1919. *The Political Scene: An Essay on the Victory of 1918*. New York: Henry Holt.

———. 1922. *Public Opinion*. New York: Harcourt, Brace.

———. 1927. *The Phantom Public*. London: Macmillan.

———. 1937. *The Good Society*. London: Allen and Unwin.

Lippmann Walter. [1947] 1972. *The Cold War*. New ed. New York: Joanna Cotler Books.

Lippmann, Walter, ed. 1932–34. *The United States in World Affairs, 1931–33*. 3 vols. New York: Harper.

Lipset, Seymour M. 1960. *Political Man: The Social Bases of Politics*. New York: Doubleday.

Lloyd George, David. 1936. *War Memoirs of David Lloyd George*. 6 vols. London: Ivor Nicholson and Watson.

Lucas, Noah. 1975. *The Modern History of Israel*. New York: Praeger.

Lyttelton, Adrian. 1987. *The Seizure of Power: Fascism in Italy, 1919–1929*. 2nd ed. London: Weidenfeld and Nicolson.

Macdonald, James. 2003. *A Free Nation Deep in Debt: The Financial Roots of Democracy*. New York: Farrar, Straus, Giroux.

MacMillan, Margaret. 2001. *Peacemakers: The Paris Conference of 1919 and Its Attempt to End War*. London: John Murray.

Mahoney, Daniel J. 1996. *De Gaulle: Statesmanship, Grandeur, and Modern Democracy*. London: Praeger.

Maine, Henry S. 1886. *Popular Government*. London: John Murray.

Manent, Pierre. 1996. *Tocqueville and the Nature of Democracy*. Lanham, MD: Rowman and Littlefield.

———. 2006. *A World beyond Politics? A Defense of the Nation-State*. Princeton, NJ: Princeton University Press.

Manin, Bernard. 1997. *The Principles of Representative Government*. Cambridge: Cambridge University Press.

Mann, Thomas. [1918] 1985. *Reflections of a Nonpolitical Man*. Edited by Walter D. Norris. New York: Frederick Ungar.

Margalit, Avishai. 2010. *On Compromise and Rotten Compromises*. Princeton, NJ: Princeton University Press.

Marquand, David. 2008. *Britain since 1918: The Strange Career of British Democracy*. London: Weidenfeld and Nicolson.

———. 2011. *The End of the West: The Once and Future Europe*. Princeton, NJ: Princeton University Press.

Marshall, Barbara. 1997. *Willy Brandt: A Political Biography*. New York: St. Martin's Press.

Masterman, C.F.G. [1908] 2008. *The Condition of England*, new ed. London: Faber and Faber.

Masterman, Lucy. 1939. *C.F.G. Masterman: A Biography*. London: Nicholson and Watson.

Maxwell, Neville. 1970. *India's China War*. New York: Pantheon.

May, Ernest, and Philip Zelikov, eds. 2002. *The Kennedy Tapes: Inside the White House during the Cuban Missile Crisis*. New York: W. W. Norton.

Mazower, Mark. 2009. *No Enchanted Palace: The End of Empire and the Ideological Origins of the United Nations*. Princeton, NJ: Princeton University Press.

McClelland, J. S. 1989. *The Crowd and the Mob: From Plato to Canetti*. London: Unwin Hyman.

McCormick, John P. 2007. *Weber, Habermas, and the Transformations of the European State*. Cambridge: Cambridge University Press.

McCullough, David. 1992. *Truman*. New York: Simon and Schuster.

McDonald, Patrick J. 2009. *The Invisible Hand of Peace: Capitalism, the War Machine, and International Relations Theory*. Cambridge: Cambridge University Press.

McNelly, Theodore. 2000. *The Origins of Japan's Democratic Constitution*. Lanham, MD: University Press of America.

Mehta, Pratap. 2003. *The Burden of Democracy*. London: Penguin Books.

Mencken, H. L. 1908. *The Philosophy of Friedrich Nietzsche*. New York: Luce.

———. 1926. *Notes on Democracy*. New York: Knopf.

———. 1961. *The Letters of H. L. Mencken*. Edited by Guy Forgue. New York: Knopf.

Merom, Gil. 2003. *How Democracies Lose Small Wars: State, Society, and the Failures of France in Algeria, Israel in Lebanon, and the United States in Vietnam*. Cambridge: Cambridge University Press.

Michels, Robert. 1915. *Political Parties: A Sociological Study of the Oligarchical Tendencies of Modern Democracy*. London: Jarrold and Sons.

Mill, John Stuart. 1963. *The Earlier Letters of John Stuart Mill, 1812–1848*. London: Routledge and Kegan Paul.

———. 1963–91. *The Collected Works of John Stuart Mill*. 33 vols. Edited by John M. Robson. Toronto: University of Toronto Press.

Miller, David. 1989. "The Fatalistic Conceit." *Critical Review* (3): 310–23.

Miller, Henry W. 1930. *The Paris Gun*. London: Harrap.

Miller, J. E. 1983. "Taking Off the Gloves: The United States and the Italian Elections of 1948." *Diplomatic History* (7): 35–56.

Mills, Robin M. 2008. *The Myth of the Oil Crisis*. Westport, CT: Greenwood Publishing.

Milward, Alan S. 1987. *The Reconstruction of Western Europe, 1945–51*. Berkeley: University of California Press.

Morgan, Kenneth. O. 1986. *Consensus and Disunity: The Lloyd George Coalition Government, 1918–1922*. Oxford: Oxford University Press.

Morgenthau, Hans. 1948. *Politics among Nations: The Struggle for Power and Peace*. New York: Knopf.

———. 1960. *The Purpose of American Politics*. New York: Knopf.

———. 1970. *Truth and Power: Essays of a Decade, 1960–70*. New York: Praeger.

Mount, Ferdinand. 2012. *The New Few; or, a Very British Oligarchy: Power and Inequality in Britain Now*. London: Simon and Schuster.

Mueller, John. 1999. *Capitalism, Democracy, and Ralph's Pretty Good Grocery*. Princeton, NJ: Princeton University Press.

Müller, Jan-Werner. 2000. *Another Country: German Intellectuals, Unification, and National Identity*. New Haven, CT: Yale University Press.

Newman, Karl J. 1971. *European Democracy between the Wars*. Notre Dame, IN: University of Notre Dame Press.

Newton, Michael. 2012. *Age of Assassins: A History of Assassination in Europe and America, 1865–1981*. London: Faber and Faber.

Nichols, Jeanette P. 1951. "Roosevelt's Monetary Policy in 1933." *American Historical Review* (56): 295–315.

Nicolson, Harold. 1933. *Peacemaking, 1919*. Boston: Houghton Mifflin.

Niebuhr, Reinhold. 1944. *The Children of Light and the Children of Darkness: A Vindication of Democracy and a Critique of Its Traditional Defenders*. New York: Charles Scribner's.

———. 1951. *The Irony of American History*. New York: Charles Scribner's.

Nietzsche, Friedrich. 2001. *The Gay Science*. Edited by Bernard Williams. Cambridge: Cambridge University Press.

———. 2002. *Beyond Good and Evil*. Edited by Rolf-Peter Horstmann and Judith Norman. Cambridge: Cambridge University Press.

———. 2006. *"On the Genealogy of Morality" and Other Writings*. Edited by Keith Ansell-Pearson. Cambridge: Cambridge University Press.

Nixon, Richard. 1971–78. *The Public Papers, 1969–74*. 6 vols. Washington, DC: US Printing Office.

North, Douglas C., John Joseph Wallis, and Barry Weingast. 2009. *Violence and Social Orders: A Conceptual Framework for Interpreting and Recording Human History*. Cambridge: Cambridge University Press.

Obama, Barack. 2007. *The Audacity of Hope*. Edinburgh: Canongate.

Ober, Josiah. 2008. *Democracy and Knowledge: Innovation and Learning in Classical Athens*. Princeton, NJ: Princeton University Press.

Ortega y Gasset, José. [1932] 1985. *The Revolt of the Masses*. Edited by Kenneth Moore. New York: W. W. Norton.

Ostrogorski, M. 1902. *Democracy and the Organization of Political Parties*. Translated by F. Clarke. London: Macmillan.

Paine, Thomas. 2000. *Political Writings*. Edited by Bruce Kuklick. Cambridge: Cambridge University Press.

Paterson, Thomas G., and William J. Brophy. 1986. "October Missiles and November Elections: The Cuban Missile Crisis and American Politics, 1962." *Journal of American History* (73): 87–119.

Paulson, Henry M. 2010. *On the Brink: Inside the Race to Stop the Collapse of the Global Financial System*. New York: Hachette.

Pierson, George Wilson. 1996. *Tocqueville in America*. Baltimore: Johns Hopkins University Press.

Pinker, Steven. 2011. *The Better Angels of Our Nature: The Decline of Violence and Its Causes*. London: Allen Lane.

Plato. 2000. *The Republic*. Edited by G.R.F. Ferrari. Cambridge: Cambridge University Press.

Posner, Richard A. 2010. *The Crisis of Capitalist Democracy*. Cambridge, MA: Harvard University Press.

Przeworski, Adam. 2010. *Democracy and the Limits of Self-Government*. Cambridge: Cambridge University Press.

Przeworski, Adam, José Antonio Cheibub, Michael E. Alvarez, and Fernando Limongi. 2000. *Democracy and Development: Political Institutions and Material Well-Being in the World, 1950–1990*. Cambridge: Cambridge University Press.

Rajan, R. G. 2010. *Fault Lines: How Hidden Fractures Still Threaten the World Economy*. Princeton, NJ: Princeton University Press.

Ranelagh, John. 1991. *Thatcher's People: An Insider's Account of the Politics, the Power, and the Personalities*. London: HarperCollins.

Reinhart, Carmen M., and Kenneth S. Rogoff. 2009. *This Time Is Different: Eight Centuries of Financial Folly*. Princeton, NJ: Princeton University Press.

Reiter, Dan, and Allan C. Stam. 2002. *Democracies at War*. Princeton, NJ: Princeton University Press.

Revel, Jean-François. 1984. *How Democracies Perish*. Garden City, NY: Doubleday.

———. 1993. *Democracy against Itself: The Future of the Democratic Impulse*. New York: Simon and Schuster.

Ridley, Matt. 2010. *The Rational Optimist: How Prosperity Evolves*. London: Fourth Estate.

Roberts, Alasdair. 2010. *The Logic of Discipline: Global Capitalism and the Architecture of Government*. Oxford: Oxford University Press.

Roberts, Jennifer Tolbert. 2011. *Athens on Trial: The Antidemocratic Tradition in Western Thought*. Princeton, NJ: Princeton University Press.

Roosevelt, Franklin D. 1938–50. *The Public Papers and Addresses of Franklin D. Roosevelt*. 13 vols. New York: Random House.

Roosevelt, Theodore. 1915. *America and the World War*. London: John Murray.

———. 1951–54. *The Letters of Theodore Roosevelt*. Edited by Elting E. Morrison. 7 vols. Cambridge, MA: Harvard University Press.

Roper, John. 1989. *Democracy and Its Critics*. London: Routledge.

Rose, Gideon. 2010. *How Wars End: Why We Always Fight the Last Battle*. New York: Simon and Schuster.

Rousseau, Jean-Jacques. 1997. *Political Writings*. 2 vols. Edited by Victor Gourevitch. Cambridge: Cambridge University Press.

Runciman, David. 2006. *The Politics of Good Intentions: History, Fear, and Hypocrisy in the New World Order*. Princeton, NJ: Princeton University Press.

Russett, Bruce. 1994. *Grasping the Democratic Peace: Principles for a Post–Cold War World*. Princeton, NJ: Princeton University Press.

Saldin, Robert P. 2011. *War, the American State, and Politics since 1898*. Cambridge: Cambridge University Press.

Samons, Loren J. 2004. *What's Wrong with Democracy? From Athenian Practice to American Worship*. Berkeley: University of California Press.

Sarotte, Mary Elise. 2009. *1989: The Struggle to Create Post–Cold War Europe*. Princeton, NJ: Princeton University Press.

Schelling, Thomas C. 1960. *The Strategy of Conflict*. Cambridge, MA: Harvard University Press.

Schlesinger, Arthur M. 1986. *The Cycles of American History*. Boston: Houghton Mifflin.

Schultz, Kenneth A. 2001. *Democracy and Coercive Diplomacy*. Cambridge: Cambridge University Press.

Schultz, Kenneth A., and Barry R. Weingast. 2003. "The Democratic Advantage: Institutional Foundations of Financial Power in International Competition." *International Organization* (57): 3–42.

Schulzke, C. Eric. 2005. "Wilsonian Crisis Leadership, the Organic State and the Modern Presidency." *Polity* (37): 262–85.

Schumpeter, Joseph A. 1951. *Imperialism and Social Classes*. Edited by Paul M. Sweezy. Oxford: Oxford University Press.

———. 1976. *Capitalism, Socialism, and Democracy*, new ed. London: George Allen and Unwin.

Sen, Amartya. 1999. *Development as Freedom*. Oxford: Oxford University Press.

Shapiro, Ian. 2003. *The State of Democratic Theory*. Princeton, NJ: Princeton University Press.

———. 2007. *Containment: Rebuilding a Strategy against Global Terror*. Princeton, NJ: Princeton University Press.

Shaw, George Bernard. 1919. *Peace Conference Hints*. London: Constable.

Shaxson, Nicholas. 2011. *Treasure Islands: Tax Havens and the Men Who Stole the World*. London: The Bodley Head.

Sheffield, Gary. 2002. *Forgotten Victory: The First World War, Myths, and Realities*. London: Headline.

Shklar, Judith N. 1957. *After Utopia: The Decline of Political Faith*. Princeton, NJ: Princeton University Press.

Shlaes, Amity. 2007. *The Forgotten Man: A New History of the Great Depression*. New York: Harper Collins.

Silber, William L. 2007. *When Washington Shut Down Wall Street: The Great Financial Crisis of 1914 and the Origins of America's Monetary Supremacy*. Princeton, NJ: Princeton University Press.

Siniver, Asaf. 2008. *Nixon, Kissinger, and U.S. Foreign Policy Making*. Cambridge: Cambridge University Press.

Skidelsky, Robert. 1967. *Politicians and the Slump: The Labour Government of 1929–1931*. London: Macmillan.

———. 1983–2000. *Keynes: A Biography*. 3 vols. London: Macmillan.

Slaughter, Anne-Marie. 2004. *A New World Order*. Princeton, NJ: Princeton University Press.

Sorkin, Andrew Ross. 2009. *Too Big to Fail: The Inside Story of How Wall Street and Washington Fought to Save the Financial System—and Themselves*. New York: Viking.

Soros, George. 1994. *The Alchemy of Finance: Reading the Mind of the Market*. New ed. New York: Wiley.

Stears, Marc. 2010. *Demanding Democracy: American Radicals in Search of a New Politics*. Princeton, NJ: Princeton University Press.

Stedman Jones, Daniel. 2012. *Masters of the Universe: Hayek, Friedman, and the Birth of Neoliberal Politics*. Princeton, NJ: Princeton University Press.

Steel, Ronald. 1980. *Walter Lippmann and the American Century*. New York: Transaction Publishers.

Stevenson, David. 2011. *With Our Backs to the Wall: Victory and Defeat in 1918*. London: Allen Lane.

Stiglitz, Joseph. 2012. *The Price of Inequality*. London: Allen Lane.

Strachan, Hew. 1997. *The Politics of the British Army*. Oxford: Oxford University Press.

Taleb, Nassim Nicholas. 2007. *The Black Swan: The Impact of the Highly Improbable*. London: Allen Lane.

Tett, Gillian. 2009. *Fool's Gold: How the Bold Dream of a Small Tribe at J. P. Morgan Was Corrupted by Wall Street Greed and Unleashed a Catastrophe*. New York: Free Press.

Thompson, Helen. 2008. *Might, Right, Prosperity, and Consent: Representative Democracy and the International Economy, 1919–2001*. Manchester: Manchester University Press.

———. 2011. *China and the Mortgaging of America: Economic Interdependence and Domestic Politics*. Basingstoke: Palgrave Macmillan.

Thompson, John B. 2000. *Political Scandal: Power and Visibility in the Media Age*. Cambridge: Polity Press.

Tilly, Charles. 2007. *Democracy*. Cambridge: Cambridge University Press.

Tocqueville, Alexis de. 1948. *The Recollections*. Edited by J. P. Mayer. London: Harvill Press.

———. 1985. *Selected Letters on Politics and Society*. Edited by Roger Boesche. Berkeley: University of California Press.

———. [1835–40] 2000. *Democracy in America*. Edited and translated by Harvey C. Mansfield and Delba Winthrop. Chicago: University of Chicago Press.

———. [1856] 2011. *The Ancien Régime and the French Revolution*. Edited by Jon Elster. Cambridge: Cambridge University Press.

Tombs, Robert, and Isabelle Tombs. 2006. *That Sweet Enemy: The British and French from the Sun King to the Present*. London: William Heinemann.

Tooze, Adam. 2006. *The Wages of Destruction: The Making and Breaking of the Nazi Economy*. London: Allen Lane.

Urban, George. 1976. "A Conversation with George Kennan." *Encounter* (47): 10–43.

Vaughn, Stephen. 1980. *Holding Fast the Inner Lines: Democracy, Nationalism, and the Committee on Public Information*. Chapel Hill: University of North Carolina Press.

Von Mises, Ludwig. [1919] 1983. *Nation, State, and Economy: Contributions to the Politics and History of Our Times*. Edited by Leland B. Yeager. New York: New York University Press.

Wall, Richard, and Jay Winter, eds. 2005. *The Upheaval of War: Family, Work, and Welfare in Europe, 1914–1918*. Cambridge: Cambridge University Press.

Warren, Mark, E., ed. 1999. *Democracy and Trust*. Cambridge: Cambridge University Press.

Warth, Robert D. 1954. *The Allies and the Russian Revolution: From the Fall of the Monarchy to the Peace of Brest-Litovsk*. Durham, NC: Duke University Press.

Watson, David. 1974. *Georges Clemenceau: A Political Biography*. London: Eyre Methuen.

Webb, Beatrice. 1952. *Diaries, 1912–1924*. Edited by M. Cole. London: Longmans.

Weber, Marianne. 1975. *Max Weber: A Biography*. New York: Wiley.

Weber, Max. 1994. *Political Writings*. Edited by Peter Lassman and Ronald Speirs. Cambridge: Cambridge University Press.

Weingast, Barry R., and Donald Wittman, eds. 2008. *The Oxford Handbook of Political Economy*. Oxford: Oxford University Press.

Weisbrot, Robert. 2001. *Maximum Danger: Kennedy, the Missiles, and the Crisis of American Confidence*. Lanham, MD: Ivan R. Dee.

Welch, Cheryl B., ed. 2006. *The Cambridge Companion to Tocqueville*. Cambridge: Cambridge University Press.

Wells, H. G. 1933. *The Shape of Things to Come*. London: Hutchinson.

Weyl, Walter. 1912. *The New Democracy: An Essay on Certain Political and Economic Tendencies in the United States*. New York: Macmillan.

White, William Allen. 1928. *Masks in a Pageant*. New York: Macmillan.

Williamson, Murray, and Jim Lacey. 2009. *The Making of Peace: Rulers, States, and the Aftermath of War*. Cambridge: Cambridge University Press.

Wilson, Woodrow. 1966–94. *The Papers of Woodrow Wilson*. 69 vols. Edited by Arthur Link. Princeton, NJ: Princeton University Press.

Winter, Jay, Geoffrey Parker, and Mary Habeck, eds. 2000. *The Great War and the Twentieth Century*. New Haven, CT: Yale University Press.

Winter, Jay, and Jean-Louis Robert, eds. 1997. *Capital Cities at War: Paris, London, Berlin, 1914–1919*. Cambridge: Cambridge University Press.

Wolin, Sheldon. 2003. *Tocqueville between Two Worlds: The Making of a Political and Theoretical Life*. Princeton, NJ: Princeton University Press.

Wright, Gordon. 1942. *Raymond Poincaré and the French Presidency*. Stanford, CA: Stanford University Press.

Wright, Quincy. 1983. *A Study of War*, 2nd ed. Chicago: University of Chicago Press.

Ypi, Lea. 2012. *Global Justice and Avant-Garde Political Agency*. Oxford: Oxford University Press.

Zakaria, Fareed. 1998. *From Wealth to Power: The Unusual Origins of America's World Role*. Princeton, NJ: Princeton University Press.

Zeckhauser, Richard, ed. 1991. *Strategy and Choice*. Cambridge, MA: MIT Press.

Zetterbaum, M. 1967. *Tocqueville and the Problem of Democracy*. Stanford, CA: Stanford University Press.

ONLINE RECORDS

"Constituent Assembly Debates," www.parliamentofindia.nic.in/ls/debates/debates.htmlc.

"Freedom in the World 2012," http://www.freedomhouse.org/report/freedom-world/freedom-world-2012.

"GB Shaw Archive," http://walterschafer.com/atimesofshaw/articles/.

"Inaugural Addresses of the Presidents of the United States: From George Washington to George W. Bush," www.bartleby.com/br/124.html.

"Nobel Acceptance Speeches," http://www.nobelprize.org/nobel_prizes/economics/laureates/.

"Parliamentary Debates since 1803," http://www.hansard-archive.parliament.uk/.

"Project for a New American Century: Statement of Principles," http://www.newamericancentury.org/statementofprinciples.html.

"Soviet Documents on Foreign Policy," http://www.marxists.org/history/ussr/government/foreign-relations/author/index.htm

INDEX